the complete book of
DIABETIC
COOKING

the complete book of
DIABETIC COOKING

the essential guide to diabetes with an expert introduction to nutrition and healthy eating – plus 170 delicious recipes shown step by step in over 650 fabulous practical photographs

BRIDGET JONES

LORENZ BOOKS

This edition is published by Lorenz Books, an imprint of Anness Publishing Ltd, 108 Great Russell Street, London WC1B 3NA; info@anness.com

www.lorenzbooks.com; www.annesspublishing.com; twitter: @Anness_Books

If you like the images in this book and would like to investigate using them for publishing, promotions or advertising, please visit our website www.practicalpictures.com for more information.

© Anness Publishing Ltd 2015

Publisher: Joanna Lorenz
Editorial Director: Helen Sudell
Executive Editor: Joanne Rippin
Photographs: Thomas Odulate, Amanda Heywood, Nicky Dowey, William Lingwood, Craig Robertson, Simon Smith, Peter Anderson, Martin Brigdale
Recipes: Alex Barker, Joanna Farrow, Nicola Graimes, Christopher Trotter, Georgina Campbell, Ysanne Spevack, Michelle Beridale-Johnson, Kate Whiteman, Maggie Mayhew, Jennie Shapter, Keith Richmond, Rena Salaman, Matthew Drennan, Becky Johnson
Production Controller: Ben Worley

PUBLISHER'S NOTE
Although the advice and information in this book are believed to be accurate and true at the time of going to press, neither the authors nor the publisher can accept any legal responsibility or liability for any errors or omissions that may have been made nor for any inaccuracies nor for any loss, harm or injury that comes about from following instructions or advice in this book.

NOTES
• Bracketed terms are intended for American readers.
• For all recipes, quantities are given in both metric and imperial measures and, where appropriate, in standard cups and spoons. Follow one set of measures, but not a mixture, because they are not interchangeable.
• Standard spoon and cup measures are level. 1 tsp = 5ml, 1 tbsp = 15ml, 1 cup = 250ml/8fl oz.
• Australian standard tablespoons are 20ml. Australian readers should use 3 tsp in place of 1 tbsp for measuring small quantities.
• American pints are 16fl oz/2 cups. American readers should use 20fl oz/ 2.5 cups in place of 1 pint when measuring liquids.
• Electric oven temperatures in this book are for conventional ovens. When using a fan oven, the temperature will probably need to be reduced by about 10–20°C/20–40°F. Since ovens vary, you should check with your manufacturer's instruction book for guidance.
• The nutritional analysis given for each recipe is calculated per portion (i.e. serving or item), unless otherwise stated. If the recipe gives a range, such as Serves 4–6, then the nutritional analysis will be for the smaller portion size, i.e. 6 servings. The analysis does not include optional ingredients, such as salt added to taste.
• Medium (US large) eggs are used unless otherwise stated.

Contents

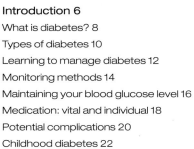

Introduction

Diabetes is unique among chronic health conditions for the importance that is now placed on self-management. With medication, professional guidance and support, the outlook for someone diagnosed with the condition is extremely good. Achieving an overall sense of wellbeing by adopting a positive, active, healthy lifestyle is important. With the right approach, diabetes will not stop anyone from doing anything; while it may make someone slightly different, it does not set them apart — having children, eating out, enjoying sport, taking part in extreme activities, travelling all over the world are all acceptable and achievable.

This book leads you through the process of understanding and self-managing diabetes, not only the physical facts, the medication and the dietary changes, but the psychological impact and the different reactions to being diagnosed and living with a life-changing condition. The first phase of diagnosis is usually the most difficult, coming to terms with the condition and understanding how to deal with it. Having some idea of what sort of medication and monitoring to expect helps. Developing a rapport with health professionals, telling those around you and building self-confidence are all important aspects of diabetes management.

There is guidance on the different ways to introduce essential changes to diet or activity, discussing ideas with the professionals, and developing individual strategies for confident control. Suddenly dealing with healthcare, especially for someone who has never before had a significant illness, can be stressful, so the support of family and friends is

essential. Carers may have to cope with children, teenagers or elderly relatives and unexpected responses. Motivating children and youngsters to work with diabetes instead of rebelling against it is quite different from encouraging older people to change the habits of a lifetime.

Careful planning is important and this book shows how to consider the impact of everyday and special occasions. We control our lifestyles without even thinking about it, but getting used to having diabetes means a higher level of planning to factor in medication, food intake and physical activity. For the best control and long-term wellbeing, planning also means being positive and active, and thinking in advance on some occasions. Diabetes affects everyone differently, and the modern approach to managing the condition is to provide each person with a unique package of medication, monitoring methods, diet and lifestyle guidelines. Managing diabetes is a continuing process, as different life phases present new challenges: from home to school, college and living alone, through the excitement of marriage or setting up home with a partner, planning a pregnancy and dealing with the stresses of work and family. The way in which diabetes is managed will vary, but there will always be support available. As well as the healthcare professionals who are involved, there are also self-help groups and publications for all ages.

This book sets out the contemporary approach to managing diabetes — to calm the inevitable concerns, discover how best to take control, realize a sense of wellbeing and develop a taste for great food. Offering lots of advice and recipes to help you eat well, manage weight, and develop a super-positive approach to food, the book will help you through every aspect of living with diabetes.

There are recipes for all occasions, from all over the world, and to suit everyone (with or without diabetes). The chapters cover Breakfasts; Snacks and Drinks; Soups; Vegetarian Main Courses; Fish and Shellfish; Meat, Poultry and Game; Salads and Vegetable Dishes; Desserts; and Cakes, Cookies and Bread. There are variations, tips on eating well, and advice on putting together delicious, health-promoting meals.

Whether you have recently been diagnosed, or have been living with the condition for a while, this book will help you manage your eating and nutrition, as well as offering lots of advice on all other aspects of a healthy lifestyle.

Left: Fish and eggs make excellent low-fat protein choices, especially when teamed with a leafy green such as spinach.

Right: Oily fish contributes valuable good fat, as well as the best kind of protein, to a healthy diet.

Above: Fresh vegetables and full-flavoured ingredients are great for positive eating habits and the enjoyment of food.

Below: Shepherd's Pie can be adapted for a healthier diet with lentils in the meat and a topping of root vegetables.

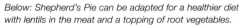

What is diabetes?

Diabetes mellitus is a condition resulting from an insufficiency of insulin, a hormone produced by the pancreas, and is a disorder of the endocrine system, which looks after the body's hormone functions. It may be caused either by a lack of insulin or because the body's ability to utilize it is reduced.

As one of the diseases that is increasing in the modern world, diabetes is the subject of much research to determine its causes and consequences and find the best ways of treating the condition. There have been many advances in understanding and dealing with diabetes in recent decades, but many areas are still unexplained. Although large numbers of individuals are diagnosed with it, it is estimated that many people who have diabetes are unaware of it, and that their long-term health may therefore at risk from the consequences and side effects of the disease.

What the pancreas does
The pancreas is an organ in the digestive system, situated near the duodenum. As well as producing insulin and other important hormones, it is responsible for producing enzymes used in the digestion of fats and proteins in the intestine. Most of the

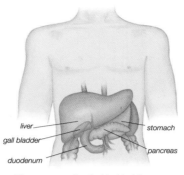

The pancreas lies just behind the stomach, but has been shown here in front so it can be seen clearly.

organ is made up of clusters of cells called ancini, which produce digestive enzymes. Interspersed among them are tiny cell clusters called pancreatic islets, or islets of Langerhans. These islets include four different types of hormone-secreting cells, about 70 per cent of which are beta cells (B cells), which are responsible for secreting insulin. Of the other three types, alpha cells (A cells) secrete glucagon, which increases blood glucose when the level falls too low; delta cells (D cells) secrete somatostatin, which is also produced in the brain and inhibits the release of

other hormones such as growth hormone and hormones that stimulate the thyroid as well as gastrointestinal hormones. Finally, F cells secrete pancreatic polypeptide, which inhibits somatostatin secretion, gallbladder contraction and the secretion of the digestive enzymes from the pancreas.

What insulin does
Insulin is important for controlling the amount of glucose (sugar) in the blood. In a system that functions properly, a high level of glucose in the blood (high blood sugar level) is the main stimulant for the release of insulin. As well as the glucose level in the blood, the level in the intestine rises as food is being digested and absorbed, and this also helps to stimulate insulin secretion. The insulin then facilitates the absorption of glucose from the blood into cells where it is used to generate energy or is converted into glycogen and stored in the liver for later use. The role of insulin is not limited to the processing of glucose: it is also important for fat and protein metabolism.

Relating insulin to eating
The body is traditionally compared to a machine, taking in fuel in order to work, but it is far more complicated than this – the human body is wired to allow individual choice and control in addition to reflexes and innate essentials. We can decide how to fuel our bodies – what to eat, how much and how often, and how active we want to be.

We eat to stay alive and to give us the energy to power all our activity. The body automatically processes the food we eat, extracting the energy, storing the excess, getting rid of unwanted waste and then accessing the stored supplies later as we need them. Having too much potential energy stored as fat can result in health problems, and there is great awareness of the importance of

Tiredness, thirst, and blurred vision are symptoms associated with diabetes.

balanced eating, both for short-term wellbeing and long-term good health. Although insulin is just one element in this chain of events, it is vital. Without sufficient insulin, the body cannot process glucose from the blood, and the glucose builds up to abnormally high levels in a condition known as hyperglycaemia.

Symptoms of hyperglycaemia

The symptoms vary, developing in different ways and at different rates. When the concentration of sugar in the blood is very high it causes huge thirst. There is frequent urination as the kidneys try to expel the excess sugar. Frequent urination tends to lead to dehydration and this can result in constipation. Tiredness and lack of energy are common. Constant hunger and increased eating may be accompanied by unexplained weight loss. Urinary infections, such as thrush and cystitis, take hold more easily when the urine contains sugar, so genital itching can be a problem. Vision may be blurred. The hands and/or feet may tingle. Coping with several such impactful symptoms can make anyone feel seriously run down.

Meals with a high vegetable content are a good choice for healthy eating.

What causes insulin disorders?

There is no clear-cut cause of diabetes, and it is likely that a number of factors lead to an inability to produce or utilize insulin. Diabetes can be a secondary condition, for example, resulting from problems or diseases of the pancreas. There may be links with an overproduction of growth hormones. These are the main contributing factors:

Ethnicity Type 2 diabetes is more prevalent among some ethnic types than others. For example, African-American, Hispanic-American and British-Asian populations display a higher incidence than the Caucasians in their respective countries.

Heredity There is a strong genetic link in cases of both types of diabetes, but this is related to a predisposition to developing the condition – a family history of diabetes does not make its development a certainty.

Viral infection It is thought that Type 1 diabetes may be triggered by a viral infection that affects the pancreas, specifically in young people. Again, this is not a direct cause but it is possible that some existing predisposition or minor condition may be accelerated or activated in this way.

Weight and diet Being overweight and having a poor diet increase the risk of developing diabetes, especially Type 2. Type 2 diabetes has traditionally been thought of as an "age-onset" disease. However, the incidence of this type of diabetes has increased

---

SYMPTOM SUMMARY

The three "Ps" or "polys":
• Polyuria (excessive urination)
• Polydipsia (excessive thirst)
• Polyphagia (excessive eating)

can be accompanied by:
• Tiredness and/or lack of energy
• Genital itching
• Constipation
• Blurred vision
• Tingling feet or hands

Having diabetes does not prevent anyone from taking vigorous exercise: it's about planning and eating right.

dramatically among younger age groups. While it must be emphasized that not everyone with diabetes is necessarily overweight, being overweight or obese increases the risk of developing diabetes.

Lifestyle Eating too much and having a badly balanced diet, combined with taking too little exercise, is also thought to contribute to the risk of diabetes.

You're not alone

Worldwide, over 170 million people have diabetes, and the World Health Organization estimates that this figure will double by 2030. While diagnosis rates have increased in the USA, it is thought that a third of those who have the condition do not realize it – this figure is not a new one but it is not decreasing as hoped with increased publicity and awareness.

Types of diabetes

There are two main types of diabetes mellitus, known as Type 1 and Type 2. The resulting symptoms vary in severity between the two.

Type 1 diabetes

In this case, also known as insulin-dependent diabetes mellitus (IDDM), there is no insulin available. Heredity factors may increase the risk of developing the condition, but are not the sole proven reason. It is an autoimmune disease, in which the body's own immune system attacks and destroys the beta cells in the islets of Langerhans in the pancreas – the tiny clusters that are responsible for producing insulin. An attack may be triggered by a viral infection, which starts the process of self-destruction of the beta cells. There is some evidence that children are more likely to develop Type 1 diabetes in autumn or winter, when viral infections are more common. It is not the virus that causes damage – it's the body response.

Type 1 diabetes usually develops before the age of 20 and becomes a lifelong condition. As the body is not able to produce any insulin at all, drugs that boost the production or uptake of the hormone are ineffective, and insulin has to be injected every day.

Regular meals and snacks are important for blood glucose control, and whenever possible it is good to sit down to a proper meal, rather than eating on the go.

Recognizing the symptoms

The symptoms that are general to both types of diabetes tend to come on suddenly and severely with Type 1, due to the complete lack of insulin. Sometimes the signs may be misssed or misunderstood, particularly if the diabetes is set off by a viral infection that could account for the symptoms experienced. Even after the initial illness has cleared up, it is easy to mistake the symptoms of diabetes for post-infection lethargy and feeling run down.

As well as controlling blood glucose levels, insulin plays an important role in

Healthy eating is particularly important for anyone with diabetes.

balancing the digestion of fats and proteins and stopping the body from breaking down muscle. When glucose from the blood cannot be absorbed for energy, the body draws first on its supplies of fat and then on protein or muscle tissue. This eventually causes wasting of the muscles.

A side effect of digesting fat is a build-up of ketones, the by-products of this process. Acetone, one of the ketones, is expelled through the lungs on the breath, giving it an acidic, fruity odour. Eventually the accumulation of ketones can reach dangerously high levels in a condition known as ketoacidosis, which can lead ultimately to a coma if untreated.

Type 2 diabetes

Also known as non-insulin dependent diabetes mellitus (NIDDM), this is more common than Type 1. It usually occurs among people over 35, but is being increasingly found in younger people, even children. Being overweight is a risk factor for developing this type of diabetes, along with poor diet and lack of exercise. Heredity is also a factor.

In this type of diabetes, insulin production is reduced (not ceased), so the rise in blood glucose levels is more gradual. The body is still releasing some insulin but not enough to process sufficient glucose for the system to function normally. Some cases show not only a low level of insulin but also a decreased ability to use it. Or there may be enough insulin but the receptor cells no longer respond to it. Type 2 diabetes can be managed by diet and exercise. Drugs may be used to boost the production or uptake of insulin, but insulin injections are not used to control the condition.

Even when the condition is temporary, such as with gestational diabetes, you should understand it properly.

Being aware of symptoms

In Type 2 diabetes the symptoms develop slowly and are less severe than in Type 1. This means that the condition may be overlooked for some time, reducing wellbeing and worsening general health. It is often diagnosed by chance, when a routine visit to a doctor or tests taken for another reason show high levels of blood glucose.

It is important to be aware of persistent unexplained symptoms and not dismiss them as the consequences of getting older. Consistent increases in the need to urinate, increased thirst regardless of activity or the weather, feeling low and losing weight without eating less or exercising more (or eating more but not putting on weight) make up a package that should be checked out by a doctor. One interesting point is that people with Type 2 diabetes often do not perceive sweetness as well as other people, so they add slightly more sugar to food and drinks to detect it.

Secondary diabetes

Insulin levels can be thrown out as a result of a separate problem, so that diabetes becomes an additional unwanted side effect. There may be problems with hormones other than insulin, problems with or damage to the pancreas, or an imbalance may be due to severe alcohol abuse. Cushing's syndrome is a condition that produces high levels of blood glucose, and impaired glucose tolerance (IGT) is characterized by blood glucose levels that are higher than normal but not high enough to be considered diabetic. High levels of blood glucose may be an indicator that diabetes will develop later.

Diabetes during pregnancy

Gestational diabetes may develop due to the hormonal changes during pregnancy, ceasing after the baby is born. It can cause complications for the unborn baby and during birth, so the symptoms should not be ignored. A dietician should advise on adjusting the mother's diet to manage the condition, and it may be necessary for her to receive insulin treatment.

Developing temporary diabetes during pregnancy can sometimes be a warning sign that the condition may develop permanently later in life, but this is not always so.

Learning to manage diabetes

Most people know someone who has diabetes, and many will have more diabetic acquaintances than they realize because, once it is supervised and controlled, diabetes is rarely a big issue. With care, experience and patience, daily monitoring and management of the condition become routine.

Adjusting to the condition, however, is not so simple, and working with your healthcare professionals is essential. Being in control is not about going it alone. You need to be proactive and positive about seeking advice and support, and check out any doubts.

The diagnosis

Any symptoms that seem to indicate diabetes should be checked out with your doctor. There are blood and urine tests, which may need to be repeated more than once, at different times of day or after a period of fasting (ask about any pre-test fasting when you arrange an appointment). When the diagnosis is confirmed, the professional response will depend on the severity of the condition, as the first priority is to bring the blood glucose level back to normal. If your case is severe you may be admitted to hospital for stabilizing.

First stages

In the first days after diagnosis, go with the flow, stick to the professional advice you are given and don't panic if you don't understand every detail. Read all the information the medical team provides and let it sink in. Work with them as they stabilize your condition, and provide all the information they need about your diet and lifestyle, being as accurate as you can.

Don't be shy about asking your questions – expect answers but do not be concerned if there are no ready, standard solutions. No two people experience exactly the same set of symptoms, consequences and concerns. Getting involved in the right way from the beginning will enable you to look after yourself effectively. Learn slowly and surely, taking advantage of all the support on offer and asking for more when in doubt. Fighting for instant independence and control is not the best way forward.

There are lots of useful sources of information and support groups, but you should avoid overloading on every

Talk to, and take advice from, the trained health professionals you meet.

MANAGING DIABETES
Learning to manage the condition depends on getting a good grip on:
- What has to be done.
- How diabetes varies, and why.
- How to recognize and respond to signs and symptoms.
- The importance of regular health check ups.

possible opinion. As you gain understanding of the condition and its implications for you, jot down your concerns and take them back to your team contact, specialist nurse or doctor. Check out any information from other sources, including well-meant advice from friends, before following it.

What the professionals do

The members of the team looking after you and the way they work will vary, depending on the facilities available locally and the severity of your condition. Once you are diagnosed you can expect prompt attention and

Local groups, national organizations and diabetes magazines are useful.

PROFESSIONAL SUPPORT

The professional team typically provides:

- On going instruction, monitoring and advice on medication or insulin injections.
- Support to ensure supplies and medication are adequate.
- Information on blood or urine tests and how to interpret them.
- Advice on how to respond to test results in terms of diet.
- Regular carer visits to ensure you are coping.
- Education and further information as required.
- Advice on how to cope with illness, from minor ailments to hospital visits.
- Support with any changes in circumstances, from moving house or a holiday to planning pregnancy.

guidance, on a one-to-one basis:

- Your individual treatment, equipment and medication will be explained.
- You will have a specific care programme, with goals to help keep you on track.
- The dietician will ask about your usual diet and eating patterns so that these can be adapted, and the importance of food and healthy eating will be explained to you.
- You will be given lots of information on why diabetes control is important.

TAKING RESPONSIBILITY

Your aims are to:

- Take control as far as possible.
- Know how to manage and when to communicate with the professionals.
- Know whom to contact, when and where.
- Learn about monitoring blood glucose.
- Learn about diet and exercise.
- Look after yourself – your general wellbeing is important.

- You will be guided on how to improve your everyday exercise, if necessary.
- All other aspects of care will be explained – feet care, for example.

Teamwork

The medical team aims to give you responsibility for managing your diabetes on a day-to-day basis whenever possible, while giving maximum support for a positive, healthy and balanced lifestyle. This works very well once everyone has settled down – you, your family and friends, work colleagues and teachers – with the professionals providing the foundation of your care. The more confident you become and the more control you take, the happier the professionals will be, because they know you won't let minor problems drift until they become major difficulties.

Be proactive about checking out new research and information on diabetes.

What about you?

Where do you fit in? When the condition is stable, familiar and manageable, you are the key operator. Gradually you will take responsibility as far as possible, but this won't happen overnight. You may not come up with the right question at the right moment, or what may seem quite straightforward in a consultation may become muddled 24 hours later when you try to think it through. Don't feel pressurized or pretend that you know more than you do – voice all your doubts and concerns. Your team of carers will help you to learn more and take control. Remember, they are used to this and have helped many other people with diabetes through the learning process.

Monitoring methods

Self-monitoring your diabetes helps you to understand it by showing how eating and insulin influence blood glucose levels, and by highlighting the consequences of a good – or bad – diet and the advantages of regular exercise. Your doctor or nurse will explain exactly how and when to monitor, how to interpret the results and how to use them to change your diet and/or lifestyle. Being able to monitor the condition yourself also gives you the confidence to be in charge of it rather than a victim of it.

When you are confident about controlling your condition on a day-to-day basis and your blood glucose levels are generally good, health professionals aim to act as mentors rather than controllers, making regular checks to ensure that your condition is stable.

Blood and urine monitoring are both used. The type you need is assessed when the diabetes is diagnosed, after it is stabilized. Self-monitoring is tailored to the individual, and the results must be understood in the same context.

Urine test

This gives retrospective blood glucose levels. By the time the urine is tested, the glucose level in the blood will have changed, and the test indicates the level about two hours earlier. Therefore testing urine is not used for short-term

There are various ways of taking a sample for a blood glucose test.

management of medication or food intake and is not immediate enough for checking the possible onset of a very low blood glucose level.

Urine tests can be useful for medium-term monitoring covering a longer period of days. They are often used by people with Type 2 diabetes who rely on diet or tablets to control their blood glucose.

Blood glucose test

Testing the blood glucose level by means of a fingerprick blood test provides current information that can be used to adjust eating patterns or medication. It can confirm low blood glucose (hypoglycaemia) if you are unsure about the symptoms.

A blood test is useful with Type 1 diabetes, especially for assessing how types and dosages of insulin are

Discuss monitoring methods, and any concerns or problems you may have with control, with the healthcare team.

working by comparing results over a period of days. This method is also helpful if your levels of activity vary.

Regular check-ups

Self-monitoring is supported by professional checks every two, three or six months, depending on the individual. Your doctor or nurse will explain the results both in general terms and interpreting them for managing your condition. The main regular check-ups are as follows:

Long-term blood glucose level Known as HbA1c, this level is taken as a percentage; ideally, it should be 6 per cent or below.

Blood pressure High blood pressure

increases the risk of coronary heart disease or stroke. Desirable blood pressure levels vary according to age, gender and the individual.

Blood fats Blood tests for fats or lipids check levels of cholesterol and triglycerides. These vary between individuals, but as a guide should be below 2.3mmol/litre for triglycerides and 5mmol/litre for cholesterol.

In addition to these three check-ups your cholesterol level and weight will be measured, and there will also be monitoring of your kidneys, eyes, feet, and a general "lifestyle" overview.

Proactive check-ups

Regular checks should be interactive: they are an opportunity for you to quiz the doctor. This applies whether you are the person with the condition or the carer of a diabetic child, parent or partner. Even if you feel your concerns are not urgent they should be dealt with, because ignoring possible problems could make them worse. Conversely, if you are really pleased with your control and monitoring, you may want to progress in some way or have ideas for improvements. You can make the most of your doctor's advice if you decide what you want to discuss before your check-up.

Go through any notes you have made since your last check-up and organize your thoughts and queries in advance. Define any problems and symptoms, including roughly when and why you were concerned and whether a problem has occurred more than once. Focus on facts.

Keeping notes

It's an excellent idea to keep a dedicated notebook to record useful information as you come across it, because it becomes personal: you don't have to search directories or information sources, you know that one book contains all the details you need, and it can become a real buddy. A neat little ring binder that you can carry around with you works well. Another way to keep a personal record is to keep a computer file into which you can download information and paste useful bits and pieces.

Diabetes information If you come across some interesting research, advice or treatment, write it down.

Personal queries Jot down points that are not urgent but you want to remember for your next check-up.

Food facts At first, you have to be absolutely honest about eating – with yourself and your healthcare team. We all kid ourselves about what we eat or drink at times, but with diabetes it is vital to know. Keeping a food diary does not have to be a weekly confession session, it is much better to make a note of what you eat when you eat it each day. Once the condition is stable and your diet is balanced, you will be able to abandon this.

Monitoring notes Keeping a checklist of your blood glucose levels, and any concerns you have, over a period of days will give you an idea of how controlled they are. You will be able to get advice at once or later at a routine check-up.

Ups and downs Notes about difficulties can give a perspective on problems, and provide a practical reference that you can check to see if you need professional help with any aspect of your everyday care. It's a good idea to make a note of the positive things too.

Eyes and feet Note any difficulties or concerns, temporary perhaps, if they are not sufficiently serious for immediate attention.

Exercise or weight review If you want to increase your exercise levels in the long term, or find weight control difficult, note why and how.

Lifestyle changes If you are moving house, travelling, getting married, planning a family, going through a rough patch in your relationship, or contemplating any event that may affect your diabetes control, make a note to find out whether you should adjust your treatment or goals.

Keeping a regular record of queries or problems is useful for when you next have a check-up.

Maintaining your blood glucose level

Achieving good diabetes control is about having balanced blood glucose levels, which may involve insulin and/or drug control, eating well and getting to grips with exercise. Blood glucose levels and the benefits of control have been the subjects of much research in the UK and USA. Balancing your blood glucose avoids the adverse effects of high and low levels, but it is not only about coping on a day-to-day basis. It is also essential for long-term health, reducing the risk of illnesses such as heart disease, stroke, atherosclerosis, kidney disease, loss of eyesight and neuropathy. This is why your healthcare team will provide realistic goals for blood glucose levels and why it is so important for you to understand them.

Blood glucose measurements

The amount of glucose in the blood is usually expressed either as millimoles per litre (mmol/litre) or as milligrams per decilitre (mg/dl). You should follow the system used by your healthcare team and the monitoring equipment they

You might find it easier to test your blood glucose level with a glucometer.

recommend or provide, but it is useful to know that different measures exist as there is so much information available and it is important not to misinterpret.

The blood glucose level varies according to the time of day and food intake. For example, it is lower first thing in the morning and higher after a meal has been digested. For someone without diabetes it may be around 5mmol/litre (90mg/dl) before breakfast, rising to about 8mmol/litre (144mg/dl) after a meal. For diabetes control, the aim is usually to keep the level between 4–6mmol/litre (72–108mg/dl) and no higher than 10mmol/litre (180mg/dl) within 1–2 hours of eating a meal.

Long-term blood glucose

Over the life of red blood cells, molecules of glucose gradually attach to haemoglobin molecules to form glycosylated (or glycated) haemoglobin. The HbA1c test is used to assess the percentage of such molecules, which reflect the average level of glucose in the blood over the previous few weeks. As a guide, non-diabetics normally show a range of 4–6 per cent glycosylated haemoglobin. For anyone with diabetes, the general aim is to

---

DEFINITIONS
Millimole One thousandth of a mole, a unit of measure that relates to molecular weight. When used to measure blood glucose, 1mmol/litre equals 18mg/dl.
Fasting blood glucose The level of glucose measured in the morning, before breakfast, and 12 hours after a light meal.
Preprandial blood glucose The level before a meal.
Postprandial blood glucose The level two hours after a meal.

---

keep the HbA1c level to 7 per cent or lower. What is important is that if the initial percentage is high, subsequent testing shows a downward progress over time. Seeing the percentage reducing is a sign of improvement and better blood glucose control.

A high blood glucose level, typically above 10mmol/litre (180 mg/dl), is known as hyperglycaemia. The symptoms are like those experienced before diabetes is diagnosed, including blurred vision, thirst, lethargy and urinary infection. Severe

Strip kits for urine testing use colour to detect the presence of ketones.

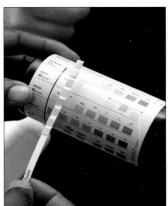

If your blood glucose levels drop you may find taking glucose tablets useful.

hyperglycaemia leads to confusion and slurred speech, so the person may appear to those around them to be drunk. You may not immediately be aware that your blood glucose level is high, and this is why regular self-monitoring is important.

Diabetic ketoacidosis (DKA)

If you have to use insulin to control your diabetes, hyperglycaemia that is not reversed can lead to ketoacidosis. This problem can arise if you are ill or off your food, when you may miss an insulin injection or think you do not need it. All cellular function in the body uses some energy, so anyone on insulin must continue to take it even though they may not be eating normally.

When glucose is not available from the blood, the body seeks an emergency supply of energy and begins to break down fat. Ketones or ketone bodies are acidic by-products of the digestion of fat, which are passed out of the body in urine and also as a gas through the lungs. They have a characteristic, slightly fruity smell, which can be detected on the breath (although not everyone is aware of the odour). As the body tries to dilute the ketones, you urinate more and become dehydrated. The skin may become dry and you may vomit and hyperventilate. This is an emergency and insulin is

needed as soon as possible. If it is not given, a diabetic coma will result.

Ketone testing strips are available to check the urine for the presence of ketones, and should be used if there are any symptoms of ketoacidosis. The emergency contact in your diabetes support team should be notified, or the doctor called. If this is not possible, you should go to the nearest hospital emergency department.

Hyperosmolar nonketotic state

This disorder may be experienced by people with Type 2 diabetes, and usually arises if you are ill with an infection and not getting enough fluid. It does not usually lead to ketone build-up in the urine but it is still a serious condition that can lead to diabetic coma if the symptoms – increased urination, thirst, feeling sick, dehydration and, eventually, drowsiness – are ignored.

Hypoglycaemia

The opposite of hyperglycaemia, this condition arises when the blood glucose level is too low. It is referred to as a "hypo" and it is important that the early symptoms are recognized. A hypo can occur if a meal is missed, insulin treatment is not stabilized or the wrong dose has been injected by accident, or too much alcohol has been consumed. Unexpected physical activity, such as dashing for a train, can also lead to a hypo. At night, a hypo can occur if the blood glucose level falls too low during sleep, resulting in a restless night and headache on waking.

Hypo symptoms These may include hunger, dizziness, trembling, sweating, palpitations, paleness, drowsiness, lack of concentration, confusion or aggression. The hypo may lead to loss of consciousness and, ultimately, fits. The symptoms vary and it is important that you learn to recognize your own early symptoms so that you can take glucose in time.

Treatment Glucose tablets, honey, a glass of fruit juice or a glucose drink

Fruit juice or a glucose drink will help to balance low blood glucose.

should be taken. If the symptoms do not subside within 15 minutes, repeat the treatment. Once the symptoms subside you should eat a more substantial snack, such as a sandwich.

If you are with someone who is experiencing a hypo, they may become drowsy or confused and may need encouragement to drink. Honey or Hypostop, a special glucose gel, can be rubbed on the gums and inside the cheek in an emergency. But don't give food or drink to someone who is unconscious as they may choke. Emergency medical assistance must be called if they lose consciousness.

Make sure that family, friends or colleagues know how to recognise or cope with a hypo.

BLOOD GLUCOSE CHECKLIST
- What are my blood glucose goals?
- How many times a day should I check my blood glucose level?
- What's my HbA1c – can I improve it?
- What are my early warning hypo symptoms?
- What are my emergency glucose supplies and where are they?
- Do those around me know how to cope with a hypo?

Medication: vital and individual

Many people with Type 2 diabetes control their condition by diet and exercise alone. Some take drugs that help to control their insulin, others may have to inject insulin. People with Type 1 diabetes need to take insulin every day. Medication is worked out to suit individual requirements – what the body needs to fit in with your lifestyle. Stabilizing diabetes is about getting treatment that balances your daily and long-term needs; it is not a one-off solution, as normal life phases will introduce changes that probably mean the medication needs modifying. Also, medication and delivery methods are always under review.

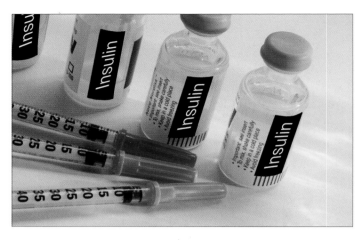

Insulin
Your insulin may be of animal origin (derived from cows or pigs) or "human", meaning it is synthesized using a bacterium, yeast or animal base and human cells. The types available vary in different localities and the many forms and combinations do not act in the same way on everyone. Suitable types, mix and dosages are prescribed to optimize individual control.

Insulin is usually classified by the length of time it takes to act. This includes the speed with which it is absorbed into the system, the duration of effect and the peak period for effectiveness. The type and number of injections a day are individual. For example, some people inject before meals with short-acting insulin and at night with an intermediate type, while others may rely on medium-, intermediate- or long-acting insulin as the basis for control. Different patterns of injections may be needed for different days. This is not as complicated as it sounds, and once you are familiar with your own patterns of activity and eating you will become aware of your insulin needs and be able to anticipate changes easily.

Rapid-acting insulin This works within 5–15 minutes and the effects last for about 2–5 hours. It is taken before meals and is usually complemented by a type that acts more slowly to control blood glucose levels between meals.

Short-acting insulin This is slower to take effect but still lowers blood glucose relatively quickly and may be taken 15–30 minutes before a meal. Its effects can last for up to 8 hours, peaking at between 2–6 hours.

The front of the thigh is a typical area for injecting insulin.

The type, mix and dose of insulin will be tailored to your individual needs.

Medium- and long-acting insulin
These may not be absorbed as quickly but are effective for longer periods, sometimes up to 24 hours or more. They may be most effective 4–12 hours after they are taken.

Insulin mixtures Prepared insulin mixtures include various types that act at different rates, for example to take effect before a meal and continue to work for some time afterwards. Some people mix their own insulin.

Insulin check
Short-acting insulin is clear, medium- and long-acting insulin is cloudy. Check your insulin carefully and never contaminate one type with another. When you have a repeat prescription, check that you have received the right product. Do not use insulin that looks unusual – if it is cloudy or has areas of cloudiness when it should be clear, or if cloudy insulin looks uneven.

Injecting
You will be shown how and where to inject. Insulin is injected under the skin, not into muscle or a blood vessel, so it is important to get the depth right. The

abdomen, thigh or buttocks are typical areas but some people inject in the arm. Do not inject in the same place all the time as this may lead to soreness, tough skin, or lumpy fat under the skin. Insulin may be effective more quickly when injected in some places; your healthcare team will help you with this.

Syringes Syringes and needles are usually disposable. The needles come in different lengths.

Pens These have disposable needles that can be changed when blunt. Some pens have replaceable cartridges while others are disposed of when the contents are used. The dose volume is selected before giving the injection. Carry a spare pen in case one breaks.

Auto-injectors These are spring-loaded syringes or pens that insert the needle into the skin, and are suitable for people who worry about injecting.

Needle-free injector This device uses a precision nozzle rather than a needle. A fine stream of insulin is forced through with enough power to penetrate the skin. The advantage is that there is no needle involved; the disadvantage is that it is not as discreet as a syringe.

Insulin pump

A pump delivers a pre-determined amount of insulin continuously, in a process known as continuous subcutaneous insulin infusion (CSII).

Discuss any possible complementary medicines with your doctor before use.

Typically, it is a small battery-operated device that can be strapped to the arm or attached to a belt. A line goes from it to a needle or fine tube in the skin, which has a cover for use when the pump is disconnected. The amount of insulin delivered does not change unless a new level is set, so frequent monitoring is important.

The pump is worn constantly but it can be disconnected for relatively short periods of time. Whether a pump is suitable or not depends on the individual. It is a relatively expensive system and may need more attention than regular injections.

Oral medication

With Type 2 diabetes, the aim is to control blood glucose levels by diet, exercise and weight management. If the blood glucose is very high at first, or it is hard to change your lifestyle sufficiently, tablets may be prescribed.

• Sulphonylureas (sulfonylureas) boost insulin production; they may also increase the body's ability to use insulin.

• Biguanides reduce sugar absorption from gut to bloodstream and reduce the release of glucose from stored glycogen in the liver; they also encourage uptake of glucose from the blood into the cells.

• Alpha-glucosidase inhibitors inhibit the digestion of sugars.

Remembering to take the right tablets at the right time of day is important, as the medication is planned to work with meals and activity. Sulphonylureas, for example, can increase the level of insulin enough to cause a hypo if taken incorrectly.

Whenever you have to take additional medication (prescribed or "over the counter"), check with your healthcare team that it will not disrupt your diabetes control. If you do have to take other medication, a pill plan is essential to keep track of what you have taken, and when. Special containers are available for organizing tablets by day and time. A chart with tick boxes showing what to take and when works for some, and can be specially helpful for older people, or those caring for them.

Everyone feels fed up about their condition occasionally, but it's not helpful to fixate on the number of tablets you need to swallow every day. Getting miserable makes it worse, asking for help makes it work.

Complementary therapies, remedies and supplements

Any complementary treatment, including herbal remedies and supplements, must be discussed in advance with the doctor. Although some may be beneficial, others (or extremely high doses) may interfere with insulin production or the body's receptiveness, or disrupt the balance of medication or insulin dosage. For example, fish oil capsules can raise blood glucose levels, and very high doses of thiamine (vitamin B1) or vitamin C can disrupt insulin activity.

Complementary therapies can assist in some ways but may disrupt the metabolism. Doctors are aware of the benefits and possible adverse effects of such treatments. An experienced therapist would be aware of the need to work with the medical team but it is important to consult your doctor first before additional treatments are used.

Potential complications

Uncontrolled diabetes results in severe complications, and it is best to understand and acknowledge this from the start. The good thing is that the complications are avoidable. We all make everyday choices to stay safe without even thinking about it – we do not knowingly put ourselves in life-threatening situations. In the same way, adopting a positive attitude to diabetes management soon becomes second nature. The information on these pages highlights why it is so very important to make this effort and never to feel that it is not worth it.

Atherosclerosis

This condition, in which a fatty plaque builds up on the inner walls of blood vessels, is often compared to the way water pipes "fur up" as mineral deposits build up inside them in hard water areas: the rough white scale gradually becomes thicker over the years, until in old pipes there is very little space left for water to pass through.

Having diabetes does not mean that you have to eat differently to others.

Cholesterol is necessary in the right amounts to build and maintain cell membranes, and is manufactured by the body. However, excess cholesterol can gradually be deposited around the inside of the blood vessels, making them rough and encouraging further deposits to build up. This reduces the space available for blood to pass through, increasing the pressure. The build up and pressure can damage the blood vessels. Bits of the deposit can subsequently break away from the walls and cause blockages. Depending on where a blockage occurs, it can cause a stroke or heart attack.

Uncontrolled diabetes increases the likelihood of developing atherosclerosis. Eating a well-balanced diet and exercising helps to keep the blood cholesterol level down and thus helps to reduce the chances of developing atherosclerosis.

High blood pressure

Hypertension, or high blood pressure, increases the chances of heart attack, stroke and the other complications that are associated with uncontrolled

NO SMOKING

As well as controlling blood glucose, it is vital not to smoke. Smoking damages and kills the body, and it is especially bad for anyone with diabetes. Look at the list of potential complications, put smoking into the equation and it is a package that adds up to sickness and premature death. Do not smoke. It smells disgusting, it will make you ill, and it will eventually kill you prematurely: all good reasons to give up. Seek all the help and support you need from your healthcare team, family, friends and work colleagues.

diabetes, including kidney failure, retinal blindness and neuropathy.

Both diet and lifestyle are influential in raising or lowering blood pressure. Exercise, in particular, is important – in combination with a balanced diet and relaxation – for improving general fitness and keeping blood pressure within healthy limits.

Coronary heart disease

Both atherosclerosis and raised blood pressure increase the chances of a heart attack. Eating a balanced diet and maintaining a healthy weight are important for a healthy heart, and so is the right sort of regular exercise. The heart is a muscle, and exercise builds up healthy, strong muscles as well as keeping blood glucose levels under control and reducing blood pressure. Cardiovascular exercise – the type that gets you moving and makes you warm (at least) or slightly sweaty, raises your

pulse rate and makes you a little bit out of breath – helps to build up the heart, gradually making it stronger and more powerful.

Retinal blindness or diabetic retinopathy

Rarely does anyone with diabetes become blind, but, sadly, it can happen. Not bothering to control diabetes, failing to have all the right checks or take care of the eyesight can lead to blindness. This is because the tiny blood vessels behind the eyes can become blocked or damaged; the body makes new vessels along the retina for blood supply, which can affect the eyesight. This does not happen suddenly, so regular eye tests and

checks mean that early signs can be detected before any symptoms are apparent. Keeping the blood glucose level under control is important to avoid this kind of deterioration and also to help avoid the formation of cataracts.

Kidney problems

Keeping blood glucose under control is important for healthy kidneys, to stop any damage that may have been caused increasing, and helping to maintain long-term health. Blood glucose levels that are out of control for many years can damage blood vessels in the kidneys in a progressive disease called diabetic nephropathy, which results in kidney failure.

Foot problems

Neuropathy is a loss of feeling in the extremities, which is particularly noticed in the feet. The loss of sensation may be very minor at first, starting with pins and needles and a lack of sensitivity, and most people do not realize they have a problem until the feet are checked for sensitivity. If the condition worsens, damage to the feet may go unnoticed: minor cuts or sores do not heal well, in-growing nails may be neglected, and relatively common infections can flourish uncontrolled.

If you have diabetes a foot examination will be part of your regular check-up, but it is also important to take good care of your feet: keep them clean, washed and dry. Wear cotton socks, tights or stockings that allow the feet to breathe, and change them at least daily. Wear comfortable shoes that are not too small and take care to avoid blisters. Keep your toenails short.

Regular exercise not only helps control blood glucose levels, it also helps to create a feeling of general wellbeing.

Take care of your feet: massage is beneficial and good for spotting any problems early on.

PROBLEMS WITH SEX

Impotence in men and difficulties with orgasm for women can be experienced by those with diabetes but there is no reason to live with these problems. Embarrassment often prevents sufferers from explaining their predicament to their doctor. It may help to realize that others have experienced similar difficulties and the team are used to treating the problem.

Sex is not a luxury but an important part of a healthy life, not necessarily in the style of media-hyped extravaganzas but as a feature of stable relationships, and the healthcare team are ready to deal with difficulties in normal sexual function.

LIMIT ALCOHOL

Alcohol is not banned, but it should be limited to occasional, small amounts, taken when eating meals. Binge drinking, or even regular drinking makes blood glucose control difficult and it can lead to severe problems.

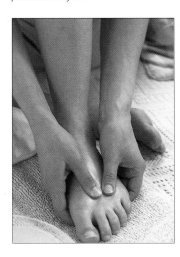

Childhood diabetes

While childhood diabetes is usually Type 1, there are increasing incidences of Type 2, which is linked with childhood obesity, poor diet and inactivity, and although the numbers are small, in percentage terms the recent increase is alarming. Specialized paediatric diabetes teams support children and their carers. From the first months and years of life through to adolescence, close and specific professional guidance is important: it should be sought and followed.

The aim is to bring up children with a positive, confident attitude to all aspects of diabetes, including the physical symptoms. As well as learning about the condition, injecting insulin and making healthy food choices the norm, they should be encouraged to interact with the professionals caring for them, tell everyone about their diabetes and enjoy an active lifestyle. Gradually, they have to learn about the effects of different types of pressures on the condition, including stress and strenuous exercise. It is essential that children and young people are not isolated or made to feel different because of their diabetes.

A dance class is a good way for children to enjoy sociable exercise.

Exercise

An active lifestyle is beneficial to everyone and essential for a youngster with diabetes. It helps to maintain a healthy weight as well as managing blood glucose. It is also fun. Playing, running about, playing ball and team games, dancing, skateboarding, cycling, rollerblading and so on are all exciting, sociable and fun. Encouraging children to take part and enjoy all sorts of activities with family and friends, in school and in clubs and groups, is the best foundation for future health. It will

Choose fun-filled types of exercise for children that they will treat as play.

also assist their social, work and physical development.

Don't force activities on your child but involve them in as many as you can as early as possible, then encourage them with the ones they enjoy. Being proficient and winning is important, but enjoying an activity is more important. Walking, cycling, garden games and outdoor family excursions will set the pattern from an early age. Sitting in front of a television or computer for hours on end does no good.

Diet

Babies, toddlers and young children with diabetes need to follow a healthy diet for growth and to provide sufficient energy resources for their frantic activity. Young children need a varied high-energy diet, with regular snacks and meals. Follow the dietician's advice and voice any concerns, no matter how minor they may seem, especially with babies and toddlers.

As babies are weaned and toddlers develop food preferences, this is the time to instil a taste for as wide a variety of foods as possible, avoiding a "sweet tooth". Rather than focusing on what cannot be eaten, this is an ideal age to develop and share a liking for good food. An inclusive, positive outlook helps, and the whole family should enjoy eating well (particularly siblings who may not have diabetes), not just the child. Everyone outside the family who looks after the child at any time should be aware of their condition and be prepared to help with the same positive outlook.

Choosing healthy food works only when the good options are readily available and attractively presented. Make it easy for your young child to pick the right food and encourage their peers to enjoy it as well.

Taking control of your child's pre-school diet is not as difficult as monitoring what is eaten once they have started school. This is why it is so important to nurture a sense of positive choice. Having diabetes does make a child different, and encouraging a positive approach to the right foods early on is important. Choice and personal decision work better than constant food bans. Getting the right perspective on confectionery and high-fat snacks is about perseverance and habit, as well as recognizing times (such as children's parties) when the boundaries have to be broadened.

Team responsibility

Children should be involved in their own diabetes management, and healthcare professionals will guide you through

Many children are quite happy eating a wide variety of fresh fruits every day.

this, making sure they are happy and confident with each step of responsibility they take for monitoring and injecting with supervision and support. You and your child are a team, working together to involve the rest of the family, friends, teachers and everyone else who needs to know about their condition.

Gradually, as with every other aspect of life, your child is being prepared for taking primary responsibility for their diabetes control. The balance between independence and having you check their diet, medication and monitoring is an important part of setting them up for life, not just until they leave home.

School and other organizations

Anyone who is responsible for your child for any period of time needs to know that they have diabetes: this includes playgroup leaders, teachers,

Homemade Prune and Chocolate cake makes a good occasional treat.

It is easy to hide wholefoods in standard family recipes such as Shepherd's Pie or homemade pizza.

activity leaders, the parents of your child's friends, and of course grandparents or other family members with whom they may stay. They should know about the child's routine, diet and medication, and should know the signs of a hypo and how to respond, as well as what to do in an emergency. They should be aware of where to find medication and emergency carbohydrate supplies, and who to contact and where.

While at school, your child must always have someone they can turn to for help, such as a class teacher or tutor, and they should be confident about asking all the other teachers. There must be somewhere for the child to inject insulin, if necessary. Snacks should be scheduled into the timetable, ideally during break times, but if your child has to eat during a lesson, the teacher should be aware of the reason.

Child support groups

Support groups for children and young people with diabetes are excellent. They provide opportunities to meet others of the same age with the condition, and swap information about monitoring and lifestyle. Such groups are a good way to show your child that there are lots of other young people out there with the same condition.

Children love risotto and it's a good source of slow-release carbohydrates.

Family meals are important for forming good eating habits early on in life.

Teenagers

Hormonal changes and the drive to be individual and independent make adolescence a phase of conflict and confusion for all young people, as they try to establish who they are. Diabetes control that may have been relatively straightforward in childhood can become difficult at this stage because of reduced activity or growth spurts, quite apart from issues of confidence or rebellion. If your child is newly diagnosed as a teenager, they may not welcome having to make adjustments to their lifestyle and may bottle up concerns about the future, all the while feeling run down and physically drained if the diagnosis has been delayed.

As a rule, boys develop in ways they find positive, but in some cases their weight gain can be unwelcome and often the embarrassment and rebelliousness of the phase makes relationships with parents fraught. The physical development of girls can be complicated. While they may enjoy appearing more grown up they have to learn to cope with menstruation, their changing body shape, and the hyper-thin female images in the mass media. For teenagers with diabetes this is a time for social and psychological guidance as well as practical diet and medication management. A trained counsellor will be part of the healthcare team and will help the young person gain confidence and establish their independence, learning, with your support, to take responsibility for the condition rather than rebel against it.

New home, new life

Leaving home presents new opportunities and circumstances that can throw diabetes out of control. Travelling, going to university, moving into a first home or setting up home with a partner are all typical scenarios. Developing a sense of responsibility for diabetes control as an adolescent prepares the young adult for living

Leaving home does not have to mean abandoning a healthy eating plan.

independently and taking the initiative with healthcare professionals. Plan ahead and consult with the healthcare team. From experience, they will highlight potential problems and how to avoid them or deal with them, especially when travelling. Establish contact with a new healthcare team, if necessary, or temporary professional contacts when travelling away from home for any length of time. Ensure that all records and details are passed on to, or available to, the new team before leaving, and find out about prescriptions and where and when to obtain medication.

Stress and lifestyle changes affect blood glucose, so be prepared for blips in control. Make sure flatmates, college tutors, travelling companions and new colleagues are aware of the diabetes. Good eating and exercise patterns need to be established early on.

RE-ESTABLISHING YOUR LIFE BALANCE

Starting university and/or moving in with a bunch of new friends of the same age puts a whole new set of pressures in place. It is important to have the social confidence and understanding to let everyone who matters know about your diabetes. Being an individual and establishing credibility with your peers is about confidence – especially on the social scene.

The healthcare team are aware of the effects this social pressure can have, and will help you prepare for it. Drugs, binge drinking, bad diet, lack of exercise, a disregard for good blood glucose control and missing regular diabetes checks can wreck your life. Self-esteem and a positive view of the future provide the motivation for a balanced approach.

Diabetes as an adult

Type 2 diabetes usually develops in those over 35. Its onset is gradual and it is associated with excess weight, poor diet and lack of exercise, although these are not the only criteria. The aim is to control the condition by diet and lifestyle, which usually means making significant changes to patterns of eating and behaviour. Changes in diet and lifestyle include:

• Looking at food and eating in a new way, and changing meal patterns.
• Trying new ingredients and developing different styles of cooking.
• Changing drinking habits.
• Giving up smoking.
• Making time for walking or cycling instead of always using the car.
• Finding out about being active, and overcoming the first difficult stages.
• Maintaining a positive outlook for the future and enlisting the support of family, friends and contacts.

Pregnancy and diabetes

Diabetes may develop temporarily during pregnancy, when it is referred to as gestational diabetes. It must be monitored closely and the woman should be checked after the pregnancy to make sure her blood glucose has returned to normal. Temporary diabetes during pregnancy can be a warning that she will develop Type 2 diabetes later, so likely symptoms should be checked.

Planning a pregnancy

Anyone with diabetes who is planning to become pregnant should talk to their healthcare team well in advance and get their blood glucose as well balanced as possible, make sure they are eating an excellent diet, and get as fit as possible. Professional guidance pays off for mother and baby, especially for the long-term health and diabetes control of the mother.

Diabetic pregnancy

If you have diabetes you must tell your doctor at once if you become pregnant. It may mean changing your existing

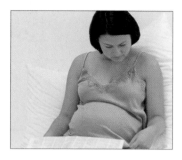

Women who develop diabetes during pregnancy will be monitored closely.

medication or going on to insulin as your blood glucose levels may fluctuate widely. Close monitoring should continue while you are breastfeeding. Babies born to mothers with diabetes may be larger than normal but they do not necessarily have diabetes, and they are usually healthy and normal.

Diabetes in the elderly

Some people develop diabetes at a stage when it is difficult to be motivated to change eating patterns or activity levels, and their reaction often impacts on their partner or carer. A spouse who takes most of the responsibility for cooking may suffer the bad temper of a partner who is loath to amend their eating habits. "Secret eating" is not uncommon, especially among those who live alone, and in this case getting an accurate account of eating habits can be a problem for the health team.

Regular yoga classes are a great way for older people to maintain fitness.

Developing a positive approach

Diabetes is not a hindrance to being active, maintaining weight balance, and feeling energetic and good. It won't stop you from doing anything. For many, the main difficulty is deciding to change and actually doing it. The healthcare team take charge at first, with tests, drugs, diet advice and a weight review. As they gradually hand over responsibility, controlling the condition for the rest of your life means moving from short-term coping to a practical plan for your long-term health and wellbeing. This is about building the confidence and mental strength to maintain control. There is significant contemporary research into diabetes from the psychological angle, especially since individuals are being given more responsibility for controlling their condition. A good attitude is vital. Express your feelings and seek help to develop a positive mental outlook.

Most people experience a range of reactions influenced by personal circumstances, character and outlook. Some they may talk about, others they may find too embarrassing to discuss. Feeling "targeted" or let down in some way, finding the diagnosis hugely unfair and trying to lay blame for the condition are all common responses.

It is easy to find links between illness or stress and the onset of diabetes. Those who have a long-standing problem with weight, lack of exercise and "unhealthy" eating may blame themselves, especially if they are run down and experiencing low self-esteem. This is futile and is also inaccurate: rarely does someone in a normal "healthy" state of mind adopt a lifestyle in order to cause ill health.

Young people may blame a parent who has diabetes. They are not being nasty, simply trying to understand why they have it, but this may be hurtful to the parent. Carers may feel responsible for the way they have fed an elderly relative, or for having an overweight child who is diagnosed with diabetes.

Anger and resentment

There may be an initial angry reaction, mixed with sadness and worry. Anger and resentment build up before there is any sense of control, especially when taking control is not easy. Going over what the diagnosis means – the assessments and appointments – and coming to terms with the commitment needed, while wondering whether it is possible to achieve results, can lead to irritation and general bad temper.

Worry, panic and fear

It is easy to start worrying about the long-term implications of diabetes for special occasions, such as holidays or major lifestyle changes. Being afraid of what the future holds is normal but many who have diabetes may not want to admit to this because, having got through the first stages and taken control, it seems silly to have been so frightened at first. Everyone worries about something, so tell someone. Bottling up concerns, unshared, makes them seem much worse than they are.

Denial

There may be a sense of denial when diabetes is first diagnosed, especially with Type 2 diabetes. Someone who is not on medication but follows a diet to control the condition can drift from the regime after a while, dismissing the problem as a temporary "blip". A sense of responsibility makes someone conform to new guidelines at first, then lose motivation and get rather fed up with the whole thing. Instead of acknowledging that the blood glucose and symptoms are controlled because of the changes, it is easier to pretend the symptoms will not return. For those who are reluctant to accept change, the diet may deteriorate, or secret eating may become a problem.

Rebellion

Fighting against the few essential restrictions may be linked with denial, especially when there is a carer involved who encourages good eating. In some ways addressing the problem of outright rebellion can be more straightforward than persuading someone to face up to the fact that they are in denial. Help is especially important when the person's relationship with their partner or carer seems to be in jeopardy.

The continuing support of a partner you can talk to is vital for developing and maintaining a positive outlook.

SECRET EATING

Changing your shopping patterns and not buying the bad food means the whole household will benefit. Secret eating can start with one covert treat but once it is established it is difficult to stop. Admitting to it is the first task, and replacing "bad" treats with good alternatives is the second. If you are a carer who suspects or knows that someone is eating secretly, you'll find that direct confrontation usually leads to denial. Instead, suggest gently that they may have had a one-off treat and then build up to getting them to admit to regular secret eating. Making treats part of the regime may be necessary if someone really cannot live without them. This way they can be balanced. However, secret eating may have more to do with rebellion. Elderly people who lose some independence through physical limitations may eat because it is something they can still do on their own. Try to re-establish their sense of control and help them regain responsibility.

Proactive and positive control

Taking responsibility helps to sort out your problems and allows you to let go of those negative feelings. A "can do" approach means searching for information and leads to a positive outlook now and in the future. It gets rid of blame. The past cannot be changed, but the future can be good.

Follow the guidelines you are given closely at first. As the weeks and months pass, the regime will become natural and successful individual interpretation is easier. Here are a few ways that you can take control.
• Get used to taking exercise, and prioritize time for activity.
• Try a bit of careful strength training to tone up your muscles.
• Find new foods that taste terrific.

• Examine your drinking habits.
• Take pride in having good-looking feet – no matter how lumpy and bumpy the rest of your body feels.
• You have more control than you realize. Once you understand that you can change what happens for the good, confidence increases and encourages a proactive approach. Your growing inner strength supports your healthy lifestyle.

Understanding stress

One reaction to stress is the "fight or flight response". Among other things, heart rate increases, blood is diverted from the essential organs to the muscles, digestion is inhibited and blood glucose levels are raised as the brain sends signals that enable the release of stored energy supplies. This is a fundamental biological reaction to stress as a physical threat, so the body automatically prepares itself for fighting an enemy or running away. In reality, the source of stress may be an exam, a fraught supermarket trip, a traffic jam or a sudden major worry about what the future holds. Such events are not usually resolved by a burst of physical activity to use up the blood glucose, so stress upsets blood glucose control. Chronic stress is bad for everyone

Allowing time for relaxation is an important part of a healthy lifestyle.

Listen to your body and allow yourself to take a rest when necessary.

because of the negative effects it has on the cardiovascular system, possibly leading to high blood pressure and heart disease. Short-term stress is also bad for anyone with diabetes because it raises the blood glucose level. Talk to your healthcare team about dealing with stress. It may mean adjusting your medication when coping with a stressful event, and being ready for swings in blood glucose levels.

All types of exercise help to relieve the symptoms of stress.

medication all contribute. Depression is not usually due to one thing but the result of a series of events over time, but one minor difficulty can finally trigger a sense of hopelessness and an inability to carry on.

The healthcare team will provide solutions to your practical problems and talk through difficulties. Getting through depression is about finding positive thoughts, taking each negative aspect and finding a positive solution or at least a neutral alternative thought. Talking about problems and/or writing them down are good ways of sorting them out. Instead of bottling up fears and frustrations, tell someone you trust. Share your feelings with your family and listen to their opinions. Alternatively, a good friend can often see a solution or understand feelings that an immediate relative is too close to notice.

When there seems to be so many overwhelming negative issues they can connect into a destructive mental net that gets smaller and tighter, preventing you from looking outwards. Listing individual problems separates them, opens the net, moves it away and breaks it down. This allows space to look outwards, consider solutions and find positive thoughts. Gradually the negative net loosens its hold.

Physical activity is an excellent antidote to negative thoughts. It also has the double value of being hugely helpful for controlling blood glucose levels. It addresses the impact of stress in the short term and provides long-term goals that will help to create a positive outlook.

Learning to relax

Progressive muscle relaxation can be helpful in any situation, especially when lying awake at night. It involves focusing on a positive thought to divert the mind from the worry – music, a radio in the background or a memory of a happy occasion work well. At the same time, tense and relax the muscles, working from the feet to the top of the head. Start with the toes, tensing and curling them, then "shaking them out" by wiggling them; then tense and relax the feet, flexing them and stretching them; work on the ankles; then the calf muscles; move up to the knees, thighs, hips, abdomen, chest and so on. The trick is to concentrate on the muscles. If the mind wanders, bring it back by focusing on the background positive thought and then re-focus on the muscles. This moves the mind on from the original source of stress. This is a relatively easy technique to learn, and once you've cracked it, it is a great way to relax. Many people who use it at night never progress beyond their knees before falling asleep.

Relaxing from toe to head is not practical in a traffic jam or supermarket queue, but the same technique can be used on one particular group of muscles, such as your hands, feet or buttocks. There are many different techniques and the psychologist with your healthcare team will help you find one that suits you.

Depression

Everyone feels a bit miserable at times, but there is a difference between "feeling down" and clinical depression. Depression is an overwhelming sense of helplessness and hopelessness, feeling that there is nothing good about the past, the present or the future, and not being able to see a way forward. Symptoms include feeling tired, sleeping too much or, conversely, not being able to sleep. Complete lack of motivation for any activity, being tearful and not feeling able to get on with life are signs of depression.

Being diagnosed with diabetes can trigger depression. Difficulties with weight and lifestyle changes and taking

---

DEAR DIARY
Keep a diary to record the good things and offload the bad bits. It doesn't have to be a daily record, but making a habit of writing means it is there to give vent to your frustrations or fears.

Feel-good fitness

Regular activity is important for everyone and especially valuable in diabetes control. Everyone who has ever had real weight problems will appreciate the impossibility of controlling weight (in the long term) by diet alone. Eating less is not easy but exercising more is. The most difficult part is getting into the routine – one activity session is relatively easy but carrying on for a month is the challenge. Finally, it becomes a habit, and you begin to miss it if you don't do any: success!

Benefits of exercise

Activity makes you feel good and happy (because the body releases endorphins, the feel-good hormones) and in the long term it has real health benefits:
• Reduced risk of coronary heart disease and heart attack
• Improved muscle, joint and bone health (reduced risk of osteoporosis)
• Better mobility, balance and flexibility
• Improved brain activity, including memory, motor skills and coordination.

This is understandable when you break the benefits down and realize that exercise promotes the following:
• Reduced blood pressure

• Reduced resting heart rate
• Improved circulation
• Improved oxygen uptake and supply
• Better muscle strength and posture
• Lower cholesterol levels
• Increased metabolic rate, improving long-term weight control
• Lower stress and increased relaxation
• An improved self image.

Everyone who has discovered fitness as the alternative to being overweight will describe the vitality and sense of wellbeing that develops. Confidence, determination, a sense of achievement and increased resilience to everyday problems are also real benefits. In addition exercise helps to improve insulin sensitivity and regulate blood glucose levels.

Exercise or activity?

Activity refers to daily movement, such as walking around the garden or up stairs, cleaning or shopping. Exercise usually describes specific times set aside to "be active", this may include walking, sport or activity programmes.

At least 30 minutes moderate aerobic activity every day is a starting point. This could be a brisk walk or a swim, ideally taken in one go but two or three separate sessions can be added up over a day.

Individual levels

Exercise is individual and you need to be honest with yourself about how active (or inactive) you are. It is important to build up slowly. The body should get warm and then a little sweaty. You should be able to talk while exercising: that should make you a little puffy, but when being slightly breathless turns to gasping, the exercise is too fierce. On the other hand, if you are swinging along without even noticing it, you are not improving your fitness.

From inactivity, working up to 30–40 minutes moderate activity a day is a

Exercise must be enjoyable, selecting the right activity for you is important.

Everyday exercise does not have to be frantic; brisk walking is excellent.

start. Moving on means aiming for 40 minutes focused cardiovascular exercise, in one go, five days a week. As the exercise becomes easier, increase the intensity to make it a little more difficult, for example by walking faster or uphill. This is the only way to get fitter.

Cardiovascular exercise

Aerobic, cardiovascular (CV) or cardio-respiratory exercise increases the heart rate and respiratory rate: in other words it gets your blood pumping and makes you breathe a little harder. It's defined as using the large muscle groups in regular rhythmic movement, and walking is the basic example as long as it is fast enough to get your system working a little harder than usual. For someone elderly or who has been seriously inactive, a gentle walk may be enough at first. Gradually lengthening the time or distance will improve fitness.

Walking Cut out car journeys to the shops, work or school. Walk up and down stairs instead of using the lift, and walk up escalators.

Swimming and aqua fitness classes Water helps to support the body and reduce pressure on joints while building up aerobic fitness, so it is excellent for someone who is very overweight or has joint problems.

Jogging In the gym or outside, this is excellent for burning fat and getting fit, but wear the right trainers and work up slowly to build muscle strength.

Cycling Use a bicycle for transport, or take rides with the family for pleasure.

Skipping Starting gently and working up from 1 minute, this can be fun, especially as part of a mixed routine.

Dancing Go to a class, go out dancing with friends or dance at home.

Around the house Mowing the lawn, washing the car, dusting, polishing, brushing and vacuum cleaning are all good aerobic exercises.

Strength for support

Building up your muscles is important, especially if you are overweight. Extra

Dancing is fun, enlivening and good excercise; do it alone or with others.

weight puts a lot of strain on the joints, especially when you are moving. Strengthening the muscles helps to relieve this, which is important before increasing the intensity of your aerobic exercise programme.

Muscle strength is also important for good posture and balance at all ages. Having good core strength – a strong girdle of muscles around the abdomen – makes it easier to improve agility, the ability to move and change direction quickly without losing balance or injuring joints. This is important for sport, exercise or any everyday activity.

Stretching

Flexibility promotes good posture and agility and helps to avoid injury, and everyone should stretch to improve or maintain their flexibility. Muscles work by tensing, becoming shorter in length to pull a load (such as a leg or arm). When they have been through a bit of a workout, they should be stretched gently again.

Warming up, cooling down

Whatever level you exercise at, it is important to warm up. Warming up lubricates joints, circulates blood to provide oxygen to the muscles and gently stretches the body into activity. It raises the heart rate slowly, avoiding any shocks to the system.

Cooling down keeps the blood flowing so that the pulse rate and breathing slowly return to normal. Stopping suddenly after exercise – lying down after a hard run – can briefly deprive the brain of blood, causing dizziness. Keeping the arms moving, walking on the spot or other gentle

No sport is excluded, and you should choose an activity that you enjoy.

Swimming is gentle on the body and an excellent form of aerobic exercise, it is particularly good for anyone who is overweight or unfit, or during pregnancy.

activity keeps the heart pumping blood around the body as it returns to normal.

The fitter you become, the faster you warm up, but take it very easy at first, allowing 10 minutes of gentle warm-up activity before upping the pace.

Aerobic exercise routine
Here's a simple routine to get you started at home: the more strenuous exercises are alternated with easier, less intensive ones. If you have not been moving about much and feel stiff, gently stretch and move your body to mobilize all your joints towards the end of your warm-up. Time your session and have some music to motivate you.

Try this programme three days a week at first, doing 30 minutes walking or other gentle exercise on the other days. Gradually work up to using the programme on five days and walking on two days. Work at your own pace – if walking up and down stairs smartly makes you slightly breathless, do it just once and increase it after two weeks or when you are slightly fitter; if you cannot complete 5 minutes of each exercise, start with 3 minutes instead, then increase it.

Warm-up
5 minutes walk
5 minutes gentle march
Cardiovascular exercise
2 x walking up a flight of stairs quite smartly, then straight back down
5 minutes stepping
5 minutes marching

5 minutes side-stepping
2 minutes jogging or skipping
5 minutes marching
2 minutes jogging or skipping
5 minutes stepping
2 x walk up stairs quite smartly, then straight back down
Cool-down
5 minutes walk

Strengthening exercises
When you have increased your general fitness with the routine above, add some specific exercises to strengthen and develop your muscles. The following exercises will begin to strengthen muscles in the lower body and arms. Add them to your workout three times a week, on alternate days after aerobic exercise and before core stability exercises.

Calf raises Stand facing a wall with your feet hip-width apart. Steady yourself with the fingers of one hand against the wall. Keeping your stomach and buttocks tight, and your legs straight (but don't lock the knees), rise on to the balls of your feet, then lower on to your heels again. Repeat slowly 10–12 times.

Squats Stand with your feet hip-width apart, stomach tight. Hold your arms in front, hands together in front of your chest. Lower your bottom to just about sitting position, keeping your back straight, then stand up again. Repeat 10–12 times. If you are afraid of falling

Becoming physically fitter will also increase your levels of wellbeing.

over, lower yourself almost on to a chair without quite sitting down. This is good for the thighs and bottom.

Biceps curls Hold a dumbbell or weight. Stand with your feet hip-width apart, stomach tight. Hold your arm at your side, with your elbow slightly away from your body (not resting against it) and lift your hand to your shoulder, palm up. Keep the upper body still – the elbow will move slightly, but don't swing your upper arm as this makes the exercise easier. Feel it down the front of your upper arm. Repeat 10–12 times on each arm.

Triceps extensions Holding a dumbbell, lift your hand straight up in the air slightly to the front of your head. Bend your arm at the elbow, dropping your hand behind your back. Straighten and lower your arm in this way 10–12 times. Feel it down the back of your upper arm. Repeat with the other arm.

Chest fly Sit in an upright chair with your back supported. With a dumbbell in each hand, hold your arms out to your sides at chest height, with elbows very slightly bent. Bring your hands together in front of your chest, then take them back. Repeat 10–12 times. Try to clench your chest muscles as you do this, keep your stomach tight and bottom well back into the chair.

Core stability

These exercises strengthen the abdominal muscles. Getting them right is all about technique – the movement is very small, especially at first when the muscles are not very strong. Use an exercise mat to protect your back.

Abdominal curls Lie with your lower back and bottom firmly against the floor, with feet hip-width apart, knees bent and apart, arms at your sides, palms upward.

Tailor your exercise to your flexibility and strength, use support when you need it, and rest if you begin to feel weary.

1 Look up at the ceiling and focus on one point.
2 Gently lift your upper body off the floor, leading with your shoulders and chest. The lift is very small. You should feel the muscles working around your belly button.
3 Lower your shoulders. Repeat slowly 10–12 times.

Your bottom should remain on the floor. If you lift your head and shoulders too far and begin to curl them towards your stomach, you stop working the stomach muscles and start to use the lower back and chest. Persevere with small lifts – it is the way to get results.

If you feel your neck tightening, relax and gently move your head from side to side, with chin to chest. As you do the exercise, try to relax your neck and allow your head to follow on, rather than straining to support it.

When you feel ready to take abdominal curls to the next level, add the following:
1 Hold your hands to your temples, elbows to the sides – this adds a little weight to your upper body, making the lift slightly harder.
2 Extend your arms behind your head, hands together – this adds more length, making the lift harder still. Don't try it until you can happily complete

three sets of 12–15 repetitions with hands by temples.

Oblique curls This is a four-stage movement, nominally higher than abdominal curls, which works the muscles around the side of the stomach. Lie with lower back and bottom firmly against the floor, with feet hip-width apart, knees bent and apart, arms at your sides, palms upward.
1 Gently lift your upper body off the floor, leading with your shoulders and chest as before.
2 Twist the upper body very slightly to one side, curving from the stomach to the shoulders, so that you are looking to one side.
3 Return to the straight position.
4 Lower the upper body back to the floor. Repeat, alternating sides.

Your bottom should remain on the floor. The lift and twist should be separate movements: pause when you have lifted and after returning to the straight posture. Do not twist too much.

HOW TO DO THE EXERCISES
Walking on the spot: lift the feet and swing the arms at your sides. Marching on the spot: lift the knees, bend the elbows, and use the arms.
Stepping: step on to the bottom stair or a step with one foot then the other, then step back down, leading with the same foot. Keep going in time to music.
Side-stepping: move the right foot to the right, then stamp the left foot next to it; move the left foot to the left, then stamp the right foot next to it. Keep going, swinging your arms rhythmically.
Jogging on the spot: use your arms with elbows bent and tucked at your side; keep knees soft, use heel-to-toe stepping as you put your feet down.
Skipping: use a running action at first and progress to jumping with both feet when you are fitter.

back but do not force it (hold your trainer laces if you can't get your hand around your foot). Put your foot on a stool if you can't lift it very high.

Back stretch Stand with your feet hip-width apart, stomach tight and knees slightly soft. Extend your arms with your hands meeting in front of your chest. Think of "hugging a tree" to get the posture right. Draw your shoulders forward, staying upright and tucking in the base of the spine.

Chest stretch Stand with your feet hip-width apart, stomach tight and knees slightly soft. Place your hands on your bottom, palms facing out. Squeeze your elbows together and feel the stretch across the chest.

Back of arms Bend your arm at the elbow and take your hand over the opposite shoulder. For a more difficult stretch, lift your arm straight up above your head, then bend it back at the shoulder taking your hand behind your back. Support your upper arm with your other hand.

The lunge is good for toning up thighs and bottom.

Once you have developed your fitness you will feel more confident about expanding your exercise regime with organized classes of various kinds.

Back extensions

This exercise is for the muscles in the lower back.
1 Lie face down on the floor, arms at your sides with palms up. Relax your feet on their sides.
2 Gently lift your upper body off the floor very slightly. The lift is from the lower back and it should be very small.
3 Hold briefly then lower the shoulders gently. Repeat 10–12 times.
   Your back should be straight – if it curves up from the waist, the lift is too high. From shoulders to lower back should be fairly level (with the normal body curve), so that the muscles in the lower back do the lifting. Do not push with your feet or hands – this will create a curve in the lower back, and take the exercise away from the muscles that should be being worked.

Stretching

Always stretch the main muscles after exercise. These are a few basic stretches to get started. Hold each for 6–8 seconds. Repeat each of the following exercises for each leg.

Calf stretch Move one leg back behind you, extending it and keeping the heel on the floor. Bend the other leg in front of you and rest your hands on that thigh for support. Keep your leg and back in a straight line. Feel the stretch in your calf muscles.

Thigh stretch (back) Stand with your feet apart and one foot in front of the other. Stretch the front leg straight and slightly to one side, bend the other leg at the knee and rest your hands on that thigh. Push your bottom out and sit back so that you feel the stretch in the thigh of the straight leg.

The lunge Keep your body straight, take your back leg down low (knee to floor) and hold for a few seconds. Do not extend the knee beyond the toes.

Thigh stretch (front) Stand facing a wall and rest one hand against it for support. Bend the opposite leg at the knee and take the foot behind you up to your bottom. Hold the foot to ease it

The right food for you

Talk diabetes and food to most people and the usual comment is, "You can't eat sugar and chocolate." This is not strictly true, and the following pages take a practical overview of how diabetes influences diet. Eating for long-term health is paramount and this is about being inclusive, not prohibitive: the more varied and interesting the diet, the better it is likely to be. Concentrate on beneficial ingredients and swing the balance away from foods that should be eaten in smaller proportions: eat well, stay healthy and live long.

It is vital for anyone with diabetes to follow simple general guidelines for well-balanced eating, but no single eating pattern suits everyone, and getting a perspective on food means interpreting healthy diet information for your own lifestyle and taste.

Maintaining your ideal weight will help your posture, add to your energy levels, and promote general wellbeing.

Weight management

For good health, "food in" has to equal "energy out". If you eat too much for your exercise levels, the excess is stored as fat, causing weight gain, and being overweight makes controlling diabetes difficult. As anyone prone to putting on too much weight knows, it can be a boring and stressful topic because good health is so closely related to not being overweight. Being overweight puts strain on organs and joints, and makes all activity harder than it should be. There is also a link between excess weight and insulin resistance. Not everyone with diabetes is overweight but most people with Type 2 diabetes are overweight, as are many with Type 1 diabetes.

Assessing weight

The World Health Organization defines obesity as "a disease state in which excess body fat has accumulated to an extent that health may be adversely affected" and the Body Mass Index (BMI) is used to assess the problem. This is a calculation of weight in relation to height: the weight divided by the height squared:

$$BMI = \frac{weight\ (kg)}{height \times height\ (m)}$$

A result of 20–25 is considered normal; below 20 is underweight and over 25 is overweight; over 30 is obese.

This is a good general guide but it does not give a complete picture. The area where fat is stored also influences health. Fat stored around the abdomen rather than around the bottom and hips is more likely to be associated with insulin resistance, so waist circumference is also measured, with results over 102cm/40in for men and 88cm/34.5in for women indicating an unhealthy level of fat.

There are exceptions to every rule, and the BMI or waist measurements do not always give an accurate assessment, although a combination of the two is a useful guide. If they indicate a problem, don't dismiss it.

An active rather than sedentary lifestyle promotes a healthy appetite.

Diet and exercise

In the management of diabetes, weight control, exercise and blood glucose control are all connected, so it is important to get advice from the dietician and follow it. Very low-calorie diets and exclusion diets that cut out whole food groups are not healthy, and are likely to interfere with blood glucose control. If the doctor and dietician recommend such a diet to reduce weight, it will be properly co-ordinated and managed, but this is not something to try unsupervised. Avoid faddy diets, meal substitutes and diet foods.

Follow the recommended proportions for different food groups, eating enough to supply your needs but not more. Regular exercise will help reduce weight and maintain a healthy weight in the long term.

Food in the right proportion

A daily balanced diet should consist of:
• A high proportion of starchy carbohydrates – 45–60% of total calorific intake
• A high proportion of vegetables and fruit – at least 5 portions a day
• A modest proportion of protein – about 10% of total calories
• A small proportion of fat – less than 35% of total calories (10–20% of total calories should be from monounsaturated, less than 10% from saturated, and less than 10% from polyunsaturated fats)
• Limited foods containing sugar – up to 10% of the total calories, distributed throughout the day
• Alcohol does not have to be cut out completely, but should be limited and consumed with food

Water

Essential for all life, the body consists of about 70% water and needs 2–3 litres/ 4½–7 pints every day. Raw vegetables and fruit contain a high percentage of water, and all drinks contribute to the intake, but it is important to drink water throughout the day.

Salt

Daily intake of salt should be less than 6g (⅙oz). Most processed foods are over-salted, but in fresh food the nuances of flavour are lost when lots of salt is used. Getting into the habit of reducing salt in cooking will soon adjust your taste for salty foods downwards.

Fibre

While not a nutrient, fibre is vital for gut health, and especially helpful in controlling blood glucose levels.

Soluble fibre, the kind that is in oats, is helpful in lowering blood cholesterol and slows down the digestion of food. Insoluble fibre is the indigestible matter that absorbs water and passes through the gut. It slows down the rate at which food is digested and, because it absorbs moisture, is good for carrying away waste products, helping to prevent constipation.

It is important to maintain a balanced diet, including the right proportion of each food group over each day. From the top: carbohydrates; animal proteins; beans and pulses; dairy; and finally refined sugars.

About sugar

There is lots of confusing information on sugar intake and blood glucose control. The disadvantage of eating chocolates, cakes and sweet desserts regularly is that it is easy to develop a taste for them. It is a good idea to get rid of a sweet tooth: as with salt, it is not difficult because the less you eat, the less you want. Instead, develop a taste for fresh fruit and zesty, sharp flavours. Instead of using sweeteners, gradually give up sweetened tea or coffee and get used to the idea of "sweet" being the natural level of sugar in fruit. Dried fruits, especially dates and figs, have a naturally high sugar content.

The problem with sugar (sucrose), syrups and honey is that they add empty calories. On their own, they do not represent brilliant food value. They are a problem for anyone who has difficulty maintaining a healthy weight, and even worse for anyone trying to lose weight. Eaten on their own, or in a high concentration, they cause blood glucose to rise high and quickly, causing fluctuations.

A moderate amount of sugary foods can be eaten when they are combined with other foods that help to slow down absorption and balanced by insulin, medication or exercise. The point of diabetes control is to make food intake work for the individual, and what works well for one person is not necessarily best for another. Banning anything that contains sugar (an elderly person's much-loved breakfast marmalade, or chocolate snacks for a teenager) is not going to help anyone moderate their intake from choice, balancing it with good ingredients, careful monitoring and exercise. But if confectionery and puddings are not a major issue, regard them as rare treats, as anyone, with diabetes or not, is advised to do.

The glycaemic index

Digestion breaks down carbohydrates into the simple sugar glucose, which is absorbed into the blood. Some carbohydrates are digested and absorbed more quickly than others, and these are the ones we should avoid or limit. The glycaemic index (GI) ranks carbohydrate absorption in comparison to glucose itself: on a scale of 0–100, glucose is rated at 100. Low GI foods are good; high GI foods should be limited or balanced with low GI foods.

GI values

These values are calculated as a percentage increase in blood glucose levels over a set time as a result of eating a particular food. Foods with a high GI value cause the largest increase in blood glucose, while those with low values cause the lowest rise.

Low GI = 55 or less
Medium GI = 56–69
High GI = 70 or more

The values are not exact measures; it is the relationship between them that is important. Extensive lists of values are available for commercial products as well as basic ingredients. If you choose to refer to a list, check that its values have been calculated in accordance with professional guidelines, such as those set out by the World Health Organization or the UN Food and Agriculture Organization. If you are interested in the GI values of specific brands, remember that internationally available products are not made to the same "recipe" in every country. Sugar and fat levels, for example, are adjusted to suit local tastes or regulations, so the value for a particular breakfast cereal, for example, may not be the same in the US, Europe or Australia.

GI and diabetes

Foods that have a high GI value make the blood glucose level rise quickly. A low GI value indicates that the food will be digested more slowly, the blood glucose level will not rise as much and the rise and fall will not be as rapid.

Foods with a high GI value normally induce the body to release more insulin, but someone with diabetes has to deal with them by adjusting their medication. Therefore, foods with low GI values are more helpful. Avoiding rapid rises in blood glucose means the body is more likely to cope with its limited insulin, without having to take drugs. For someone with Type 2 diabetes it is easier to maintain control by diet alone.

Factors influencing the GI value

Individual carbohydrate foods vary and the GI value is not identical for all ingredients of the same type.

Type of carbohydrate Different

TYPES OF SUGAR
Starch is broken down into sugar as the first stage of digestion – in fact, the process starts as the food is chewed – and all sugars have the highest GI values of all. In older diabetic recipes, especially for baking, powdered fructose (found in fruit and honey) was used instead of sucrose (ordinary white or brown sugar) because it tastes sweeter, so less is needed. But refined or unrefined, as syrup or honey, sugar is essentially a source of empty calories and should not be eaten to such an extent that any small benefits of one type over another are useful.

---

types of basic foodstuffs contain different starches and sugars, whose chemical structures vary, so they do not always have the same GI value. For example, ordinary white rice has a high GI value but basmati rice does not break down as quickly, so it has a medium GI value.

Refining and processing

Processed and highly refined foods are digested more quickly and therefore have a higher GI value.

Fibre content Both soluble and insoluble fibre reduce the rate at which food is digested, giving a lower GI value. Insoluble fibre (found in whole grains and cereals, beans and pulses, vegetables and fruit) is not digested but slows down the rate at which food is broken down as it passes through the gut. Soluble fibre (found in oats and fruits containing pectin, such as gooseberries, currants and apples) slows down the rate of absorption because it is gelatinous and tends to line the walls of the gut.

Preparation and cooking The preparation of basic ingredients influences their GI value; for example, boiled potatoes in their skins have a lower value than mashed potatoes, and boiled new potatoes have a lower value than main crop types, which are softer in texture. Rice, grains and vegetables cooked until soft are easier to break down (so have a higher GI value) than those that retain some bite. Pasta is quite a "solid" starch product that is not digested as quickly as potatoes, for example, especially when it is cooked *al dente*.

Acid content Acids, such as lemon juice or vinegar, reduce the GI value.

Context and accompaniments Carbohydrates are broken down more slowly when they are eaten with protein or fat, such as animal fat in oily fish or meat, or vegetable fat in oils, nuts, seeds or avocado. Combining low GI-value foods with high GI-value foods also reduces the overall GI value of the whole meal.

GI VALUES

Use the following list as a guide to how quickly food will make your blood glucose levels rise. Different sources give different values, and they are usually an average of several results. Remember that with diabetes you have to be aware of how different foods affect you personally, and your medication. For example, on the GI index carrots have a low GI value and corn has a medium GI value, yet both are known among those with diabetes to be foods that can make blood glucose rise significantly. Use this table as a guide, therefore, and tailor it to suit you.

LOW: 55 OR LESS

Apples 38
Apricots, dried 31
Barley, pearl or pot 25
Black-eyed beans (peas) 42
Buckwheat (groats) 54
Bulgur wheat 48
Butter (wax) beans 31
Carrots, boiled 47
Carrots, raw 16
Cherries 22
Chickpeas 36
Grapefruit 25

Grapes, green 49
Haricot (navy) beans 38
Kidney beans 28
Kiwi fruit 53
Lentils, red 26
Lentils, green 30
Marrowfat peas, boiled 39
Mung beans, boiled 31
Oat bran 55
Oats, raw (rolled, not
 instant) 51
Oranges 44
Noodles, instant 47

Noodles, mung bean 33
Noodles, rice 40–90
Pasta, wheat with egg 40
Pasta, spaghetti 40
Pasta, wholemeal (whole-
 wheat) spaghetti 37
Pasta, macaroni 45
Peaches 42
Peaches, canned in juice
 38–45
Pears 38
Pears, canned in juice 44
Peas 39–54

Pinto beans 39
Plums 39
Porridge (made with
 rolled oats and
 water) 42
Prunes 29
Semolina 55
Soya beans 18
Split peas 32
Strawberries 40
Wheat 41
Wholemeal (whole-wheat)
 bread, stoneground 53

MEDIUM: 56–69

Apricots, fresh 57
Bananas 56
Basmati rice 58
Beetroot (beets) 64
Corn 55
Couscous 65
Mangoes 56
Melon, cantaloupe or
 honeydew 67
Papaya 59
Pineapple 66
Pitta bread 57
Potatoes, new (boiled in
 their skins) 62
Raisins 64
Rye bread 58

Sourdough bread 53
Sultanas (golden raisins) 56
Sweet potatoes 61

HIGH: 70 OR MORE

Apricots, canned in light
 syrup 64
Bagels 72
Baguette 95
Broad (fava) beans 79
Dates 100
Parsnips 97
Potatoes, baked 85
Potatoes, boiled and
 mashed 74
Pumpkin 75
Rice cakes 77
Rice, white 98
Swede (rutabaga) 72
Watermelon 72
White bread 70

Food in the right proportion

Taking control of diabetes means adjusting to a normal healthy, well-balanced way of eating. This is no different from what everyone else should be doing – it's just more important when you have diabetes. Controlling blood glucose means balancing the amount of carbohydrate you eat with the energy you use up and your medication.

No food bans

Foods are not banned completely, but sugar and foods that raise blood glucose should be avoided in all but small amounts. For example, you might eat an occasional chocolate but it is important to differentiate between a "rare treat" and a "regular indulgence", and to avoid the latter. A very small amount of sugar in a product such as marmalade can be accommodated in your planned diet and balanced by medication, the time of day or the food it is eaten with. Desserts and sweet products such as cakes and biscuits, with high sugar content, are the ones to avoid. Ultimately, most people find it easier to cut out sweet stuff completely.

How important is food?

Remember that it really is not that important to be able to eat exactly what you want, when you want. Food is

Give meals proper time and attention, don't just grab food and eat on the go.

Activity and an energy-promoting diet help to create a positive outlook.

essential and enjoyable, but it is just one part of a great big life that has lots of other pleasures to offer.

It's too easy to fixate on food, fretting about what you do and don't eat. There is an amazing choice of wonderful things to eat and having a widely varied diet is one of the best ways to achieve a healthy balance. The less you eat the foods that are likely to mess up your blood glucose levels, the less you miss them. The more you begin to enjoy good foods, the better you will feel. Instead of mourning lost sugar, get excited about feeling brilliant and energized – a really good diet will make you feel and look fantastic: from inside out you will begin to zing and glow, with great hair, glossy nails and skin better than ever before.

Food and flavour

A good approach is to think of food not as a filler but as a source of flavour. Instead of responding only to hunger, try to develop a sense of needing flavour and texture. If you have to cut back on overall food intake to lose

weight, try to focus on the first part of eating as the best, satisfying your need for intense flavour. This helps to reduce the dependence on "feeling full" as a sign to stop eating and makes it easier to get used to smaller portions. Lighter food, bursting with flavour, is what you want. Recognize it, feel good about it and look for it every time.

Building a good diet

A variety of foods have to be eaten regularly to make up a balanced diet. Different foods provide different nutrients and including all sorts supplies the body with the range it needs. While some nutrients can be stored, others have to be eaten daily. There are many models of an ideal diet based on a high proportion of carbohydrates with a low GI value, a high proportion of fruit and vegetables, a modest amount of protein and a relatively small amount of fat, mainly vegetable fat. The following guide is a good starting point for building a good diet.

Eat plentifully

Plan your eating around the following ingredients, especially lots of fresh vegetables. If you need to lose weight, or have a tendency to eat too many carbohydrates, make vegetables the focus of main meals and add balanced amounts of carbohydrate and protein. **Low GI Carbohydrates** barley,

Eggs are versatile and nutritious, full of protein and other nutrients.

pearl or pot; basmati rice, especially
brown; bulgur wheat; butter beans;
pasta, especially whole-wheat and egg;
rolled oats, especially large flakes;
stoneground wholemeal bread.
Fruit apples; canned peaches or pears
in juice; dried apricots; firm bananas;
grapefruit; kiwi fruit; oranges; peaches;
plums; strawberries.
Beans, peas and lentils chickpeas;
haricot (navy) beans; all types of lentils;
mung beans; red kidney beans; soya
beans.
Vegetables and salads aubergine
(eggplant); broccoli; cabbage – white,
red, green, Chinese; cauliflower;
carrots; courgettes (zucchini); green
beans; onions – garlic, ordinary, spring,
leeks, shallots, scallions; peas; (bell)
peppers of all colours; tomatoes.

Eat in moderate amounts
These lower-fat protein foods go with
the carbohydrates and vegetables.
Nuts and seeds are good sources of
protein and "good" vegetable fat;
avocado is also rich in vegetable fat.
The high GI fruits and vegetables also
fall into this group: be aware that they
can raise blood glucose levels quickly,
depending on what they are eaten with.
Tofu or beancurd.
Meat lean beef; lamb; pork.
Game venison; rabbit; pheasant.
Poultry chicken; turkey; duck (without
the skin).
Dairy eggs; cheese; milk; yogurt.
Nuts and seeds (unsalted and

*Unroasted, unsalted nuts are good for
you in moderate amounts.*

unroasted) walnuts; brazil nuts;
hazelnuts; sunflower seeds; sesame
seeds; pumpkin seeds.
Fish and seafood of all kinds.
High GI fruit and vegetables
avocados; ripe bananas; parsnips;
swedes (rutabaga); dates; broad (fava)
beans; watermelon.

Eat only occasionally
Large amounts of high-fat and/or highly
processed foods should not feature
largely in any individual's daily diet.
Butter; cream; crisps (US potato chips)
and other high-fat savoury snacks,
including roasted and salted nuts;
mayonnaise; processed meat and
poultry, such as sausages, salami,
bought burgers; fried foods; savoury
pastries and pies.

*Vegetables are versatile and delicious,
everyone should eat plenty of them.*

*Eating a wide variety of food promotes
a healthy balance.*

Eat very seldom
Sugars are no longer excluded
completely from a diabetic diet. It is
quite likely that, when diagnosed,
someone with Type 1 diabetes who is
not overweight will not be asked to
exclude confectionery and chocolate,
though the importance of balancing the
medication with the diet may be
emphasized. However, these foods
should be "planned" and acknowledged
as occasional treats. Those with Type 2
diabetes, aiming to control the
condition with diet, must be particularly
careful about avoiding sugar, and
should avoid cakes and sweet pastries;
sweet biscuits (cookies); chocolate and
confectionery; ice cream; flavoured or
sweetened yogurt; sweetened drinks
and juices; jams, jellies and conserves.

Buying and storing food

Buy vegetables and fruit often, they hold far more vitamins when fresh.

This is about shopping for health. Eating a balanced diet is easier when you have plenty of the right food in store. While changing the outlook of the entire household may not be easy, it is the best route to a healthy life and the easiest way to control diabetes. Other family members may eat different foods but they should all be supportive and positive about eating a good diet.

You have to be motivated to adopt a different attitude to food and shopping. Everyone can do it if they want to, and wanting to feel terrific – to have a great sense of wellbeing – provides the motivation. There are other motivating factors, especially sharing life with, and caring for, the people close to you.

Everyone needs some help, and changing your outlook on eating is major, because eating is not only about providing the body with energy, but a source of pleasure and comfort, and a social tool. Make the most of positive moments, when motivation is high, to start new regimes.

How well do I eat?

Listing what you eat is the only way to find out how your diet works. This means keeping a food diary and writing down everything you eat and drink. If your life falls into a regular pattern, you will be able to assess your diet over a couple of weeks; if you have a less predictable life, it may take longer to get a complete overview. It is also about mood swings and eating patterns – the foods you eat when life is hectic compared to when it is calm, when you are at home compared to work. A food diary can be very revealing and provide clear pointers for change. Don't cheat. Write everything down, with a guide to quantities, and do it after each meal or at the end of each day. Think of it as positive reinforcement: as you make changes, you can use it to keep track of how well things are going.

Sorting out your stores

Start by sorting out the food you have in store, because it is the foundation of good eating. Make a list of everything in your food cupboards, refrigerator and freezer. Apart from the basics like onions and eggs, are you well stocked with good stuff, or do you have lots of ingredients that are going to hinder,

Educate your palate to enjoy fresh, home-made food, and high-fat, processed food will not be tempting.

Spicy hummus made with canned chickpeas takes just minutes to make.

CONVENIENCE FOODS

Get a perspective on bought prepared food: there is nothing wrong with eating it occasionally but doing so regularly is not good. The interesting thing is that when most of your meals are full of punchy flavours from fresh ingredients, convenience foods start to taste very inferior. The starches and fats used to stabilize them for chilling and reheating give them a different texture, and they lack the distinct and refreshing tastes of home cooking. The portions are usually tiny. If they are satisfying, it is because the high fat content and mix of ingredients induces a feeling of "fullness". The proportion of vegetables in prepared meals is very small.

Changing your taste doesn't happen overnight, and weaning taste buds off highly seasoned commercially prepared food can be difficult. But avoiding processed foods is one of the best steps towards a good diet. They contain more salt, sugar and fat than most homemade meals, have a lower fibre content and tend to be digested more easily, so do not help balance blood glucose levels.

Canned fish is quick and versatile, good for toast-toppers, fast meals and snacks.

rather than help, balanced eating? Does your food store encourage control or is it likely to disrupt it?
1 Assess the store list and make a list of the positive items that are missing.
2 Make a plan of action to use up the negative items.
3 Go shopping.

The refrigerator
There should always be good sources of instant flavour in the refrigerator, such as lemons, fresh ginger, chillies, plain low-fat yogurt, low-fat soft cheese, homemade peanut butter and oil and vinegar dressing, and plenty of fresh fruit and vegetables.

The freezer
Stock the freezer with essential good things and occasional treats. Store lots of the positive foods in easy-to-thaw form, so they can be cooked from frozen or thawed quickly in the microwave. Freeze foods that should be limited in small portions, rather than keeping them in the refrigerator. Butter, cheese (grated, sliced, in wedges or diced) and low-fat soft cheese (quark or curd cheese) can all be frozen.

Keep a wide range of frozen vegetables and summer fruits. Freeze portions of puréed fruit, sweetened with dried fruit (such as apple and apricot, and fig) for flavouring yogurt.

Freeze bread of all kinds ready cut in slices or small portions, and meat and poultry as lean boneless strips, minced (ground), diced, cut in chunks or fine slices, so that you can remove small amounts and cook them from frozen. Stock up with peeled prawns (shrimp) and skined, boned fish fillets.

Store-cupboard (pantry)
These are the good foods that have a long shelf life.
Canned foods: fish, beans, peas and lentils for protein, fibre and carbohydrate; tomatoes for vitamins and phytochemicals; fruit in juice.
UHT cartons: unsweetened fruit juices; firm tofu.
Dried foods: whole wheat and white pasta, noodles (egg, buckwheat or soba) and instant couscous; grains such as basmati rice, bulgur, oats and barley; seeds such as pumpkin and sunflower seeds; ready-to-eat dried fruit and plain unroasted, unsalted nuts.
For cooking and flavouring: olive, sunflower and sesame oil; cider vinegar; capers, mustard, tomato paste, herbs and spices.

Quick storecupboard meals
Having a super store is no good if you don't have ideas for mixing and matching the ingredients for instant snacks or meals. Here are a few ideas for quick meals. These all go well added to a base of onion softened in olive oil, or with lots of chopped spring onions (scallions) and/or with an oil and vinegar dressing. Grated lemon or lime rind, chopped fresh herbs and chopped garlic are good flavouring additions.
• Chickpeas and frozen spinach, served with basmati rice and a side dish of yogurt and cucumber and mint
• Cannellini beans with tinned tuna and

Dried fruits are alternatives to sugar for sweetening desserts and bakes.

Fresh root ginger adds a punchy flavour and keeps well in the refrigerator.

frozen green beans
• Red kidney beans with chopped hard-boiled eggs and couscous
• Broad (fava) beans and chopped hard-boiled egg, served with pasta
• Sliced peppers and anchovies, served with pasta
• Frozen peas and spinach and Puy lentils, served with yogurt and chives
• Chopped frozen spinach with shredded omelette or poached eggs

For dessert:
• Diced apple, diced orange, finely chopped thin-skinned lemon and raisins
• Diced orange and chopped dried apricots with ginger and apple juice
• Canned peaches and diced orange with toasted flaked (sliced) almonds
• Chopped dried apricots, with crushed walnuts and sliced banana.

Lemons, limes and oranges bring zing to savoury and sweet dishes.

Vitamins and minerals

Fruits and vegetables are key sources of many vitamins and minerals. Traditionally, the vitamin content of fresh produce has set it apart as essential for wellbeing. Fruit and vegetables are important sources of other specific plant substances.

Protective plants

Recent and ongoing research is gradually revealing the huge importance of plant foods. With grains, beans peas and lentils, fruits and vegetables are essential for helping the body to fight infection and disease, especially cancer and heart disease. Not only do antioxidant vitamins help to prevent damage caused by diet and environment, but plants also contain thousands of substances known as phytochemicals, which play protective roles. Among those considered to make positive contributions are:

• Flavonoids (found especially in sweet-tasting vegetables and fruit such as berries and citrus fruit)
• Quercertin, which may protect against a range of conditions including heart disease and cataracts
• Carotenoids (beta-carotene and lycopene, from coloured fruit and vegetables), which have valuable antioxidant properties
• Glucosinolates (from the cabbage family), which appear to suppress cell division in some cancers
• Saponins (from the soya family) may help to control cholesterol levels.

Berries contain flavenoids.

Red, orange and yellow vegetables contain carotenoids.

Fruit and vegetable focus

For weight control fruit and vegetables provide satisfying bulk without necessarily being high in calories. They add texture and flavour, transforming bland carbohydrates and staid-flavoured proteins into dishes we enjoy. There are lots of ways to increase the amount you eat every day. Make a big pot of mixed vegetable soup, enough for one or two meals, and freeze some in individual portions that you can have for lunch or follow with a salad for a more substantial meal. Include a raw salad with every meal – something basic such as coarsely grated courgette (zucchini), carrot or celeriac with chopped fresh herbs. Add lots of vegetables to sandwiches. Wide strips of (bell) pepper, coarsely grated carrot, strips of celery and slices of cauliflower, fennel bulb all fit well between thick chunks of wholemeal (whole-wheat) bread. Add peanut butter, low-fat soft cheese, parsley and basil.

When you feel like a snack, go for vegetable sticks, baby carrots, cauliflower florets or cherry tomatoes, and eat at least one piece of fruit at breakfast, after lunch and for at least one snack a day. Include fresh and dried fruit in savoury salads that are an accompaniment to protein.

Vitamins

Nutritionists group vitamins into two; water-soluble (C and B) or fat-soluble (A, D, E and K).

Vitamin A Important for good vision, as an antioxidant and for good skin, vitamin A is found primarily in animal foods – liver and fish liver oils, dairy produce and eggs. It can be generated in the body from beta-carotene, the substance in red and deep green coloured fruit and vegetables, such as carrots, pumpkin, apricots, peaches, mango, spinach, kale and watercress.

B complex vitamins These are important for the release of energy, nerve and brain function, healthy muscles, blood cell production and to help alleviate depression.

• Vitamin B1 (thiamin) is found in offal, meat, milk, wholegrain cereals, nuts, beans, peas, lentils and yeast extract.
• Vitamin B2 (riboflavin) is found in meat, offal, eggs, cheese, leafy green vegetables and yeast extract.
• Vitamin B3 (niacin or niacinamide) is found in meat, offal, fish, broccoli, carrots, peanuts, tomatoes and wholefoods.
• Vitamin B5 (pantothenic acid) is found in a wide variety of foods, including meat, offal, eggs, yeast extract, mushrooms, nuts and vegetables.
• Vitamin B6 (pyridoxine) is found in many foods, including fish, meat, offal, eggs, wholegrains, sunflower seeds, beans, peas, lentils and vegetables.
• Vitamin B12 (cyanocobalamin) is

Leafy greens contain glucosinolates.

Mushrooms provide minerals and can be used to bulk out meat casseroles.

Broccoli and other vegetables in the cabbage family provide vitamin K.

Blueberries have high levels of manganese and low GI levels.

found in animal foods including offal, meat, oily fish, milk (and cheese) and eggs. Deficiency can be a problem for vegans as the only non-animal sources are yeast extract, sea vegetables such as kelp, kombu and nori, and soya beans and their products.
• Folate or folic acid is found in eggs, liver, leafy green vegetables, beans, peas and lentils, whole grains, nuts, oranges and grapefruit.
• Biotin is found in yeast extract, meat, poultry, egg yolk, fish, soya beans and whole grains.
Vitamin C Found in fruit and vegetables, vitamin C is essential for growth and protection, and is an important antioxidant.
Vitamin D This fat-soluble vitamin is essential for a healthy nervous system and for the absorption of calcium. Some Vitamin D is produced in the body from chemicals activated by ultraviolet radiation from sunlight, but dietary sources are also important. It is found in fish liver oils, oily fish, milk, eggs, butter and margarine (fortified).
Vitamin E In fact this is a number of substances, and is an important antioxidant, helpful for preventing heart disease, cardiovascular health, fertility in men and healing. It is found in vegetable oils, nuts, seeds, avocados, whole grains and spinach.
Vitamin K Important for the production of prothrombin (for blood clotting), bone formation and repair,

Home-made vegetable soup is packed with protective nutrients.

vitamin K also has a role in the conversion of glucose to glycogen. There are three forms of vitamin K, one found in foods such as broccoli, cabbage, spinach, milk and vegetable oils, the other two generated by bacteria in the gut.

Minerals

Fruit and vegetables contribute essential minerals. The minerals are divided into those required in significant quantities (macrominerals) and those needed in small, but still essential, amounts (microminerals).

Macrominerals

• Calcium – from dairy produce, fish eaten with their bones and leafy dark green vegetables.
• Chloride – from table salt.
• Magnesium – from whole grains, peas, green vegetables, dried fruit and unroasted nuts.

• Sodium – mainly from salt.
• Potassium – from bananas, citrus fruit, nuts, potatoes, beans, peas and lentils (needed to counterbalance sodium in the body).
• Phosphorus – from dairy produce, fish, eggs, red meat and poultry.

Microminerals

Many microminerals are needed by the body, but in small amounts, including those listed here.
• Boron – from apples, pears, carrots, dark green leafy vegetables, nuts and whole grains
• Chromium – from liver, meat, dairy produce and whole grains
• Copper – from offal, shellfish, mushrooms, avocados, nuts and seeds
• Iodine – from seafood and vegetables
• Iron – from offal, red meat, eggs, dried apricots, raisins and prunes
• Manganese – from nuts, blueberries, wholegrains and cereals
• Molybdenum – from offal, leafy green vegetables, pulses and whole grains
• Selenium – this is widely distributed in foods according to the soil content where they are grown or where animals are reared, it is found in fish, meat, dairy produce, brazil nuts, avocados, lentils and whole grains
• Silicon – from beetroot (beet), brown rice, green leafy vegetables, soya beans and whole grains
• Vanadium – from fish, meat, whole grains and vegetable oils
• Sulphur – from fish, meat, Brussels sprouts, cabbage, turnips
• Zinc – from red meat, peanuts and sunflower seeds

Protein choices

All living things are made up of protein, and in the diet it is essential for growth and development, maintenance and repair, for producing hormones, antibodies and enzymes.

Sources of protein

Proteins are obtained from both animal and vegetable sources. Fish and seafood, chicken, turkey, beef, lamb, pork, eggs and milk all provide complete sources of protein, but most vegetable proteins do not provide all the essential amino acids; the exception is soya beans and their products (such as tofu and soya milk). Matured beans, peas and lentils, nuts, seeds (sunflower, sesame, pumpkin) and whole grains all provide vegetable proteins. Mixing different vegetable proteins together will provide all the essential amino acids. For example, you can eat beans with brown rice, wheat, nuts or corn; or combine nuts and/or seeds with brown rice.

How much, how often?

We need protein every day but the average Western diet includes too much, especially from animal sources (and often in high-fat products).

Seeds provide good fat, minerals and protein to the diet.

High-protein diets that exclude carbohydrates and reduce the variety and quantity of fresh fruit and vegetables are not good. Protein should make up a moderate proportion of the diet. Small amounts of protein in each meal mount up to provide enough over the day. On some days you may have more protein than others but try not to have too many high-protein days.

Low-fat animal proteins

For day-to-day eating, small portions of lean poultry (without skin) and red meat (pork, beef or lamb without visible fat) are suitable. Fish is either naturally lean (white) or oily, and the oily fish contain

Brown rice and pulses combine to provide a good source of protein.

good fats that make a positive contribution. However, for a healthy diet, vegetable proteins and eggs or dairy sources should be eaten on several days a week.

Dairy sources of protein

Eggs are a good source of protein, and are often incorporated into dishes such as omelettes or baked custards (savoury or sweet). Milk, yogurt and cheese contribute to the daily protein intake; the trick is to avoid eating too much cheese, which can push the fat content of the diet up too high.

Vegetable proteins

Beans, peas, lentils, nuts and seeds all contribute protein, especially when combined with rice and whole grain breads. Tofu is versatile and it is worth discovering how tasty it can be when seasoned and grilled (broiled).

Eating vegetable-based meals does not necessarily mean keeping them completely vegetarian – for example, wholemeal (whole-wheat) pasta, beans and mixed vegetables are delicious topped with pine nuts, chopped boiled eggs and a small amount of anchovies, cold chicken, ham or cheese for flavour. Most of the protein content of the meal will come from the mixture of beans and wheat.

Mix a moderate amount of chicken with wholemeal (whole-wheat) pitta and lots of salad for a well balanced lunch.

Protein and carbohydrates together

Eating proteins with carbohydrates (through the courses of a meal as well as together on the same plate) slows down the rate of absorption, so relatively high-GI foods, such as carrots, parsnips or corn, do not have as dramatic an effect on blood sugar levels when eaten with protein (especially high-fibre foods such as beans, peas and lentils). This does not mean you have to stick to traditional meat-and-two-veg meals. Risottos, pasta dishes, stir-fries with noodles, savoury bakes, tortillas (Spanish omelettes made with potato), healthy pizzas and hearty mixed salads are all premium choices.

A few fat facts

Fat is important in a healthy diet, in the right proportion. Fats are made up of fatty acids, grouped into three main types: saturated, polyunsaturated and monounsaturated. Animal fats have a high percentage of saturated fats, but

Add plenty of vegetables to all your meat dishes.

vegetable fats are less saturated. Coconut and palm oil are exceptions to this: both are highly saturated.

Cholesterol

Saturated fats are used in the liver to manufacture cholesterol. This is essential in the body and is transported to the cells attached to low-density lipoproteins (LDLs). Any excess is carried away by high-density lipoproteins (HDLs), and taken back to the liver for breakdown and disposal. The body needs a balance of enough LDLs to distribute the cholesterol and enough HDLs to take away the excess; an excess of LDLs will raise cholesterol

Spinach and pine nuts are delicious in an omelette.

levels and, if there are not enough HDLs, the excess will be deposited on the blood vessel walls. A high-fat diet can lead to increased blood cholesterol, particularly the "bad" kind with a high level of undesirable low-density lipoproteins. Polyunsaturates (such as sunflower oil) can help to lower blood cholesterol but they also tend to lower the levels of "good" cholesterol. Monounsaturated fats (such as olive oil) are thought to lower "bad" cholesterol without reducing the "good" type.

This nutrition-packed moussaka has vegetables and Puy lentils added to the meat, and an egg and yogurt topping.

QUALITY NOT QUANTITY
A sensible approach to eating poultry and meat is to buy the best quality organic type available, in smaller amounts, and keep it for occasional or special meals. For example, you may be surprised to discover that you and your family prefer to have a really special roast once a week rather than eating meat every day.

Beans, peas and lentils

For diabetes control, it is an advantage to make the most of high-fibre foods that contribute slow-release carbohydrate and low-fat protein. Find a taste for meals full of beans, grains, herbs and spices and you'll be doing your diet (and diabetes) and your family a favour.

Freezing dried beans, peas and lentils
The canned versions are brilliant, but cooking and freezing dried beans and pulses is rather clever. Soak and boil whole bags of chickpeas, red kidney beans and soya beans , then drain and pack them immediately in portion-sized polythene bags. Seal, cool, chill and freeze. When you want to use them they need only a few seconds in the microwave and they're ready to serve.

All kinds of beans make hearty, full-flavoured salad dishes – delicious served with a homemade dressing spiked with fresh herbs, spices, garlic and ginger.

Dips, spreads and pâtés
Dark-coloured beans purée well with strong flavours and tomatoes to make hot, spicy dips, while light cannellini, butter (wax) beans and chickpeas are delicious with herbs, garlic and spices. Add finely grated vegetables or

A can of beans can be quickly whizzed in the food processor to make a delicious and nutritious dip.

chopped nuts for extra colour, flavour and texture.

These mixtures are delicious with stir-fried vegetables in pancakes or wraps. Make them thicker, add grated lemon rind, lots of chopped fresh herbs and low-fat soft cheese and serve with toast as pâtés or nutritious sandwich spreads (instead of butter). Red lentils make a great pâté when cooked and beaten into low-fat soft cheese with lemon rind, spring onions (scallions) and garlic, then cooled and chilled.

Soups and stews
Grains and beans contribute protein and fibre to dishes such as minestrone, vegetable soups with lentils or pearl barley, and chilli con carne. Chickpeas or soya beans are great in ratatouille, cauliflower cheese, or layered in a casserole with potatoes, leeks and a little diced bacon or ham.

Stir-fries
Pale green flageolet beans are delicious with stir-fried cabbage, peas and spinach, flavoured with lots of chopped fresh mint and sprinkled with pine nuts. Add red kidney beans to vegetable

stir-fries moistened with canned chopped tomatoes, or add soya beans to a little chorizo with broccoli and green beans.

Pearl barley
With a lower GI value than ordinary rice, pearl barley is a good alternative as an accompaniment. It cooks quickly, retaining a bit of bite, and is terrific hot, with rice, wheat or bulgur wheat in a pilaff. With onions, garlic, vegetables, nuts and chopped dried apricots, lots of chopped fresh parsley and coriander (cilantro), pearl barley is exotic, delicious and nutritious. Cooked and cooled, it is great in a salad mixed with diced mixed (bell) peppers, olives and chopped spring onions, topped with a little crumbled feta cheese.

Salads
Beans, pulses and grains are very good accompaniments to canned tuna or salmon, or with chopped hard-boiled eggs, for instant salads. Add chopped mixed peppers, onions, leaves and celery, or use blanched frozen vegetables – peas, broad (fava) beans or green beans.

Poached eggs and lentils make a great protein combination.

Bean burgers

Chickpeas, flageolet beans and/or green lentils make good burgers. Combine them with fresh wholemeal (whole-wheat) breadcrumbs (or rye breadcrumbs are especially good), lots of chopped spring onions, garlic, chopped parsley and lemon rind. Finely chopped celery and grated carrot are good additions, and chopped fresh sage and thyme give a deep, warm flavour. Add an egg to bind, shape with wet hands and place on a flameproof dish to grill (broil) or bake in the oven. These burgers are all-round winners, fantastic in buns with salad, with potato wedges, or served on a salad.

• Use crushed red kidney beans for a coarser mix
• Add ground cashews or walnuts
• Add a small amount of chopped smoked bacon
• Mix canned beans or pulses and wholemeal (whole-wheat) breadcrumbs with minced (ground) beef to double the quantity of normal burgers, making them higher in fibre and lower in fat.

Try tofu

Tofu can intimidate those who are unfamiliar with its bland flavour and smooth texture. The classic Chinese approach is to deep-fry it, which

These spicy lentil and lamb patties make a good alternative to burgers.

Tofu is a versatile ingredient that can be grilled or stir-fried.

creates a crisp, golden skin but tends to be rather high in fat. It's better to grill it until crisp and golden on both sides, then cut it up.

Firm tofu grills wonderfully. Trickle a little oil on a flameproof dish, place the tofu on top and add seasoning: soy sauce, sesame oil, crushed garlic, lemon rind, chopped herbs, dried chilli flakes, ground spices and/or sherry. Cover and marinate for up to 24 hours, turning in the marinade. Grill until well browned on both sides. Slice and serve on salad with new potatoes, or with stir-fried vegetables and noodles, on rice or pearl barley, or in warmed pitta with salad or as a topping for pizza.

• Use tofu in soups or with vegetables
• Whiz it into a purée for a dip or pâté
• Place it on filo pastry, top with a mix of wholemeal (whole-wheat) breadcrumbs, spring onions (scallions), garlic and lemon rind, enclose in pastry and bake until crisp and golden.

Sauces, spreads and dressings

Extras and asides can complement or wreck a well-planned diet, making diabetes control relatively easy or extremely difficult. These ideas highlight why it is important to read labels and how to adopt a different approach to classic condiments.

Hidden fats and sugars

Bought sauces, dressings and spreads can be a problem when controlling diabetes because the fat and sugar content are not always obvious. The problem with hidden fat is not only the level but the type – it may be a polyunsaturated or hydrogenated oil that contains trans fatty acids, or trans fats, and these are thought to have a similar effect to saturated fat in terms of blood cholesterol.

Sugar is a natural preservative, used in jam to preserve fresh fruit and with vinegar in chutneys, pickles and ketchup to preserve the vegetables. Salsas, marinades, dressings and cook-in sauces may also include lots of sugar. It can be avoided by using homemade alternatives.

Salsa instead of sauce

Homemade salsas and fresh relishes are good alternatives to bottled sauces. They will keep in a covered container in the refrigerator for 2–3 days, or you can freeze them in small pots, ready for thawing in the microwave in minutes.

Simple tomato salsa

Chop lots of parsley and/or fresh coriander (cilantro) leaves, 1 garlic clove, 1 onion, 1 seeded red (bell) pepper and a few celery sticks in a food processor. Add a good squeeze of concentrated tomato pureé (paste) and 3–4 fresh tomatoes and chop. Season to taste, stir in a little olive oil and leave to stand for 1 hour before serving.
• For a spicy salsa, add seeded fresh chilli, dried chilli flakes or Tabasco.

Add fresh herbs and red onion to ripe tomatoes in a flavour-packed salsa.

• Add paprika for a deeper flavour.
• For piquancy add a little cider vinegar.
• Add capers and mint.

Zesty herb salsa

Chop spring onions (scallions), garlic, peeled fresh root ginger, green pepper, fennel or celery, seeded green chilli, fresh coriander leaves and parsley together in a food processor. Season to taste, add olive oil, lime rind and juice.
• Add finely diced cucumber or grated courgette (zucchini).
• Add some torn basil leaves at the last minute.
• Add chopped dried apricots and apple for a fruit salsa.

Good basic dressings

Homemade dressings are far superior to bought dressings on salads and have many other uses.

Avocado is packed with goodness; mix it with red pepper and chilli for a salsa.

Oil and vinegar dressing

Keep a jar of good basic olive oil and vinegar dressing in the refrigerator. It's a great alternative to butter for dressing vegetables or grilled (broiled) or pan-fried foods. It also makes an excellent marinade for meat, fish, tofu or vegetables before grilling or pan frying.

5ml/1 tsp Dijon mustard
2.5ml/$\frac{1}{2}$ tsp sugar
100ml/3$\frac{1}{2}$fl oz cider vinegar
200ml/7fl oz extra virgin olive oil
salt and ground black pepper

Mix the mustard, sugar, salt and pepper in a bowl. Add the vinegar and whisk well. Pour in the oil and whisk again until emulsified. Alternatively put everything in a screw top jar and shake.
• Finely chop 1 garlic clove and mix with the vinegar.
• Add chopped herbs such as chives, parsley, tarragon, thyme or oregano.
• Add some chopped capers.
• Add dried chilli flakes for a spicy dressing.
• Add a little toasted sesame oil and a generous pinch of ground ginger.

Yogurt dressing

Use mild, natural (plain) low-fat yogurt. Stir in mustard, seasoning and snipped chives or spring onions (scallions).

Make double quantities of French dressing and store it in the refrigerator.

- Add a little crumbled blue cheese
- Add torn basil and/or chopped mint
- Add finely chopped green chilli.

Soft cheese dressing

This is a delicious alternative to mayonnaise, cream sauces or toppings. Use a mild-flavoured cheese.

225g/8oz packet low-fat soft cheese
15ml/1 tbsp chopped parsley
15ml/1 tsp snipped chives
5ml/1 tsp Dijon mustard
15ml/1 tbsp olive oil
a little milk
salt and ground black pepper

Beat the cheese and stir in the herbs, mustard and oil. Thin the mixture slightly with milk and season to taste.
- Add grated lemon or lime rind
- Add chopped spring onions.

Home-made nut butter

As long as you have a sturdy food processor, this is easy to make in a large quantity. It is useful for spreading instead of butter, dipping vegetables, dressings (add to yogurt or French dressing to thin it) or for stir-fries.

Use plain peanuts or cashew nuts, skinless almonds, or a mixture. Roast in the oven at 180°C/350°F/Gas 4 for about 40 minutes, or until they are browned, stirring occasionally.

Homemade chutney and pickle is much better than store-bought as you can control the sugar and salt content.

Sterilize and dry screw-top jars. Process the roasted nuts in batches until finely ground. Add a little salt and continue grinding until the nuts begin to clump, then trickle in a little olive oil with the motor running. Process until creamy. The hot nut butter should have a thick pouring consistency.

Pour or spoon it into the jars. Tap the jars so that air bubbles in the mixture rise to the surface. Top with a little olive oil, cover loosely and leave until completely cold before covering tightly and storing in the refrigerator. It will keep for at least 9 months.

Cashew cream

This is an excellent alternative to dairy cream for desserts, dips and savoury toppings or dressings.

Grind plain unsalted, unroasted cashew nuts to a powder in a food processor or blender. With the motor running, gradually trickle in a little unsweetened natural apple juice. Do this slowly, allowing time for the nuts to combine with the juice. The mixture will gradually become pale and creamy as it emulsifies. The consistency should be similar to that of whipped cream. The trick is to make sure the nuts are thoroughly ground before adding any juice and then to add it very slowly – otherwise the mixture will separate and become grainy.

The cashew cream will keep in the refrigerator for up to 5 days.

Low-fat soft cheese with fresh herbs makes a lovely creamy dressing.

Pickles and chutneys

Bought pickles and relishes have a high sugar content, as do many recipes for homemade preserves. However, the recipes can be adapted to fit in with a diet for diabetes control.

Recipes with a high vinegar content do not depend on sugar for keeping quality but for a balanced sweet-sour flavour. Cook the ingredients (usually onions, vegetables and fruit) in the vinegar and omit the sugar. Pot and cover them as usual (sterilizing the pots), then sweeten individual portions to taste, if necessary, before use, either with sugar or a little sweetener.

Use sweet dessert apples instead of cooking apples. They do not soften as easily, so chop them. Use dried fruit for sweetening – apricots, raisins, sultanas (golden raisins) or dates, which can also sweeten vinegar-based preserves.

Snack attack

Cutting out sugary and high-fat snacks is one good way of improving your diet and helping good blood glucose control. Having alternatives and achieving a balance are important for long-term success. An occasional sweet treat is not necessarily a problem when the sugar increase can be balanced by insulin, but regular swings in blood sugar should be avoided. It is best to develop a taste for fruit snacks and alternatives to confectionery, especially for children.

Nuts and seeds not sweets
A balanced diet should not include sweets (candy) on a daily basis for the simple reason that they encourage weight gain without contributing goodness. Dried fruit, seeds and nuts are far better than confectionery. Make up your own mix of lightly roasted cashew nuts, walnuts, brazil nuts and hazelnuts, with quartered dried apricots and raisins. Roast the nuts gently and slowly in the oven, then allow them to cool completely before storing with the fruit in an airtight jar.

Keep some home-made oatcakes in an airtight container for an instant snack.

For a savoury snack, finely chop a garlic clove and add to the nuts with a sprinkling of ground coriander, several sprigs of thyme and a couple of bay leaves. Mix well, cover and leave to stand for 30 minutes before roasting. Discard the bay leaves and thyme sprigs before storing the nuts.

Roast sunflower and pumpkin seeds with almonds. Sprinkle them with a little salt at the end of cooking and mix well. Cool completely.

Ideas for popcorn
Popcorn is popular and does not have to be coated with sugar or salt to taste good. Cook it according to the packet instructions in a little oil in a heavy, covered pan.
• Toss hot popcorn with snipped chives and a little grated Parmesan cheese.
• Cook a 2.5cm/1in piece of fresh root ginger, finely chopped, and a thickly sliced onion in the oil before adding the popcorn. Keep the temperature low until the onion has softened. Remove the onion and ginger from the pan – discard the onion and reserve the ginger. Cook the popcorn in the flavoured oil, then sprinkle with a little sesame oil and stir in the ginger.

Easy-to-eat, bananas are the ultimate convenience food; avoid if over-ripe.

• For sweet cinnamon and apple popcorn, cook a cinnamon stick in the oil before adding the popcorn. Add chopped dried apple rings to the cooked popcorn.
• Mix chopped dried dates and ready-to-eat dried apricots with popcorn for a sweet snack.

Fruit and vegetable snacks
Grown-ups know that easy-to-eat fruit and vegetables are healthy, practical and good for snacking. Introducing children to fruit and vegetable snacks is standard and especially important for cultivating palates that prefer savoury and sharp tastes to super-sweet. Little

Mixed roasted seeds can be added to sweet and savoury snacks.

Dried fruit goes very well with a low-fat soft cheese dip.

pieces of fruit or vegetable are perfect for small fingers and all of the following make great snacks for adults and children alike. For family parties, mini breadsticks and potato wedges baked in their skins go down well alongside bowls of vegetables and fruit.

• Baby carrots, baby courgettes (zucchini) and mini cauliflower florets are good plain or with dips.

• Physalis, grapes and mandarin segments are juicy with plain yogurt mixed with chopped nuts.

• Small bananas, strawberries, stoned halved plums and apricots are good for lunch boxes.

• Dried apricots are good with low-fat soft cheese and walnut halves.

• Spread oatcakes with low-fat soft cheese and top with dried apple rings.

Sandwich suggestions
Small sandwiches are good for children's snacks, and can replace salty, high-fat nibbles with drinks. Cut them into little fingers that are easy to eat. Use stoneground wholemeal (whole-wheat) bread spread with soft cheese or homemade nut butter, or for tiny round sandwiches, slice French bread across and sandwich together in pairs or make little open sandwiches.

• Make mini wraps by spreading wheat tortilla wraps with savoury or sweet fillings, rolling them up and then cutting into sections.

• Spread slices of French bread with

Use a spicy nut dip to add protein and flavour to a big pile of freshly prepared vegetable crudités.

soft cheese and press a thick layer of roasted sunflower, pumpkin and sesame seeds on top.

• Vegetable pancakes make a delicious change from bread: add finely chopped spring onion (scallions), grated carrot, grated courgette and shredded basil to the batter. Roll up the cold pancakes with low-fat soft cheese or other filling, then slice into pinwheels or into short lengths for a lunch pack.

• For sweet fillings, remember sliced or mashed banana, chopped dried apricots or raisins with soft cheese.

Crunchy snacks
Cut French bread into thin slices, rub a peeled garlic clove on both sides, and spread them out on a baking sheet. Bake in the oven at 160°C/325°F/Gas 3

for about 20 minutes until crisp and lightly browned. Rub with a peeled garlic clove, cool on a wire rack and store in an airtight container. These are good as nibbles or with dips or pâté. Plain or flavoured bagels are also good sliced and baked until crisp. Their close texture works particularly well.

Home-made energy bars
These are simple and good to eat – great for children to make, too.

225g/8oz can pineapple pieces in juice
30ml/2 tbsp sunflower oil
50g/2oz sultanas (golden raisins) or raisins
115g/4oz mixed roasted seeds (sunflower, sesame, pumpkin, linseed)
grated rind and juice of 1 orange
150g/5oz rolled oats

Mix all the ingredients in a bowl. Grease a 17.5cm/7in square shallow cake tin (pan) and line the base with baking parchment. Press the mixture into it, then bake at 200°C/400°F/Gas 6 for about 30 minutes, until well browned on top. Cut the mixture into eight fingers while still warm, cool in the tin.

Canned fish are easy to adapt into a quick and nutritious snack.

Sweet but not sugary

Unsweetened fruit juices and smoothies can be satisfying snacks.

The idea of cutting out sugar may seem a little severe at first but it really is no big deal. Anyone with a taste for sweet dishes will appreciate alternatives and there are plenty of naturally sweet foods that don't affect blood glucose levels. A healthy, well-balanced diet does not include a significant amount of sweet foods – sweetened desserts, cakes and biscuits should be an occasional treat, not a regular habit.

It is not essential to exclude sugar entirely, but it should be limited to a

Dried dates are good as a sugar substitute in small amounts.

small amount a day (about 25g/1oz) and it should be part of a dish, not sprinkled on food or stirred into drinks.

Specialist foods and sweeteners

Dieticians no longer recommend specialist foods for a diabetic diet because they tend to encourage a taste for sweet foods without making a positive contribution. Some tend to be high in fat and all are relatively expensive. Also, some have unpleasant laxative side effects.

There are many commercial sugar-free diet foods and drinks, including ice creams, available that can be useful occasionally, but generally it is not a good idea to consume lots of artificial sweeteners and far better to develop a liking for unsweetened drinks and foods that rely on naturally sweet ingredients such as fruit.

Aspartame is widely used as a sweetener in drinks and diet foods. It includes two amino acids and methanol, and although the amino acids should be broken down in the

same way as those that occur naturally in proteins, there is evidence that they build up in the body. People who suffer from phenylketonuria, a condition related to the lack of an enzyme needed to convert the amino acid phenylalanine, should avoid aspartame. Some people with kidney disorders and iron deficiencies may also be prone to problems with it. Adding a little artificial sweetener to special desserts is acceptable, but it is sensible to avoid eating significant and regular amounts.

Sweet ingredients

Dried fruits are the obvious ingredients for sweetening desserts and baking. Of course, their natural sugar content will influence blood sugar levels but they also contribute food value and fibre.

Chopped dried apricots, dates, figs, raisins and sultanas (golden raisins) are good sweeteners for yogurt, rice pudding, porridge (oatmeal), plain biscuit (cookie) mixtures such as oatcakes or shortbread, or scones. A small quantity of dried fruit will sweeten a sauce, and you can purée dried apricots or dates with tart fruit or juices.

Relatively sweet fresh fruits such as grapes, mangoes, strawberries, dessert apples, melons and ripe peaches are excellent in desserts, including tarts, jellies (made with fresh juice), pancakes,

Developing a taste for sharp fruit is better than craving for sugar.

Red berries make zingy purées that can be used instead of sweet sauces.

cheesecakes and mousses. Thoroughly cooked dessert apples can be mixed with citrus rind and juice to make a spread to use in place of marmalade, or as a base for berries and chopped sharp fruit (plums, physalis, raspberries, blackberries) to make fruit spreads or fillings for tarts, pancakes or crumble.

Freeze fruit purées and spreads in small amounts (ice cube trays are ideal) ready for thawing rapidly in the microwave and serving with scones (with low-fat soft cheese instead of clotted cream for a light cream tea) or toast, or stirring into porridge.

What about cake?

It is still possible to enjoy cakes without using recipes loaded with sugar if you yearn for comforting teatime bakes.

Teabreads made with yeasted dough or self-raising (self-rising) flour are semi-sweet and work well without added sugar. Add dried fruit to the mixture and serve plain or spread with butter. Unsweetened drop scones are also good with a little butter or a puréed fruit sauce or spread. As a rule, rubbed-in mixtures will work without sugar, so these recipes can be adapted relatively easily – adding dried fruit to a plain scone dough, for example. Or serve pancakes as a treat instead of cake: make them plain, fill them with low-fat soft cheese and serve with fruit sauce.

Whisked sponges rely on whisking sugar with the eggs to incorporate the air that makes them rise during cooking. They cannot be made without sugar; however, they can contain a relatively small proportion compared to creamed mixtures. Boiled fruit cake works well without sugar: for this type of mixture, dried fruit is soaked overnight and then self-raising flour is added. The mixture should be very soft and batter-like, rather than creamed. It

Unsweetened 70% cocoa powder is useful for sauces and baking.

can contain a large quantity of fruit, spices and citrus rinds and is therefore a good alternative to traditional Christmas and celebration cakes.

Sauces and purées

Sweet sauces need not be a problem. Here are a few low sugar ideas.
• Custards and other milk sauces can be sweetened with a little sweetener after cooking.
• Unsweetened fruit juices make good sauces and glazes (for fruit tarts): thicken with arrowroot for a clear glaze or with cornflour (cornstarch) for an opaque sauce.
• Purée fresh fruit with a little dried fruit to make a sweet, smooth sauce: dried apricots are versatile for sweetening different types of fruit.
• Purée unsalted, unroasted nuts with fruit and juices to make sauces that taste creamy – grind the nuts finely first, then add the fruit and juice gradually.
• Purée bananas with fruit juices and fruit to make creamy, sweet sauces.
• For chocolate sauce, blend cocoa powder with cornflour and a little apple juice or milk. Simmer with more juice or milk to make a syrup-style or creamy sauce. Add vanilla extract and purée with prunes to sweeten.
• Low-fat soft cheese or Greek (US strained plain) yogurt can be used instead of cream.

Unsweetened teabreads are good alternatives to high-sugar cakes.

Eating out

Diabetes does not limit opportunities for dining out. Understanding how to adjust insulin doses to suit different eating patterns is part of learning about control under the guidance of your healthcare team. Remember to retain a sense of balance and see the occasional bad eating day as normal, not the end of a good eating regime but a temporary blip.

Make sure your host know of your dietary preferences in plenty of time.

Visiting or staying over
Eating at friends' houses is not a problem but it is considerate and important to let them know in advance that you have diabetes and about foods you limit or prefer not to eat. They will then understand if you prefer to opt for fruit or cheese instead of a super-sweet dessert, or just eat a very small amount.

Have a snack to avoid a hypo if you are eating later than usual. It's wise to take a suitable snack with you when staying over – for example if you need to eat something early in the morning or before going to bed at night.

Eateries and restaurants
Depending on your lifestyle, eating out may well be a regular part of the week, for social or work reasons. Regular take-aways and inexpensive, high-fat, fast-food meals are not for you. Run through take-away menus and figure out how many dishes are deep-fried or contain lots of fat. Stir-fries and sauces often quite obviously contain a lot of oil, and the large rotating spits of compacted meat in kebab shops ooze

Menus offer so much choice that eating out should not be a problem.

fat. Bacon sandwiches and fry-ups clearly contain lots of fat. Hot, fresh, well-drained chips are not the worst choice – battered and crumbed foods soak up more fat. Large chunky chips made from real potatoes are not as bad as fine fries or re-formed chips (the sort that are more like mashed potato inside).

Most restaurants can offer dishes that fit perfectly well into a balanced diet. Chain restaurants with standard menus are rarely flexible because everything is prepared for standard cooking (often deep-frying), but establishments that cook fresh ingredients will often happily make you something that is not on the menu, for example, by leaving off a rich sauce or grilling (broiling) food rather than deep-frying it. Whereas the big food chains may not even be able to offer a salad without the standard high-fat dressing, independent cafés and restaurants can be far more flexible.

When you're choosing from the menu, select salsas, raitas and relishes instead of creamy or oily salad dressings and sauces and go for grilled (broiled) dishes instead of fried. Foods

Unsweetened fruit pancakes are delicious with fromage frais.

An occasional glass of wine with a meal will do no harm.

served with a sauce are often lighter than bakes and pastries with fillings cooked in sauces (especially in individual dishes). New potatoes or baked potatoes are healthier than fries as long as they are not served with lots of butter; roast potatoes in restaurants are often deep-fried. Choose wholemeal (whole-wheat), rye, mixed grain or nut bread (no butter), and remember that breads with cheese and other toppings will be higher fat.

Many menus include fresh fruit desserts that are not laced with too much sugar, or it is perfectly reasonable to order one portion of dessert to share between two. When eating somewhere that takes a pride in its cooking, quiz the staff about the desserts – which are less sugary, can the sauces be varied, and so on. Explain why and they will be helpful. Bear in mind that ice creams, sorbets and all frozen desserts contain more sugar because they do not taste as sweet when frozen. Set custards can be less sugary, and pancakes are usually made without sugar and sweetened by their fillings or accompaniments.

Holidays and breaks
When you're planning a holiday, discuss any medication needs and changes to your usual routine with your healthcare team in advance.

Self-catering obviously allows most flexibility, especially when there are plenty of restaurants around for eating some meals out. Full board in small hotels can be a limiting option: it's better to go for half board or bed and breakfast. Large hotels usually have extensive breakfast buffets, so making good eating choices is simply a matter of decision and willpower, but if you book with a small hotel or guest house, check that they have a choice of sugar-free cereals and other healthy breakfast options. (You can eat the occasional fried breakfast as a treat but not every day for a week.)

If you're flying, tell the airline of your special diet needs when booking. If you think standard food products may not be available at your destination, take some sensible ingredients with you. Rolled oats travel well and are good with fruit and milk for breakfast or a snack. Pack suitable snacks, such as oatcakes, and emergency glucose supplies to last through your stay.

Prepare thoroughly for any more adventurous excursions and activity or sporting holidays. Let the organizers know about your condition, and check they are happy to take your booking.

Drinking alcohol
Alcohol does not make a positive contribution to a diabetes diet as it encourages weight gain (it is high in calories), and in excess it causes liver damage. Most importantly, it does not help with diabetes control as it has the effect of lowering blood glucose, which is important for anyone on insulin. Alcohol is not banned but it should be consumed with food (and you should eat before you drink) to avoid hypos. Have several – at least three – days a week that are alcohol-free and limit your intake on other days. Never ignore problems with blood glucose control, especially in relation to alcohol. Check the recommended limits for alcohol consumption with your healthcare team, as guidelines change.
• Avoid binge drinking and drinking without eating.
• Think of alcohol as the drink you have with dinner – a glass of wine, a small beer – and alternate it with water.
• Be especially aware of waiters or friends who top up wine glasses. If your glass is refilled before it is empty, it is easy to lose track of your intake.

Make sure formal occasions are enjoyable and relaxed by planning ahead and adapting your diet and medication accordingly.

Good eating through the day

Everyone is different and no one can tell you exactly what to eat and when. Taking control of diabetes is about learning what's best for you. Take advantage of the help available during the trial-and-error stage. This section offers inspiration for good eating.

Plan your daily menus

Always start with a balanced breakfast, including at least one piece of fruit. Stick to one or two regular weekday cereals if that is easy and healthy – homemade muesli or bran flakes, for example. Wholemeal (whole-wheat) toast is good but not with lots of butter – reserve that for a weekend treat.

Working lunches can be high in fat and low in food value when relying on bought sandwiches. Make your own: have lots of thick-cut bread or split rolls ready in the freezer. It's easier to handle frozen bread, it keeps the filling cool and fresh, and thaws by lunchtime. Spread with low-fat soft cheese or nut butter, include lots of vegetables and make it a doorstep sandwich for slow-release energy and lots of vitamin value.

Milk is nutritious with cereal or in drinks, especially as a start to the day.

Oats are versatile raw or cooked, providing slow-release energy and fibre.

Breakfast suggestions

Check out the ingredients lists on cereal packets as many high-fibre, apparently healthy products contain significant amounts of sugar.
• Rolled oats or jumbo oat flakes are good raw or cooked for breakfast. For speedy muesli mix them with dried fruit and sliced almonds or chopped nuts.
• Milk that is semi-skimmed (low-fat) or skimmed contains less fat. Balance this out with the rest of your diet – if you generally have a low-fat diet, a small amount of whole milk may not be a problem for you.
• Low-fat natural (plain) yogurt is great

for breakfast: add diced fresh fruit, drained canned fruit in juice, dried fruit, nuts and/or seeds.

Light meals

Here are a few reminders of satisfying small meals that make a positive contribution in a balanced diet. Served morning, noon or evening, for all ages, these light meals are very adaptable.

Baked potato with baked beans and a little grated cheese Fibre from the beans and fat and protein from the cheese help to slow down the carbohydrate absorption from the potato. You don't need butter.

Toasted ham sandwich with sliced courgette and spring onions Use wholemeal (whole-wheat) bread and lean cooked ham. Courgette (zucchini) and spring onions (scallions) are delicious with ham and great instead of cheese.

Scrambled eggs with asparagus and peas For low-fat but really creamy scrambled eggs, cook them without butter then whisk in low-fat soft cheese just as they set. Stir in some

Fruit salad is good to eat for breakfast or for a snack.

A little cheese slows down energy absorption from a baked potato.

FRUIT SALAD IN STYLE
Serve it on small thick pancakes (drop scones without sugar) and top with thick yogurt for a clever dessert. Or spread split warm wholemeal (whole wheat) scones with low-fat soft cheese, arrange on large plates and spoon over generous portions of fruit salad – great for breakfast or a slightly different take on lunch. Tender fruits best complement the scones (for example, berries, mango, banana, canned peaches).

Poached eggs are healthy alternatives to high-fat fried eggs.

par-boiled asparagus tips and peas, serve with multi-grain bread, toasted one side, then brushed lightly with olive oil before toasting the second side.

French toast with stir-fried peppers Stir-fry a mixture of red and yellow (bell) peppers with crushed garlic and chopped spring onions, then remove from the pan. Dip slices of rye bread into beaten egg and cook in a non-stick pan, with just a little olive oil, until golden on both sides. Serve topped with the peppers.

Cheese crumpets Toast the crumpets' undersides and top with thin slivers of grated cheese, then grill (broil) until crisp and golden. Good with lots of cherry tomatoes on the side.

Poached eggs on toast Use multi-grain toast and have this with grilled (broiled) bacon for breakfast.

Mushroom omelette Couscous is delicious in omelettes and adds useful carbohydrate. Pour boiling water over some instant couscous and set aside for 5–10 minutes. Stir-fry lots of sliced mushrooms and add chopped spring onions. Add beaten eggs and cook the omelette. When it is almost set, sprinkle the cooked couscous over before folding. Canned flageolet beans in place of couscous are good too, and contribute fibre. Serve the omelette with chunks of whole-wheat soda bread.

Main meal ideas

Instead of thinking of the protein element first, focus on the carbohydrate and vegetables. For example, pasta, couscous or gnocchi barley, rice, bulgur wheat, new or baked potatoes

Add the vegetable element:
• Roasted mixed vegetables: onions, aubergines, (bell) peppers, fennel
• Baked pumpkin or squash
• Stir-fried sugarsnap peas, green beans, baby sweetcorn
• Stir-fried white cabbage, carrots, onions and apples
• Lightly steamed cauliflower and broad (fava) beans, plus cherry tomatoes
• Diced cooked beetroot, shredded red cabbage and chopped red onion
• Stir-fried celery, carrots, Chinese cabbage and baby spinach.

Then add the protein:
• Cooked diced bacon
• Canned tuna
• Hard-boiled egg
• Stir-fried chicken, turkey or pork
• Sliced grilled (broiled) bratwurst or other sausage
• Grilled salmon or tuna
• Baked white fish
• Grilled tofu
• Sprinkle with pine nuts, chopped nuts or seeds

All the combinations above rely on cooking juices to moisten meals, but you can also drizzle with a light dressing rather than coating foods with sauce. Serve a salsa on the side.

Super snacks

Replace crisps (US potato chips), salted nuts and confectionery with breadsticks, pretzels and rice crackers. Plain unsalted nuts provide good fat, protein and other nutrients. Make a big bowl of mixed nuts, quartered dried apricots, raisins, roasted pumpkin seeds and oat flakes. Store in an airtight container ready for snacking. Make up little packs of this for children.
• Top dried apricots with dollops of home-made nut butter and apple.
• Spread rice cakes with low-fat soft cheese and press on roasted seeds.

Eggs, asparagus and peas are delicious with pasta or new potatoes.

Emergency snacks

Always have emergency snack foods in store, carry them in the car and have some with you when you are out, to counteract low blood glucose: glucose sweets, honey, semi-sweet biscuits (cookies), special hypo-counteracting gel. Make sure that all the family know how to cope if you experience a hypo.

Seeds and grains

This mix is a healthy-eating essential for breakfast, snacks, light lunches and main meals. Use whole bagfuls of individual seeds and grains, and roast enough to last for 6–8 months. About three-quarters of the mixture should be seeds to about one quarter oats/rye.

• Spread a mixture of sunflower, sesame and pumpkin seeds with linseeds, a few jumbo oatflakes and dark rye flakes in one or two large roasting pans and roast in the oven at 180°C/350°F/Gas 4 for 20–30 minutes, until lightly browned. Stir and turn the seeds two or three times for even cooking. When completely cold, store in an airtight jar.

• Use to flavour plain scone or soda bread mixture.

• Good as a snack with fruit and nuts.

• Pile on wholemeal (whole-wheat) bread spread with low-fat soft cheese.

Fruit salad is delicious made with fresh, canned and dried fruit and nuts.

Cabbage with sesame seeds and cumin is packed with vitamins.

• Mix with porridge oats and dried fruit for instant home-made muesli.

• Sprinkled over salads or home-made soup instead of croûtons.

• Mix with yogurt and sliced banana.

Fruit salad options

At any time of day, fruit salad is real feel-good food. Make a huge bowlful every couple of days and have it with porridge, yogurt or bran cereal for breakfast. It's great for snacking, as a quick lunch with lots of nuts and seeds, and good for dessert, of course. A basic salad, with lemon added, will keep well for three days, covered in the refrigerator. Diced apple, diced orange and canned pineapple or peaches in juice make a basic mix. Select a thin-skinned lemon, scrub it well and chop

it, skin and all, then add it to the salad. This prevents discoloration and gives the salad a delicious zingy flavour.

• Berries (strawberries, raspberries, blueberries) do not keep for more than 2 days before softening. Pears should be added on the same day, bananas at the last minute.

• Peeled and finely chopped fresh root ginger is fabulous in fruit salad, especially with grapes, mango or pear.

• Chopped dried apricots or raisins and grated orange rind add lots of flavour to a salad of apples, pears and banana. This is very good stirred into yogurt.

• Cook peeled, sliced or diced pears in apple juice with a little chopped lemon and fresh root ginger (if you like), cool, chill and use as a delicious base for fruit salad. Cooked pears will keep for several days in the refrigerator.

• Add frozen raspberries, blueberries or strawberries about 30 minutes before serving, leaving enough time for them to soften and chill the salad.

Changing recipes

Some recipes can be adapted to suit healthy eating and sugar-free cooking. Here are a few guidelines:

• Use low-fat yogurt instead of cream in sauces or soup, but add right at the end and warm gently to avoid curdling.

• Only cook in butter at very special

Salmon is a good source of protein and good fat. It can be grilled or baked.

occasions. Use a little olive oil when you are pan-frying, stir-frying, and dressing plain cooked vegetables.
• Reduce the proportion of minced (ground) meat in recipes such as cottage pie, and increase the fibre content by adding lentils, beans or cooked wheat.
• Add two large handfuls of rolled oats to a 450g/1lb quantity of meat mixture for burgers, meatballs and meatloaf. Reduce a couple of slices of wholemeal (whole-wheat) bread to crumbs and add them too, with grated carrot and chopped mushrooms and onion. The oats and crumbs give texture, the vegetables keep it moist.
• Reduce the proportion of meat in casseroles and stir-fries, and increase that of vegetables, beans or lentils.
• Make pastry with half wholemeal (whole-wheat) and half white flour. For a reduced-fat pastry, use self-raising (self-rising) flour and one-third butter to flour (rather than half), then make the pastry slightly more moist and roll it thinly.
• Use filo pastry instead of high-fat puff pastry and melt a little butter with sunflower oil, or olive oil for savoury dishes, and brush this very sparingly over the pastry.
• Omitting the sugar from scones, batters, rubbed-in cake mixtures and American muffins will not spoil the mixture – it will still rise and bake well.
• Whisked sponge cake recipes will work with 50g/2oz sugar and 50g/2oz flour to each egg.
• Use low-fat soft cheese instead of cream for filling cakes.

Kids will love dipping mini crudités into a creamy bean and garlic dip.

Add vibrant flavours like garlic and chilli to make vegetables more appetizing.

• For set (uncooked) cheesecakes use quark or curd cheese; omit the sugar and sweeten the mixture with fruit, fruit juice and/or a little sweetener; top with lots of fruit.
• Blancmanges, sauces or custards can be sweetened with fruit purées.
• In cooked apple recipes, use sweet chopped or grated dessert apples instead of sharp cooking apples.

Children's lunch boxes
Catering for a child throughout the day means that you will often be making up lunch boxes and portable snacks for him or her to take along, not only to school, but on trips and days with friends. Be sensitive to the peer pressure a child will be subjected to, and make sure that they have things that they enjoy eating. Involve them in making choices. Try the following ideas:
• Individual unsweetened fruit juices

Grilled canned sardine and tomato toast fingers are quick and tasty.

• Mini bananas
• Ready-prepared apple segments, soaked in lemon water to prevent browning, in a mini tupperware tub
• Mini crudites with a low-fat cheese spread or creamy bean and garlic dip
• Home baked mini bagel crisps
• Little packs of dried fruit and nuts
• Small home-made crackers
   Tie labels on the snacks reminding the youngsters when they should be eaten. Snack packs are also a good idea for children's parties.

Teenage Snacks
Update the snack pack idea for older children and teenagers:
• Fruit and nut bran muffins
• Fresh tropical fruit, dried fruit, nuts
• Home-made energy bars
Make up chill packs and leave them in the refrigerator for teenagers who want to have occasional independent suppers with their friends.
• Home-made pizza
• Mini meatballs with tomato salsa
• Pasta salad
• Wraps spread with low fat soft cheese, shredded vegetables and tuna
• A couple of salsas and dips
   Keep portion-sized healthy meals in the freezer for emergency late night meals. But remember that inclusive meals at the table are best and should be encouraged as the routine. Also, young adults should be learning how to prepare and cook fresh food for themselves, rather than beginning to rely on "convenience" foods, even if they are made by you.

Use left-over bean casserole in tortilla wraps for the next day's packed lunch.

Breakfasts

Breakfast is about fuelling up to get going after the night's fast — everyone needs something, especially anyone with diabetes. There are lots of alternatives to bought sugary cereals or old-fashioned fry-ups, and this chapter is packed with ideas for everyday eating, fast-track first meals of the day, weekend specials or occasional indulgences.

Luxury muesli

Most bought muesli is too sweet and many types have added milk or cream powder, making it heavy and high fat. This healthier version is delicious and satisfying, and provides slow-release carbohydrate with natural sugar from the dried fruit for a great start to the day.

Serves four

50g/2oz/½ cup sunflower seeds
25g/1oz/¼ cup pumpkin seeds
115g/4oz/1 cup rolled oats
115g/4oz/heaped 1 cup wheat flakes
115g/4oz/heaped 1 cup barley flakes
115g/4oz/1 cup raisins
115g/4oz/1 cup chopped hazelnuts, roasted
115g/4oz/½ cup dried apricots, chopped
50g/2oz/2 cups dried apple slices, halved

1 Put the sunflower and pumpkin seeds in a dry frying pan and cook over a medium heat for 3 minutes until golden, tossing the seeds regularly to prevent them burning.

2 Mix the toasted seeds with the remaining ingredients and leave to cool. Store in an airtight container.

EAT WELL
This muesli can be sprinkled over salads – use instead of high-fat croûtons. For a snack or dessert, eat with plain yogurt, strawberries, grapes, diced apple or mango.

Tips and twists
• For a crunchy roasted mix, use jumbo oat flakes instead of rolled oats and roast them with barley and rye flakes in a large roasting pan in the oven until lightly browned. Roast the seeds in the oven in a separate pan. Mix and leave to cool completely before adding the nuts.
• Make muesli in a huge batch, making sure it is completely cool before storing in an airtight container. In a cool, dark cupboard it will keep for a year.

Light granola

Bought granola, like most breakfast cereals, has a high sugar content. This version has dried fruit for sweetness, so it won't send blood glucose levels soaring.

Serves four

115g/4oz/1 cup rolled oats
115g/4oz/1 cup jumbo oats
50g/2oz/½ cup sunflower seeds
25g/1oz/2 tbsp sesame seeds
50g/2oz/½ cup hazelnuts, roasted
25g/1oz/¼ cup almonds, roughly chopped
600ml/1 pint/2½ cups orange juice
50g/2oz/½ cup raisins
50g/2oz/½ cup dried cranberries

1 Preheat the oven to 160°C/325°F/Gas 3. Mix together the oats, seeds and nuts in a large bowl.

2 Pour the orange juice into the oat mixture and stir well so that all the ingredients are equally moist. If you have plenty of oranges, use freshly squeezed juice. You can also use a mix of oranges, lemons and grapefruits.

3 Spread out on one or two baking sheets. Bake for about 1½ hours, until crisp and well browned, stirring occasionally.

4 Remove from the oven and mix in the raisins and cranberries. Leave to cool, then store in an airtight container.

EAT WELL
For a super-healthy breakfast, spoon a generous portion of low-fat yogurt into a bowl. Top with a generous layer of fruit salad and then add a portion of granola.

Energy 813kcal/3411kJ; Protein 20.8g; Carbohydrate 100.9g, of which sugars 33.4g; Fat 39g, of which saturates 5.5g; Cholesterol 0mg; Calcium 145mg; Fibre 12.4g; Sodium 55mg.
Energy 638kcal/2674kJ; Protein 14.4g; Carbohydrate 72.3g, of which sugars 27.9g; Fat 34.3g, of which saturates 2.9g; Cholesterol 0mg; Calcium 132mg; Fibre 6.9g; Sodium 39mg.

Porridge with apple-date purée

Fresh dates and sweet apples bring great flavour and natural sweetness to porridge instead of straight sugar. They also contribute fibre and fruity food value.

Serves four

175g/6oz/1¼ cups fresh dates
2 eating apples, peeled, cored and cubed
225g/8oz/2 cups rolled oats
475ml/16fl oz/2 cups semi-skimmed
  (low-fat) milk
pinch of salt
50g/2oz/½ cup shelled, unsalted pistachio
  nuts, roughly chopped

Tips and twists
When fresh dates are available, purée a big batch with fresh pineapple or mango as well as the apple. Freeze the purée in ice cube trays, then push the cubes out into bags for storage. Use to top yogurt, rice pudding or pancakes.

1 First make the date purée. Halve the dates and remove the stones (pits) and stems. Cover the dates with boiling water and leave to soak for about 30 minutes, until softened. Strain, reserving 30ml/2 tbsp of the soaking water.

2 Remove the skin from the dates and place them in a food processor with the reserved soaking water and apples. Process to a smooth purée.

3 Place the oats in a pan with the milk, 300ml/½ pint/1¼ cups water and salt. Bring to the boil, then reduce the heat and simmer for 4–5 minutes until cooked and creamy, stirring frequently.

4 Serve the porridge in warm serving bowls, topped with a spoonful of the date purée and sprinkled with chopped pistachio nuts.

Apricot and ginger compote

Serve lots of low-fat yogurt with the fruit, either by spooning the yogurt into the bowl first (the everyday in-a-hurry method) or adding more at the table.

Serves four

200g/7oz/1½ cups dried apricots
4cm/1½in piece fresh root ginger, peeled and
  finely chopped
500g/1¼lb/2½ cups natural (plain) yogurt or
  low-fat fromage frais

1 Cover the apricots with boiling water, then leave to soak overnight.

Tips and twists
If you don't use fresh ginger very often, try freezing it. Peel the root and store it in a plastic bag in the freezer. You can grate it while still frozen, then return the rest to the freezer. Alternatively, grate or chop it before you freeze it.

2 Place the apricots and their soaking water in a pan, add the ginger and bring to the boil. Reduce the heat and simmer for 10 minutes until the fruit is soft and plump and the water becomes syrupy. Strain the apricots, reserving the syrup.

3 Serve the apricots warm with the reserved syrup. Spoon on the yogurt or fromage frais.

EAT WELL
Adapting to healthy eating is easier when emphasizing zingy flavour to take the focus away from sweetness, richness and bulk.
• Fresh root ginger is traditional for calming stomachs and nausea, and aiding digestion. For anyone finding a new way of eating, it is a brilliant, feel-good ingredient. It is enlivening and stimulating, in savoury and sweet dishes, especially when combined with citrus (lemon, lime or orange rind and juice).
• For a substantial breakfast of slow-release carbohydrates, round off with toasted wholemeal (wholewheat) muffins or a thick slices of stoneground wholemeal toast.

Energy 436kcal/1843kJ; Protein 14.1g; Carbohydrate 67.9g, of which sugars 26.7g; Fat 14g, of which saturates 2.2g; Cholesterol 7mg; Calcium 201mg; Fibre 6.6g; Sodium 141mg.
Energy 166kcal/708kJ; Protein 6.1g; Carbohydrate 35.7g, of which sugars 35.7g; Fat 1g, of which saturates 0.3g; Cholesterol 1mg; Calcium 159mg; Fibre 5.5g; Sodium 54mg.

Big breakfast smoothie

This fruit smoothie is full of natural sugar to raise early morning blood glucose levels, as well as vital nutrients from fruit for a great start. Have it with porridge, muesli or stoneground wholemeal toast for additional slow-release carbohydrate.

Makes two glasses

½ mango
1 banana
1 large orange
30ml/2 tbsp wheat bran
15ml/1 tbsp sesame seeds

EAT WELL
Fruit smoothies make good snacks or accompaniments for a light lunch. Try this drink with tomatoes, mushrooms or a little peanut butter on stoneground toast, or in a lean ham sandwich.

1 Using a small, sharp knife, skin the mango, then slice the flesh off the stone (pit). Peel the banana and break it into short lengths, then place it in a blender or processor with the mango.

2 Squeeze the orange and add the juice to the blender or food processor with the bran and sesame seeds. Whizz until smooth, and serve immediately.

Tips and twists
This drink makes a great breakfast, but is so delicious you could serve it as a dessert after a summer meal.

Raspberry and oatmeal smoothie

Just a spoonful or so of oatmeal gives substance to this tangy, invigorating drink, providing slow-release carbohydrates to balance the fruit. The smoothie will thicken up in the refrigerator so you might need to stir in a little extra juice or mineral water just before serving.

Makes one large glass

25ml/1½ tbsp medium oatmeal
150g/5oz/scant 1 cup raspberries
45ml/3 tbsp natural (plain) yogurt

1 Put the oats in a blender and add all but two or three of the raspberries, and about 30ml/2 tbsp of the yogurt. Whiz until smooth, scraping down the side of the blender if necessary. Pour in 120ml/4fl oz/½ cup very cold water. Blend briefly to mix.

EAT WELL
• For a sweeter drink, add half-and-half strawberries or a pear or apple, instead of all raspberries.
• Add unroasted, unsalted nuts, like almonds or walnuts, for protein to complement the fruit and oats.

2 Pour the raspberry and oatmeal smoothie into a large glass, swirl in the remaining yogurt and top with the reserved raspberries.

Tips and twists
If you don't like raspberry pips (seeds) in your smoothies, press the fruit through a sieve (strainer) with the back of a wooden spoon to make a smooth purée, then process with the oatmeal and yogurt as before, or try using redcurrants instead of the raspberries.

Although a steaming bowl of porridge can't be beaten as a winter warmer, this smooth, oaty drink makes a great, light alternative in warmer months. It is a good way to make sure you get your fill of wholesome oats for breakfast.

Energy 172kcal/726kJ; Protein 4.9g; Carbohydrate 27.6g, of which sugars 23.1g; Fat 5.5g, of which saturates 0.9g; Cholesterol 0mg; Calcium 102mg; Fibre 8.5g; Sodium 11mg.
Energy 186kcal/793kJ; Protein 7.5g; Carbohydrate 34.6g, of which sugars 16.4g; Fat 3.1g, of which saturates 0.4g; Cholesterol 1mg; Calcium 137mg; Fibre 5.4g; Sodium 51mg.

Muesli smoothie

This can be made the night before and chilled ready for breakfast in a glass. A drink that boosts slow-release carbohydrate is great for complementing foods that are not starchy, such as omelettes, boiled or poached eggs that are not served on hunky pieces of wholemeal toast.

Makes two glasses

1 piece preserved stem ginger
50g/2oz/¼ cup ready-to-eat dried apricots,
    halved or quartered
40g/1½oz/scant ½ cup muesli (granola)
about 200ml/7fl oz/scant 1 cup
    semi-skimmed (low-fat) milk

1 Chop the preserved ginger and put it in a blender or food processor with the apricots, muesli and milk.

2 Process until smooth. If the texture is a little too thick for your taste, add more milk. Serve in wide glasses.

Tips and twists
If you don't have any home-made muesli, use rolled oats. Look out for muesli base in healthfood shops – it's a mix of grains (unsweetened, without added milk powder) and useful for this type of recipe. Unsweetened apple juice is a good substitute to use instead of milk or, for a tangy drink, opt for orange juice. For a fresh-fruit boost, add a cored apple or stoned (pitted) peach, cut into chunks. A handful of blueberries or a peeled kiwi fruit also go well.

Grapefruit and pear breakfast juice

This deliciously refreshing, rose-tinged blend of grapefruit and pear juice will keep you bright-eyed and bushy-tailed. It's perfect for a quick breakfast drink, especially with pear, that provides slow-release carbohydrate. For more carbohydrate, have a barely ripe banana or cereal.

Makes two tall glasses

1 pink and 1 white grapefruit, halved
2 ripe pears
ice cubes

1 Take a thin slice from one grapefruit half and cut a few thin slices of pear. Roughly chop the remaining pear and push through a juicer.

2 Squeeze all the juice from the grapefruit halves. Mix the fruit juices together and serve over ice. Decorate with the grapefruit and pear slices.

Tips and twists
Whiz a peeled orange or 4–6 ripe plums in a blender with the pears for different versions of this juice.

Energy 204kcal/864kJ; Protein 6.6g; Carbohydrate 39.1g, of which sugars 28.8g; Fat 3.4g, of which saturates 1.4g; Cholesterol 6mg; Calcium 150mg; Fibre 3.1g; Sodium 97mg.
Energy 71kcal/304kJ; Protein 0.5g; Carbohydrate 18.2g, of which sugars 18.2g; Fat 0.2g, of which saturates 0g; Cholesterol 0mg; Calcium 21mg; Fibre 0g; Sodium 9mg.

Egg-stuffed tomatoes

This simple dish is quick and easy to prepare and makes a nutritious breakfast with wholemeal bread, toast or warm rolls. It also makes a good brunch dish that can be prepared in advance.

Serves four

175ml/6fl oz/¾ cup low-fat crème fraîche
30ml/2 tbsp chopped fresh chives
30ml/2 tbsp chopped fresh basil
30ml/2 tbsp chopped fresh parsley
4 hard-boiled eggs
4 ripe tomatoes
salt and ground black pepper
salad leaves, to serve

EAT WELL
Eating eggs (protein and fat) at the same time as crusty white bread helps to slow down the time taken for the carbohydrate to be digested and absorbed.

1 In a small bowl, mix together the crème fraîche and herbs, and then set aside. Using an egg slicer or sharp knife, cut the eggs into thin slices.

2 Make deep cuts to within 1cm/½in of the base of each tomato. (There should be the same number of cuts in each tomato as there are slices of egg.)

3 Fan open the tomatoes and sprinkle with salt, then insert an egg slice into each slit.

4 Place each stuffed tomato on a plate together with a few salad leaves, season with a little salt and pepper, and serve with a dollop of the herb crème fraîche mixture on the side.

Energy 309kcal/1276kJ; Protein 7.6g; Carbohydrate 3.6g, of which sugars 3.4g; Fat 29.6g, of which saturates 5.2g; Cholesterol 214mg; Calcium 62mg; Fibre 1.5g; Sodium 223mg.

Frittata with sun-dried tomatoes

This Italian omelette, made with tangy Parmesan cheese, can be served warm or cold.
For a filling breakfast, serve it with chunks of warm ciabatta or wholemeal toast.

Serves four

6 sun-dried tomatoes
30ml/2 tbsp olive oil
1 small onion, finely chopped
pinch of fresh thyme leaves
6 eggs
25g/1oz/⅓ cup freshly grated Parmesan
   cheese, plus shavings to serve
salt and ground black pepper
thyme sprigs, to garnish

1 Place the sun-dried tomatoes in a
bowl and pour over enough boiled
water from the kettle to just cover.
Leave to soak for 15 minutes.

2 Lift the tomatoes out of the hot water
and pat dry on kitchen paper. Reserve
the soaking water. Use a sharp knife to
cut the tomatoes into thin strips.

3 Heat the olive oil in a frying pan. Cook
the onion for 5–6 minutes. Add the
thyme and tomatoes and cook for a
further 2–3 minutes.

Tips and twists
Omit the Parmesan and instead
add diced red (bell) pepper with the
onion for a lower-fat version.

4 Break the eggs into a bowl and beat
lightly. Stir in 45ml/3 tbsp of the tomato
soaking water and the Parmesan and
season to taste. Raise the heat under
the pan. When the oil is sizzling, add
the eggs. Mix quickly into the other
ingredients, then stop stirring. Lower
the heat to medium and cook for
4–5 minutes, or until the base is golden
and the top puffed.

5 Take a large plate, invert it over the
pan and, holding it firmly with oven
gloves, turn the pan and the frittata
over on to it. Slide the frittata back into
the pan, and continue cooking for
3–4 minutes until golden brown on the
second side. Remove the pan from the
heat. Cut the frittata into wedges,
garnish with thyme sprigs and
Parmesan, and serve immediately.

Energy 170kcal/705kJ; Protein 5.7g; Carbohydrate 3g, of which sugars 2.6g; Fat 15.2g, of which saturates 4.1g; Cholesterol 13mg; Calcium 158mg; Fibre 0.6g; Sodium 167mg.

Scrambled eggs with smoked salmon

A special treat for weekend breakfasts, eggs served this way are a good alternative to the traditional fry-up. Thin wholemeal toast and butter make a good accompaniment.

Serves one

3 eggs
15ml/1 tbsp single (light) cream or milk
knob (pat) of butter
1 slice of smoked salmon, chopped or whole
salt and ground black pepper
sprig of fresh parsley, to garnish
triangles of hot toast, to serve

EAT WELL
Try scrambled eggs and smoked salmon with baked potatoes, they slow down the rate at which the carbohydrate is broken down.

1 Whisk the eggs well in a bowl, together with half the cream or milk, season with a generous grinding of black pepper. Don't add any additional salt as the smoked salmon will probably be quite naturally salty.

2 Melt the butter in a pan, then add the egg mixture and stir until nearly set. Add the rest of the cream, which prevents the eggs from overcooking.

3 Either stir in the chopped smoked salmon or serve the whole slice alongside the egg. Serve immediately on warmed plates.

Tips and twists
Scrambled eggs with tomatoes and mushrooms are delicious for breakfast, lunch or supper. Halve some button mushrooms and brown them in a little olive oil over high heat for a few minutes. Add some halved cherry tomatoes and a good sprinkling of pepper, with chopped fresh tarragon or parsley. Toss well until hot. Serve the eggs on toasted muffins or crumpets, with the tomatoes mixture.
   Try scrambling the eggs with some crisply grilled bacon pieces, or chopped lean, cooked ham, and some grated Cheddar cheese.

Energy 447kcal/1862kJ; Protein 37.3g; Carbohydrate 0.4g, of which sugars 0.4g; Fat 33.6g, of which saturates 13.1g; Cholesterol 734mg; Calcium 128mg; Fibre 0g; Sodium 1370mg.

Smoked haddock with spinach and egg

This is a really special breakfast treat. Use young spinach leaves in season and serve a carbohydrate on the side – warm rolls, for example – or have an oaty fruit drink.

Serves four

4 undyed smoked haddock fillets
milk for poaching
45ml/3 tbsp low-fat Greek (US strained plain)
    yogurt or crème fraîche
30ml/2 tbsp olive oil
250g/9oz fresh spinach, tough stalks removed
white wine vinegar
4 eggs
salt and ground black pepper

1 Place the fish in a frying pan and pour in just enough milk to come half way up the fish. Over a low heat, poach the haddock fillets, shaking the pan gently to keep the fish moist on top, for about 5 minutes.

2 When cooked, remove the fish from the pan and keep warm. Increase the heat under the milk, bring to a steady simmer, and allow to reduce by about half, stirring occasionally.

3 Stir the yogurt or crème fraîche into the milk, and heat through without letting the sauce boil. Season to taste with pepper and remove from the heat.

4 Heat a frying pan then add the olive oil. Add the spinach, stirring briskly for a few minutes. Season lightly then set aside, keeping it warm.

5 To poach the eggs, bring 4cm/1½in water to a simmer and add a few drops of vinegar. Gently crack two eggs into the water and cook for 3 minutes. Remove the first egg using a slotted spoon and rest in the spoon on some kitchen paper to remove any water.

6 Repeat with the second egg, then cook the other two in the same way.

7 Place the spinach over the fillets and a poached egg on top. Pour over the cream sauce and serve immediately.

Energy 350kcal/1455kJ; Protein 27.5g; Carbohydrate 1.5g, of which sugars 1.4g; Fat 26.3g, of which saturates 14g; Cholesterol 277mg; Calcium 170mg; Fibre 1.3g; Sodium 969mg.

Herrings in oatmeal with bacon

With an oatmeal coating, these herrings make a delicious, sustaining breakfast for a special treat, but the fried bacon and fish make it too high in fat for everyday eating. Any other oily fish, such as mackerel, is also good cooked this way. Use cherry tomatoes for extra flavour, and grill or bake them in the oven while the herring is cooking.

Serves four

50g/2oz/½ cup medium oatmeal
10ml/2 tsp mustard powder
4 herrings, about 225g/8oz each, cleaned,
   boned, heads and tails removed
30ml/2 tbsp sunflower oil
8 rindless bacon rashers (strips)
salt and ground black pepper
grilled (broiled) tomatoes and lemon, to serve

1 In a shallow dish, combine the oatmeal and mustard powder and season. Press the herrings in the mixture to coat.

2 Heat the oil in a large frying pan and fry the bacon. Remove from the pan.

3 Lay the herrings in the pan. Cook the fish for about 3–4 minutes on each side, until crisp and golden.

4 Using a spatula, lift the herrings from the pan, serve with the bacon, grilled (broiled) tomatoes and lemon wedges.

Tips and twists

For a lower-fat, traditional-style breakfast, cook the herrings without a coating under the grill (broiler), skin sides up, until crisp. Turn, brush with a little oil, and sprinkle with oatmeal, then grill on a lower heat, until well browned. Omit the bacon and serve with grilled mushrooms and tomatoes.

Energy 700kcal/2917kJ; Protein 51.9g; Carbohydrate 20.9g, of which sugars 0g; Fat 46g, of which saturates 11.2g; Cholesterol 139mg; Calcium 153mg; Fibre 2g; Sodium 1050mg.

Jugged kippers

Most often grilled with butter, kippers are a little too indulgent (and quite salty) for everyday eating but make a good occasional breakfast or brunch treat instead of a high-fat mixed grill. Serve with wholemeal soda bread or toast, for carbohydrate, and follow with fresh fruit or a vegetable juice for a well-balanced breakfast.

Serves four

4 kippers (smoked herrings), preferably
   naturally smoked, whole or filleted
25g/1oz/2 tbsp butter
ground black pepper
butter and lemon wedges, to serve

1 Select a large jug (pitcher), or a bowl big enough for the kippers to be entirely immersed when the water is added. If the heads are still on the kippers, remove them, but leave the tails on.

2 Put the fish into the jug, tails up, and then cover them with boiling water. Leave for about 5 minutes, until tender.

3 Drain well and serve on warmed plates with lemon, a pat of butter and a little black pepper on each kipper.

Energy 248kcal/1025kJ; Protein 15.9g; Carbohydrate 0.1g, of which sugars 0.1g; Fat 20.4g, of which saturates 5.8g; Cholesterol 68mg; Calcium 49mg; Fibre 0g; Sodium 776mg.

Oatmeal pancakes with bacon

These pancakes are high in slow-release carbohydrate – what a great way to replenish low blood glucose at the beginning of the day. Grilling the bacon helps to keep the fat levels down. Serve with poached eggs (or fry them in a non-stick pan with very little olive oil) and grilled tomatoes.

Makes eight pancakes

115g/4oz/1 cup fine wholemeal
  (whole-wheat) flour
25g/1oz/¼ cup fine pinhead oatmeal
pinch of salt
2 eggs
about 300ml/½ pint/1¼ cups buttermilk
butter or oil, for greasing
8 bacon rashers (strips)

Tips and twists
When whole oats are chopped into pieces they are called pinhead or coarse oatmeal. They take longer to cook than rolled oats, which are in larger, thin flakes but have a chewier texture.

1 Mix the flour, oatmeal and salt in a bowl or food processor, beat in the eggs and add enough buttermilk to make a creamy batter of the same consistency as ordinary pancakes.

2 Thoroughly heat a non-stick or cast-iron griddle or frying pan over a medium-hot heat. When very hot, grease lightly with butter or oil, using kitchen paper for an even application.

3 Pour in the batter, about a ladleful at a time. Tilt the pan around to spread evenly and cook for about 2 minutes on the first side, or until set and the underside is browned. Turn over and cook for 1 minute until browned.

4 Keep each of the pancakes warm while you cook the others. Grill (broil) the bacon. Roll the pancakes with a cooked rasher to serve.

Energy 177kcal/740kJ; Protein 10.4g; Carbohydrate 11.5g, of which sugars 1.7g; Fat 10.3g, of which saturates 4.2g; Cholesterol 76mg; Calcium 52mg; Fibre 1.3g; Sodium 573mg.

Kidney and mushroom toasts

Devilled kidneys are a traditional English breakfast, and they pair up with mushrooms beautifully for a traditional dish that doesn't contain a huge amount of fat. Mustard is the essential seasoning for this dish, and olive oil is a delicious alternative to butter for healthy cooking.

Serves two to four

4 large, flat field (portobello) mushrooms, stalks trimmed
45ml/3 tbsp olive oil
10ml/2 tsp Irish wholegrain mustard
15ml/1 tbsp chopped fresh parsley
4 lamb's kidneys, skinned, halved and cored
4 thick slices of stoneground wholemeal (whole-wheat) bread, cut into rounds and toasted, or halved, warm scones
sprig of parsley, to garnish
tomato wedges, to serve

Tips and twists
Do not overcook the kidneys as they become unpleasantly tough.

1 Wipe or rinse the tops of the mushrooms thoroughly and gently remove the stalks.

2 Rinse the prepared lamb's kidneys well under cold running water, and pat dry with kitchen paper. Heat the oil, with the mustard and half the parsley in a large frying pan.

3 Add the mushrooms and kidneys to the pan and fry for about 3 minutes on each side. When the kidneys are cooked to your liking, sprinkle with the remaining parsley.

4 Serve the mushrooms and kidneys with the tomato, garnished with parsley, on top of the hot toast or scones.

Energy 297kcal/1240kJ; Protein 19.6g; Carbohydrate 13.2g, of which sugars 1.3g; Fat 18.9g, of which saturates 10.8g; Cholesterol 323mg; Calcium 72mg; Fibre 2.2g; Sodium 387mg.

Snacks and Drinks

When you need regular food to keep your body happy and healthy, it's good to have a collection of delicious snack ideas. Dips, pâtés and savoury toast-toppers are brilliant for snack-meals, while hard-working drinks are brilliant for revitalizing. Forget salty, high-fat, artificial-flavoured commercial snack packs — enjoy these feel-good fillers instead.

Smoked mackerel pâté

Traditional smoked fish pâté is laden with butter and cream, sending the saturated fat content soaring, but this recipe uses low-fat soft cheese instead. The pâté provides useful good fat from oily fish and makes a tasty sandwich filler for packed lunches.

Serves six

4 smoked mackerel fillets, skinned
225g/8oz/1 cup low-fat soft cheese, such as
    quark or curd cheese
1–2 garlic cloves, finely chopped
juice of ½ lemon
30ml/2 tbsp chopped fresh chervil, parsley
    or chives
15ml/1 tbsp Worcestershire sauce
salt and cayenne pepper
fresh chives, to garnish
warmed Melba toast, to serve

EAT WELL
For a healthy lunch, serve with
carrot and celery sticks, tomatoes
and a baby potatoes in their skins.

1 Break up the smoked mackerel fillets, discarding any remaining bones. Put the pieces in a food processor. Add the soft cheese, the chopped garlic and lemon juice.

2 Process the mixture for a few seconds, just long enough to mix the ingredients, then add the chopped chervil, parsley or chives.

3 Process the mixture until it is fairly smooth but still slightly chunky, then add Worcestershire sauce, salt and cayenne pepper to taste. Process the pâté again to mix.

4 Spoon the pâté into a dish, cover with clear film (plastic wrap) and chill. Garnish with chives and serve with Melba toast.

Energy 344kcal/1421kJ; Protein 10.7g; Carbohydrate 0.5g, of which sugars 0.4g; Fat 33.3g, of which saturates 14.3g; Cholesterol 88mg; Calcium 57mg; Fibre 0.1g; Sodium 518mg.

Artichoke and cumin dip

This aromatic dip with a powerful garlic punch is a great alternative to high-fat pâtés and mayonnaise-based dips. Serve it with wholemeal pitta and add a crunchy side salad of fennel, perhaps with some fresh orange segments, for a delicious lunch.

Serves four

2 x 400g/14oz cans artichoke hearts, drained
2 garlic cloves, peeled
2.5ml/½ tsp ground cumin
olive oil
salt and ground black pepper

Tips and twists

Canned artichoke hearts make a good store-cupboard (pantry) standby, useful for adding to pizza toppings, and for a pasta sauce, as well as this quick and easy dip.

1 Put the artichoke hearts in a food processor with the garlic and ground cumin, and a generous drizzle of olive oil. Process to a smooth purée and season with plenty of salt and ground black pepper to taste.

2 Spoon the artichoke dip into a serving bowl and fork the top lightly. Serve topped with an extra drizzle of olive oil swirled over the dip, with slices of warm pitta bread, or wholemeal (whole-wheat) toast fingers for dipping.

Energy 76kcal/315kJ; Protein 2g; Carbohydrate 3.8g, of which sugars 2g; Fat 6g, of which saturates 0.8g; Cholesterol 0mg; Calcium 84mg; Fibre 2.7g; Sodium 121mg.

Tzatsiki with courgettes and aubergines

This classic yogurt and cucumber dip is an excellent alternative to mayonnaise or cream-based sauces, and is especially good with mixed pan-fried vegetables. If you are making the tzatsiki in advance do not add the salt until serving, as it makes the yogurt watery.

2 Trim the courgettes and aubergine, then rinse them and pat them dry. Cut them lengthways into long, thin slices and coat them lightly with the flour.

3 Heat the oil in a large, heavy or non-stick frying pan and add as many courgette slices as the pan will hold in one layer. Cook for 1–2 minutes, until light golden, then turn them over and brown the other side. Lift the slices out, drain them on kitchen paper and keep them hot while cooking the remaining courgette slices followed by the slices of aubergine.

4 Pile the fried slices in a large warmed bowl, sprinkle with salt and pepper and serve immediately, together with the bowl of chilled tzatsiki, garnished with a few mint leaves.

Serves four

3 courgettes (zucchini)
1 aubergine (eggplant)
25g/1oz/¼ cup plain (all-purpose) flour
sunflower oil, for frying
salt and ground black pepper

For the tzatsiki
15cm/6in piece of cucumber
200g/7oz Greek (US strained plain) yogurt
1 or 2 garlic cloves, crushed
15ml/1 tbsp extra virgin olive oil
30ml/2 tbsp thinly sliced fresh mint leaves,
   plus extra to garnish

1 Start by making the tzatsiki. Peel the cucumber, grate it coarsely into a colander, and press out most of the liquid. Add the cucumber to the yogurt with the garlic, olive oil and mint. Stir in salt to taste, cover and chill.

Energy 236kcal/977kJ; Protein 6.7g; Carbohydrate 9.9g, of which sugars 4.2g; Fat 19.6g, of which saturates 4.5g; Cholesterol 0mg; Calcium 135mg; Fibre 2.4g; Sodium 40mg.

Aubergine dip

Adjust the amount of garlic and lemon juice in this richly flavoured aubergine dip depending on how garlicky or tart you want it to be. The dip can be served with a garnish of chopped fresh coriander leaves, olives or pickled cucumbers. It's good in mini pitta or served with crispbread.

Serves two to four

1 large or 2 medium aubergines (eggplants)
2–4 garlic cloves, chopped
90ml/6 tbsp tahini
juice of 1 lemon, or to taste
salt and ground black pepper
pitta, olives, fresh coriander (cilantro) to serve

1 Place the aubergine(s) directly over the flame of a gas stove or on the coals of a barbecue. Turn the aubergine(s) frequently until the skin is charred. Remove from the heat with tongs.

2 Put the aubergine(s) in a plastic bag and seal the top tightly, or place in a bowl and cover with plenty of sheets of crumpled kitchen paper. Leave to cool for 30–60 minutes.

3 Peel off the blackened skin from the aubergine(s), reserving the juices. Chop the aubergine flesh, either by hand for a coarse texture or in a food processor or blender for a smooth purée. Put the aubergine in a bowl and stir in the reserved juices.

4 Add the chopped garlic and tahini to the aubergine and stir until smooth. Stir in the lemon juice. If the mixture becomes too thick, stir in 15–30ml/ 1–2 tbsp water. Season the dip with a little salt and plenty of ground black pepper to taste.

5 Spoon the dip into a serving bowl. Serve at room temperature. Garnish with a few sprigs of fresh coriander or fresh mint, and olives. Serve with pitta.

EAT WELL
• Toss cooked pasta with canned tuna, chopped hard-boiled egg and spring onion. Serve topped with generous dollops of aubergine dip – delicious instead of a cream sauce.
• Serve the dip as a delicious filling for baked potatoes instead of butter. It's also good with hard-boiled eggs and chopped olives.

Energy 129kcal/535kJ; Protein 3.3g; Carbohydrate 1.9g, of which sugars 1.6g; Fat 12.2g, of which saturates 1.6g; Cholesterol 0mg; Calcium 85mg; Fibre 2.5g; Sodium 4mg.

Hummus

This classic Greek chickpea dip is flavoured with garlic and tahini – sesame seed paste. For a full flavour, a little ground cumin or a seeded, roasted red pepper can be added. It is delicious with pitta bread or crudités as a delicious dip, and great in sandwiches instead of butter.

Serves four to six

400g/14oz can chickpeas, drained
60ml/4 tbsp tahini
2–3 garlic cloves, crushed
juice of ½–1 lemon
salt and ground black pepper

EAT WELL
Hummus makes a good filling for baked potatoes, lowering their overall GI value and adding protein, especially served with a mixed salad or followed by fresh fruit.

1 Reserving a few for garnish, coarsely mash the chickpeas in a mixing bowl with a fork. If you like a smoother purée, process the chickpeas in a food processor or blender until a smooth paste is formed.

2 Mix the tahini into the bowl of chickpeas, then stir in the crushed garlic cloves and the lemon juice, to taste. Season with salt and ground black pepper to taste and garnish the top with the reserved chickpeas. Serve the hummus at room temperature.

Energy 140kcal/586kJ; Protein 6.9g; Carbohydrate 11.2g, of which sugars 0.4g; Fat 7.8g, of which saturates 1.1g; Cholesterol 0mg; Calcium 97mg; Fibre 3.6g; Sodium 149mg.

Cannellini bean bruschetta

More lunch than between-meal snack, this dish is a sophisticated version of beans on toast. Canned beans can be used instead of dried; use 275g/10oz/2 cups drained, canned beans and add to the tomato mixture in step 3. Rinse and drain them well before use.

Serves four

150g/5oz/⅔ cup dried cannellini beans
5 fresh tomatoes
45ml/3 tbsp olive oil, plus extra for drizzling
2 sun-dried tomatoes in oil, drained and
    finely chopped
1 garlic clove, crushed
30ml/2 tbsp chopped fresh rosemary
salt and ground black pepper
a handful of fresh basil leaves, to garnish

To serve
12 slices Italian-style bread, such as ciabatta
1 large garlic clove, halved

1 Place the beans in a large bowl and cover with water. Leave to soak overnight. Drain and rinse the beans, then place in a pan and cover with fresh water. Bring to the boil and boil rapidly for 10 minutes.

2 Reduce the heat and simmer the beans for 50–60 minutes or until tender. Drain and set aside. Meanwhile, place the tomatoes in a bowl, cover with boiling water, leave for 30 seconds, then peel, seed and chop the flesh.

3 Heat the oil in a frying pan, add the fresh and sun-dried tomatoes, the crushed garlic and rosemary. Cook for 2 minutes until the tomatoes begin to break down and soften.

4 Add the tomato mixture to the cannellini beans, season to taste and mix well.

5 Rub the cut sides of the bread slices with the garlic clove, then toast lightly. Spoon the cannellini bean mixture on top of the toast. Sprinkle with basil leaves and drizzle with a little extra olive oil before serving.

EAT WELL
Cannellini beans have a low GI value, and balance the higher value of white breads. They are high in protein and low in fat. They are also a valuable source of B vitamins and minerals.

Energy 479kcal/2026kJ; Protein 19.9g; Carbohydrate 74.8g, of which sugars 10.3g; Fat 13.3g, of which saturates 2g; Cholesterol 0mg; Calcium 173mg; Fibre 10.2g; Sodium 563mg.

Scrambled eggs with tomatoes

This Greek-style version of a classic combination makes a delicious lunch or supper, and is very easy to make for a quick meal or snack. To make for just one person, use two eggs and reduce the quantities of all the other ingredients by two-thirds.

Serves four

30ml/2 tbsp extra virgin olive oil
2 or 3 shallots, finely chopped
675g/1½lb tomatoes, roughly chopped
pinch of dried oregano or 5ml/1 tsp chopped
   fresh thyme (optional)
6 eggs, lightly beaten
salt and ground black pepper
fresh thyme, to garnish

1 Heat the olive oil in a large frying pan and cook the chopped shallots, stirring occasionally, until they are glistening, translucent, and completely softened but not browned.

2 Stir in the chopped tomatoes, and dried or fresh herbs, and season with salt and ground black pepper to taste. Cook over a low heat for about 15 minutes, stirring occasionally, until most of the liquid has evaporated and the sauce is thick.

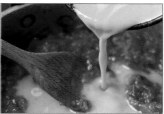

3 Add the beaten eggs to the pan and cook for 2–3 minutes, stirring continuously with a wooden spatula in the same way as when making scrambled eggs. The eggs should be just set, but not overcooked. Serve garnished with fresh thyme.

Energy 245kcal/1020kJ; Protein 10.8g; Carbohydrate 7g, of which sugars 6.6g; Fat 19.9g, of which saturates 4.1g; Cholesterol 285mg; Calcium 59mg; Fibre 1.9g; Sodium 121mg.

Feta with lemon and oregano

The longer the cheese is left to marinate, the better the flavour will be. Serve with tomato and red onion salad and lots of warm stoneground bread. Use a good-quality feta cheese and drain before using. This recipe can also be made with mozzarella instead of feta.

Serves four

200g/7oz Greek feta cheese
1 lemon
a small handful of fresh oregano sprigs
60ml/4 tbsp olive oil

1 Drain the feta and pat dry with kitchen paper. Cut it into cubes and arrange in a non-metallic bowl or dish. Grate the rind from about half the lemon and finely chop a few oregano leaves. Add these to the feta, with the remaining oregano sprigs and the lemon cut into wedges.

2 Drizzle the olive oil over the cheese and turn the mixture gently to coat all the cubes. Cover the bowl with clear film (plastic wrap).

3 Chill overnight, then serve with a selection of flat breads and salads.

Energy 225kcal/930kJ; Protein 7.9g; Carbohydrate 0.9g, of which sugars 0.8g; Fat 21.1g, of which saturates 8.4g; Cholesterol 35mg; Calcium 185mg; Fibre 0g; Sodium 721mg.

Baked eggs with creamy leeks

This simple but delicious dish is good for a supper, a snack or light lunch, and can be partially made in advance and kept in the fridge up to the point of baking. Garnish the baked eggs with crisp, freshly fried sage leaves and serve with toasted finger rolls or seeded bagels.

Serves four

olive oil, for greasing
15g/½oz/1 tbsp butter
225g/8oz small leeks, thinly sliced
75–90ml/5–6 tbsp milk
4 small-medium (US medium-large) eggs

1 Preheat the oven to 190°C/375°F/ Gas 5. Grease the base and sides of four ramekins with olive oil.

2 Melt the butter in a frying pan and cook the leeks over a medium heat, stirring frequently, for 3–5 minutes, until they are softened and translucent, but not browned.

3 Add 45ml/3 tbsp of the milk and cook over a low heat for 5 minutes, until the leeks are very soft and the milk has thickened a little. Stir occasionally to prevent the mixture from catching. Season to taste.

4 Place the ramekins in a small roasting pan and divide the cooked leeks among them. Break an egg into each, spoon over the remaining milk and season with salt and pepper.

5 Pour boiling water into the roasting pan to come about halfway up the sides of the ramekins. Transfer the pan to the preheated oven and bake for about 10 minutes, until just set. Serve piping hot.

Energy 149kcal/614kJ; Protein 4.4g; Carbohydrate 2.2g, of which sugars 1.8g; Fat 13.7g, of which saturates 7.5g; Cholesterol 123mg; Calcium 39mg; Fibre 1.3g; Sodium 64mg.

Pink grapefruit and avocado salad

Creamy avocado, peppery rocket leaves and the zesty tang of citrus fruits combine beautifully in this refreshing salad. Avocados turn brown quickly when exposed to the air, but the grapefruit juice will prevent this from occurring.

Serves four

2 pink grapefruits
2 ripe avocados
30ml/2 tbsp chilli oil
90g/3½oz rocket (arugula)

1 Slice the top and bottom off one of the grapefruits, then cut off all of the peel and pith from around the side – the best way to do this is to cut down in wide strips.

2 Working over a small bowl to catch the juices, cut out the segments from between the membranes and place them in a separate bowl. Squeeze any juices remaining in the membranes into the bowl, then discard them. Repeat with the remaining grapefruit.

3 Halve, stone (pit) and peel the avocados. Slice and add to the grapefruit. Whisk a pinch of salt into the grapefruit juice, followed by the chilli oil.

4 Pile the rocket leaves on to four plates and top with the grapefruit segments and avocado slices. Pour over the dressing and toss gently with your fingers. Serve immediately.

EAT WELL
For added carbohydrate, the salad is delicious with pasta or pearl barley. Sprinkle with finely chopped walnuts and snipped fresh chives.

Energy 151kcal/625kJ; Protein 1.1g; Carbohydrate 5.6g, of which sugars 5.2g; Fat 13.9g, of which saturates 2.4g; Cholesterol 0mg; Calcium 24mg; Fibre 1.9g; Sodium 13mg.

Chopped eggs and onions

Quick and easy to make, this is a speedy lunch that you could also pack up and take to work.
An egg-based lunch is a satisfying meal that will see you through until the evening meal.

Serves four to six

8–10 eggs
6–8 spring onions (scallions) and/or 1 yellow
    or white onion, very finely chopped, plus
    extra to garnish
60–90ml/4–6 tbsp mayonnaise or
    low-fat soft cheese
mild French wholegrain mustard,
    to taste (optional)
15ml/1 tbsp chopped fresh parsley
salt and ground black pepper
rye bread, pumpernickel or rye crispbreads,
    to serve

1 Put the eggs in a large pan and pour
in cold water to cover. Heat the water.
When the water is boiling, reduce the
heat to a simmer and cook the eggs for
10 minutes. Turn the eggs twice so
they cook evenly.

2 Drain the eggs, hold them under cold
running water, then remove the shells,
dry the eggs and chop roughly.

Tips and twists
Holding a freshly boiled egg under
cold running water helps to prevent
the yolk from acquiring a greenish
tinge where it meets the white.

3 Place the chopped eggs in a large
bowl. Add the onions, season with salt
and pepper and mix well. Gradually add
enough mayonnaise to bind the
ingredients together.

4 Stir in the mustard, if using, and the
chopped parsley, or sprinkle the parsley
on top to garnish. If you have time, chill
the mixture before serving with rye
bread or crackers.

Energy 170kcal/706kJ; Protein 8.7g; Carbohydrate 0.5g, of which sugars 0.5g; Fat 15.1g, of which saturates 3.2g; Cholesterol 261mg; Calcium 48mg; Fibre 0.3g; Sodium 140mg.

Pea and mint omelette

Serve this deliciously light omelette with crusty bread and a green salad for a fresh and tasty lunch. For extra carbohydrate, add halved boiled baby new potatoes.

Serves two

4 eggs
50g/2oz/½ cup frozen peas
30ml/2 tbsp chopped fresh mint
a knob (pat) of butter
salt and ground black pepper

1 Break the eggs into a large bowl and beat with a fork. Season well with salt and pepper and set aside.

2 Cook the peas in a large pan of salted boiling water for 3–4 minutes until tender. Drain well in a colander and add to the eggs in the bowl. Stir in the chopped fresh mint and swirl with a spoon until thoroughly combined.

3 Heat the butter in a frying pan until foamy. Pour in the egg and cook over a medium heat for 3–4 minutes, drawing in the cooked egg from the edges, until the mixture is nearly set.

4 Finish off cooking the omelette under a hot grill (broiler) until set and golden on top. Carefully fold the omelette over, transfer to a warmed plate, cut it in half and serve immediately.

EAT WELL
• Vegetable omelettes are delicious and full of goodness: try a mixture of tiny fresh or frozen broccoli or cauliflower florets, fresh peas, skinned broad (fava) beans and sliced spring onions. Cook diced red or green (bell) peppers in a little olive oil until softened.
• Canned cannellini beans or chickpeas go well with the vegetables, adding carbohydrate as well as protein.
• Add cooked small pasta shapes.

Energy 205kcal/851kJ; Protein 14.3g; Carbohydrate 2.9g, of which sugars 0.6g; Fat 15.6g, of which saturates 5.8g; Cholesterol 391mg; Calcium 63mg; Fibre 1.2g; Sodium 171mg.

Beansprout and broccoli boost

Beansprouts are a highly nutritious food, bursting with vitamins B and C. Although mild in flavour, their juiciness works well in any nourishing blend. Mixed with broccoli and naturally sweet fruits. This blend includes low GI pear and is a real tonic for general wellbeing.

Makes two small glasses

90g/3½oz broccoli
1 large pear
90g/3½oz/scant ½ cup beansprouts
200g/7oz green grapes

1 Using a small, sharp knife cut the broccoli into small pieces.

2 Quarter the pear and carefully remove the core, then roughly chop the flesh into small chunks.

3 Push all the ingredients through the juicer. Pour into glasses and serve poured over ice cubes.

EAT WELL
Vegetable juices can seem strange at first, but it takes no time to acquire a taste for fruit-and-veg drinks. Orange, apple, kiwi, grapes and mango all go well with vegetables – especially yellow and red (bell) peppers, cucumber, celery, fennel and watercress.

Wheatgrass tonic

The nutritional benefits of wheatgrass are enormous. It is grown from wheat berries and is a concentrated source of chlorophyll, which combats tiredness and fatigue, and also provides enzymes, vitamins and minerals. It has a distinctive flavour so in this juice it is blended with mild white cabbage, but it is just as tasty combined with other vegetables instead.

Makes one glass

50g/2oz white cabbage
90g/3½oz wheatgrass

1 Using a large sharp knife, cut the core from the cabbage and roughly shred the leaves. Push through a juicer with the wheatgrass. Pour the juice into a small glass and serve immediately.

Energy 119kcal/505kJ; Protein 3.9g; Carbohydrate 25.5g, of which sugars 24.6g; Fat 0.8g, of which saturates 0.2g; Cholesterol 0mg; Calcium 56mg; Fibre 4.2g; Sodium 10mg.
Energy 36kcal/149kJ; Protein 3.2g; Carbohydrate 3.9g, of which sugars 3.8g; Fat 0.8g, of which saturates 0.1g; Cholesterol 0mg; Calcium 178mg; Fibre 2.9g; Sodium 130mg.

Pumpkin seed, kelp and spinach

This energizing drink contains spinach, apricots, carrots and pumpkin seeds, which are all rich in iron, as well as kelp, a type of seaweed, to give you an invigorating lift. Iron is essential for carrying oxygen in the blood and a shortage can quickly lead to tiredness and anaemia.

Makes one glass

50g/2oz/¼ cup ready-to-eat dried apricots
15ml/1 tbsp pumpkin seeds
250g/9oz carrots
50g/2oz spinach
15ml/1 tbsp lemon juice
10ml/2 tsp kelp powder
mineral water
spinach leaf and pumpkin seeds, to decorate

Tips and twists
Sea vegetables are packed with minerals, protein and other valuable nutrients. Kelp is often sold in powder form, along with spirulina, a similarly nutrient-packed seaweed.

1 Chop the apricots finely, cover with 100ml/3½fl oz/ scant ½ cup boiling water and leave for 10 minutes.

2 Using a large, sharp knife, carefully chop the pumpkin seeds into small pieces. (Take it slowly at first as the whole seeds have a tendency to scatter.) Roughly chop the carrots.

3 Drain the apricots. Push the spinach through a juicer, followed by the apricots and carrots. Stir in the lemon juice, pumpkin seeds and kelp powder.

4 Pour the juice into a glass, top up with a little mineral water, decorate with a spinach leaf and pumpkin seeds, then serve immediately for maximum benefit.

Wheatgerm and banana smoothie

Wheatgerm, the most nutritious part of the wheat grain, is packed with B and E vitamins, protein and minerals. Combined with a firm, not-too-ripe, banana, it makes a great carbohydrate-rich drink that is boosted by the goodness of citrus juice and linseeds. It makes a satisfyingly good mid-morning or afternoon snack.

Makes one large glass

30ml/2 tbsp wheatgerm
1 large banana, chopped
130g/4½oz/generous ½ cup yogurt
15ml/1 tbsp linseeds (flax seeds)
juice of 1 lime
juice of 1 large orange
mineral water (optional)
linseeds and grated lime zest, to decorate

1 Put the wheatgerm, two-thirds of the banana, the yogurt and linseeds in a blender or food processor.

2 Blend until smooth then, using a plastic spatula or spoon, scrape down the side of the bowl if necessary. Blend again or stir well.

3 Add the lime and orange juice to the yogurt mixture and blend again until evenly mixed.

4 Pour the juice into a large glass and top up with mineral water. Decorate with linseeds, lime zest and the remaining banana, then serve.

EAT WELL
• Unsalted, unroasted cashew nuts are good in fruit drinks, especially with banana.
• For a super-fruity drink, instead of squeezing the juice from the orange, peel it, remove the pith and pips (seeds), cut it into chunks, and blend with the other ingredients.

Energy 301kcal/1261kJ; Protein 8.5g; Carbohydrate 49.5g, of which sugars 45.2g; Fat 8.9g, of which saturates 1.1g; Cholesterol 0mg; Calcium 226mg; Fibre 13.5g; Sodium 165mg.
Energy 361kcal/1520kJ; Protein 18.8g; Carbohydrate 48.9g, of which sugars 35.9g; Fat 11.5g, of which saturates 1.8g; Cholesterol 2mg; Calcium 290mg; Fibre 6.5g; Sodium 116mg.

Orange and avocado

Avocados are a valuable source of vitamin E and 'good' fat. Combined with parsley, asparagus and orange, this is a feel-good drink that is quite luxurious. In general, blended vegetable and fruit drinks are good to drink with a plain carbohydrate snack, such as a wholemeal scone, savoury American style bran muffin, or a toasted English muffin.

Makes two glasses

1 small avocado
small handful of parsley
75g/3oz tender asparagus spears
2 large oranges
squeeze of lemon juice
ice cubes
mineral water
orange wedges, to decorate

1 Halve the avocado and discard the stone (pit). Scoop the flesh into a blender or food processor. Remove any tough stalks from the parsley and add.

2 Roughly chop the asparagus spears and add to the avocado. Blend thoroughly until smooth, scraping the mixture down from the side of the bowl, if necessary.

3 Juice the oranges and add to the mixture with the lemon juice. Blend briefly until the mixture is very smooth.

4 Pour the juice into two glasses until two-thirds full, then add ice cubes and mineral water.

5 Serve immediately, decorate with chunky orange wedges.

Tomato and carrot boost

Carrots are naturally sweet and they can make blood glucose levels rise sharply, so drink this with a low GI snack for good balance. Along with tomatoes and oranges, carrots are full of valuable antioxidants and vitamins. Non-organic carrots contain lots of chemicals, so wash and peel before using if you are not using fresh organic produce.

Makes two glasses

3 tomatoes
1 fresh red or green chilli
250g/9oz carrots
juice of 1 orange
crushed ice

1 Quarter the tomatoes and roughly chop the chilli. (If you prefer a milder juice, remove the seeds and white pith from the chilli before chopping.)

2 Scrub the carrots if organic, peel if non-organic, trim the tops and bottoms, and chop them roughly.

3 Push the carrots through a juicer, then follow with the tomatoes and chilli. Add the orange juice and stir well to mix. Fill two tumblers with crushed ice, pour the juice over and serve.

EAT WELL
For an early morning mix of fast and slow energy sources, have this juice with slow-release carbohydrates, such as a sandwich made with thick-sliced stoneground bread and filled with homemade nut butter, or porridge (oatmeal) topped with dried fruit and nuts.

Energy 123kcal/507kJ; Protein 2.3g; Carbohydrate 6.1g, of which sugars 5.4g; Fat 10g, of which saturates 2.1g; Cholesterol 0mg; Calcium 21mg; Fibre 2.4g; Sodium 9mg.
Energy 28kcal/121kJ; Protein 1.1g; Carbohydrate 6.3g, of which sugars 6.3g; Fat 0.1g, of which saturates 0g; Cholesterol 0mg; Calcium 18mg; Fibre 0.7g; Sodium 211mg.

Tofu and strawberry whizz

This energizing blend is bursting with goodness – just what you need to get the morning off to a good start. Not only is tofu a perfect source of protein, it is also rich in minerals. With seeds and strawberries, this creamy blend should see you through until lunchtime, if drunk with cereal, or a slice of toast. Store in the refrigerator for later in the day or the following morning.

Makes 2 glasses

250g/9oz firm tofu
200g/7oz/1¾ cups strawberries
45ml/3 tbsp pumpkin or sunflower seeds,
  plus a few extra for sprinkling
juice of 2 large oranges

1 Roughly chop the tofu, then hull and roughly chop the strawberries. Reserve a few strawberry chunks.

Tips and twists
Almost any other fruit can be used instead of the strawberries. Those that blend well, such as mangoes, bananas, peaches, plums and raspberries, work particularly well.

2 Put all the ingredients in a blender or food processor and blend until completely smooth, scraping the mixture down from the side of the bowl, if necessary.

3 Pour the smoothie into tumblers and sprinkle the top with extra seeds and a few strawberry chunks.

Butternut and cinnamon squash

Lightly cooked butternut squash makes an unusual but vitamin-packed smoothie. Butternut squash's wonderfully rich, rounded flavour is lifted by the addition of tart citrus juice and a pinch of warm, spicy cinnamon. Imagine pumpkin pie in a glass and you're halfway to experiencing the flavours of this sweet, superfood treat.

Makes two glasses

1 small butternut squash,
  about 600g/1lb 6oz
2.5ml/½ tsp ground cinnamon
1 large lemon
2 oranges
1 pink grapefruit
ice cubes

1 Halve the squash, scoop out and discard the seeds, peel and cut the flesh into chunks.

2 Steam or boil the squash for 10–15 minutes until just tender. Drain well and leave to stand until cool.

3 Put the cooled squash in a blender or food processor and add the ground cinnamon.

4 Squeeze the lemon, the oranges and the grapefruit and add all the juice to the blender.

5 Process the ingredients until they are very smooth. If necessary, pause to scrape down the side of the food processor or blender and then process again.

6 Put a few ice cubes in two or three short glasses and pour over the smoothie. Serve immediately.

Energy 267kcal/1112kJ; Protein 15.7g; Carbohydrate 15.5g, of which sugars 11.2g; Fat 16.1g, of which saturates 1.7g; Cholesterol 0mg; Calcium 684mg; Fibre 2.5g; Sodium 17mg.
Energy 45kcal/192kJ; Protein 2g; Carbohydrate 8.6g, of which sugars 7.3g; Fat 0.5g, of which saturates 0.2g; Cholesterol 0mg; Calcium 77mg; Fibre 2.9g; Sodium 6mg.

Soups

Life would be sad without soup! Light to eat, but with a substantial food value; warming for a lunch-box vacuum-flask drink, great when you need homely comfort food on a chilly day, and fabulous when hot, chunky and deliciously filling. Soup can be cooked ahead, made in big batches, chilled for several days or frozen for months — it is practical, delicious and very good for you.

Asparagus and pea soup

This bright and tasty soup uses every inch of the asparagus, including the woody ends, which are usually discarded but are used here for making the stock.

2 Chop the remainder of the leeks. Heat the oil in a large pan and add the leeks, asparagus spears, carrot and celery. Cook for 10 minutes.

3 Add the peas and chopped parsley to the pan. Pour in 1.2 litres/2 pints/ 5 cups of the asparagus stock. Bring to the boil, reduce the heat and cook for 10 minutes, until all the vegetables are tender. Season well. Cool the soup slightly, then purée until smooth.

4 Cook the asparagus tips in boiling water for about 2–3 minutes until just tender. Drain and refresh under cold water. Reheat the soup, do not let it boil. Stir in the yogurt and lemon rind.

5 Ladle the soup into bowls, garnish with asparagus tips, shavings of Parmesan cheese and black pepper.

Serves six

350g/12oz asparagus
2 leeks
1 bay leaf
1 onion, chopped
leaves from 1 head of celery
few stalks of fresh parsley
1 carrot, chopped
2 celery sticks, chopped
1.75 litres/3 pints/7½ cups cold water
30ml/2 tbsp olive oil
150g/5oz fresh or frozen peas
15ml/1 tbsp chopped fresh parsley
120ml/4fl oz/½ cup natural (plain) yogurt
grated rind of ½ lemon
salt and ground black pepper
shavings of Parmesan cheese, to serve

1 Cut the woody ends from the asparagus, and place the ends in a pan. Cut the tips from the spears and set aside. Cut the tough green trimmings from the leeks and add to the pan with the asparagus ends, add the bay leaf, onion, celery leaves, parsley stalks and water. Bring to the boil and simmer for 40 minutes.

EAT WELL
For a special occasion, you may like to sieve (strain) the soup before reheating, making it silky smooth, but for good eating everyday, and to slow down carbohydrate digestion as much as possible, keep all the valuable fibre.

Energy 221kcal/912kJ; Protein 8.1g; Carbohydrate 7.1g, of which sugars 4.3g; Fat 18g, of which saturates 10.8g; Cholesterol 45mg; Calcium 151mg; Fibre 3.8g; Sodium 129mg.

Roast vegetable soup

Thickening this full-flavoured soup with a little oatmeal provides some low GI carbohydrate to help balance the high GI values of the parsnips and swede.

Serves four

2 small parsnips, quartered lengthways
4 red onions, cut into thin wedges
4 carrots, thickly sliced
4 leeks, thickly sliced
1 small swede (rutabaga), cut into chunks
4 potatoes, cut into chunks
30ml/2 tbsp olive oil
few sprigs of fresh thyme
1 bulb garlic, broken into cloves, unpeeled
1 litre/1¾ pints/4 cups vegetable stock
90ml/6 tbsp rolled oats
salt and ground black pepper
fresh thyme sprigs, to garnish

For the sun-dried tomato bread
1 ciabatta loaf (about 275g/10oz)
60ml/4 tbsp olive oil
1 garlic clove, crushed
4 sun-dried tomatoes, finely chopped
30ml/2 tbsp chopped fresh parsley

1 Preheat the oven to 200ºC/400ºF/ Gas 6. Cut the thick ends of the parsnip quarters into four, then place them in a large roasting pan. Add the onions, carrots, leeks, swede and potatoes, and spread them in an even layer.

2 Drizzle the olive oil over the vegetables. Add the thyme and unpeeled garlic cloves. Toss well and roast for 45 minutes, until all the vegetables are tender and well browned in places.

3 Meanwhile, to make the sun-dried tomato bread, cut diagonal slits along the loaf, taking care not to cut right through it. Mix the olive oil with the garlic, chopped sun-dried tomatoes and parsley.

4 Spread the mixture into each slit, then press the bread back together. Wrap the loaf in foil and bake in the hot oven for 15 minutes, opening the foil for the last 4–5 minutes so that the top of the loaf crisps up slightly.

5 Discard the thyme from the roasted vegetables. Squeeze the garlic cloves from their skins over the vegetables.

6 Process about half the vegetables with the stock and oats in a food processor or blender until smooth.

7 Pour into a pan, bring to the boil and season to taste. Add the remaining vegetables.

8 Ladle the soup into bowls and garnish with fresh thyme leaves. Serve the hot bread with the soup.

> **EAT WELL**
> If you find that parsnips, carrots and swede (rutabaga) tend to send your blood glucose levels up, add cooked pearl barley or wholemeal (whole-wheat) pasta to the soup to help slow down digestion.

Energy 113kcal/475kJ; Protein 3.1g; Carbohydrate 15.1g, of which sugars 10.4g; Fat 4.9g, of which saturates 0.8g; Cholesterol 0mg; Calcium 105mg; Fibre 6g; Sodium 18mg.

Wild mushroom soup

Piling up polenta in thin, but full-flavoured, soups is a great way of making a satisfying light meal with useful carbohydrate. Pasta shapes, macaroni, pearl barley or a mixture of wild rice and basmati rice are also good in soups and offer the same benefits.

Serves six

20g/¾oz/scant ½ cup dried porcini
   mushrooms
175ml/6fl oz/¾ cup hot water
30ml/2 tbsp olive oil
1 large red onion, chopped
3 garlic cloves, chopped
115g/4oz/1¾ cups mixed wild
   mushrooms, trimmed
120ml/4fl oz/½ cup light red wine
1.2 litres/2 pints/5 cups vegetable stock
2.5ml/½ tsp wholegrain mustard
salt and ground black pepper
chopped fresh parsley, to garnish

For the polenta
750ml/1¼ pints/3 cups milk
175g/6oz/1 cup quick-cook polenta
50g/2oz/¼ cup butter
50g/2oz/⅔ cup freshly grated Parmesan
   cheese, plus extra to serve

1 Put the porcini in a bowl and pour over the hot water. Leave them to soak for about 30 minutes. Drain, and reserve the liquid and the mushrooms.

2 Heat the oil in a large pan. Add the onion and garlic and cook for 4–5 minutes. Add the wild mushrooms and cook for a further 3–4 minutes.

3 Add the dried mushrooms and strain in the soaking liquid through a muslin-lined sieve (strainer) or coffee filter. Pour in the wine and stock, and cook for 15 minutes or until reduced by half. Remove from the heat and cool slightly.

4 Ladle half the soup into a food processor or blender and process until almost smooth. Pour the processed soup back into the soup remaining in the pan and set aside.

5 To make the polenta, bring the milk to the boil and pour in the polenta in a steady stream, stirring continuously. Cook for about 5 minutes, or until the polenta begins to come away from the side of the pan. Beat in the butter, then stir in the Parmesan.

6 Return the soup to the heat and bring just to the boil. Stir in the wholegrain mustard and season well.

7 Divide the polenta among six bowls and ladle the soup around it. Sprinkle with grated Parmesan and parsley.

Tips and twists
Many supermarkets now sell a range of wild mushrooms. If you can't find fresh porcini mushrooms, then substitute a mixture of well-flavoured cultivated varieties, such as shiitake and chestnut.

Energy 149kcal/618kJ; Protein 3.1g; Carbohydrate 9g, of which sugars 0.5g; Fat 11.4g, of which saturates 6.9g; Cholesterol 28mg; Calcium 25mg; Fibre 1.5g; Sodium 79mg.

Butter bean and sun-dried tomato soup

This soup is easy to make for a quick lunch or supper. The key is to use a good-quality home-made or bought fresh stock with good-quality pesto and sun-dried tomato purée. Follow on with a couple of pieces of fresh fruit for dessert.

Serves four

2 x 400g/14oz cans butter (lima) beans,
   drained and rinsed
900ml/1½ pints/3¾ cups chicken
   or vegetable stock
60ml/4 tbsp sun-dried tomato purée (paste)
75ml/5 tbsp pesto

Tips and twists
Try using chickpeas instead of butter beans, omit the sun-dried tomato purée (paste) and add chopped fresh parsley, spring onions (scallions) or chives, and finely grated lemon rind. Process all the soup for a smoother texture. Swirl yogurt into the soup to serve.

1 Put the butter beans in a pan. Pour in the stock and stir well. Bring the beans to the boil over a medium heat, stirring once or twice.

2 Stir in the tomato purée and pesto. Lower the heat and cover, and cook gently for 5 minutes.

3 Transfer six ladlefuls of the soup to a blender or food processor, scooping up plenty of the beans. Process until smooth, then return to the pan.

4 Heat gently, stirring frequently, for 5 minutes, then season if necessary. Ladle into four warmed soup bowls and serve with warm crusty bread or breadsticks.

Energy 269kcal/1130kJ; Protein 15.6g; Carbohydrate 28.3g, of which sugars 4.5g; Fat 11.2g, of which saturates 2.5g; Cholesterol 6mg; Calcium 111mg; Fibre 9.7g; Sodium 944mg.

Roasted pumpkin soup

The pumpkin is roasted whole, then split open and scooped out to make this delicious soup; topped with crisp strips of fried pumpkin, it is a real treat. The soup can also be made using butternut squash, or a mixture of sweet potato and pumpkin.

Serves six to eight

1.5kg/3–3½lb pumpkin
30ml/2 tbsp olive oil
2 onions, chopped
3 garlic cloves, chopped
7.5cm/3in piece fresh root ginger, grated
5ml/1 tsp ground coriander
2.5ml/½ tsp ground turmeric
pinch of cayenne pepper
1 litre/1¾ pints/4 cups vegetable stock
salt and ground black pepper
15ml/1 tbsp sesame seeds and fresh
    coriander (cilantro) leaves, to garnish

For the pumpkin crisps
wedge of fresh pumpkin, seeded
120ml/4fl oz/½ cup olive oil

1 Preheat the oven to 200°C/400°F/ Gas 6. Prick the pumpkin around the top several times with a fork.

2 Bake the whole pumpkin in the hot oven for 45 minutes or until tender. Leave until cool enough to handle.

3 When the pumpkin has cooled sufficiently, cut it in half and scrape off and discard the seeds. Take care when cutting the pumpkin as there may still be a lot of hot steam inside.

4 Cut the pumpkin flesh into slices, and then into chunks, discarding the skin. Set aside.

5 Heat the oil (you may not have to use all of it) in a large pan and add the onions, garlic and ginger, then cook gently for 4–5 minutes.

6 Add the coriander, turmeric and cayenne, and cook for 2 minutes. Stir in the pumpkin flesh and stock. Bring to the boil, reduce the heat and simmer for 20 minutes.

7 Cool the soup slightly, then purée it in a food processor or blender until smooth. Return the soup to the rinsed-out pan and season well.

8 Meanwhile, prepare the pumpkin crisps. Using a swivel-blade potato peeler, pare long thin strips off the wedge of pumpkin.

EAT WELL
Save the fried pumpkin crisps for special occasions; for everyday slow-release carbohydrate top the soup with chunky wholemeal croûtons and pumpkin seeds.
  Lightly brush thick slices of stoneground wholemeal (whole-wheat) bread with olive oil, cut them into croutons, spread in a single layer on a baking tray, and in a medium oven bake until crisp and brown, sprinkle with unsalted pumpkin seeds about halfway through cooking.

9 Heat the oil in a small saucepan and fry the strips in batches for 2 minutes, until crisp. Drain on kitchen paper.

10 Reheat the soup and ladle it into bowls. Top with the pumpkin crisps and garnish each portion with sesame seeds and coriander leaves.

Tips and twists
If only very large pumpkins are available, simply cut off two or three large wedges weighing 1.5kg/3–3½lb in total. Roast the remainder as above for 20–30 minutes or until tender.

Energy 203kcal/839kJ; Protein 2.3g; Carbohydrate 8.3g, of which sugars 6.2g; Fat 18.1g, of which saturates 2.7g; Cholesterol 0mg; Calcium 82mg; Fibre 2.8g; Sodium 2mg.

Golden chorizo and chickpea soup

Small, uncooked chorizo sausages are available from Spanish delicatessens, but ready-to-eat chorizo can be cut into chunks and used instead. The advantage of using highly flavoured sausages is that a small amount goes a long way, keeping the fat content in control.

Tips and twists

For a low-fat version, cook diced skinless, boneless chicken in the minimum of olive oil instead of the chorizo sausage.

3 Add the chilli flakes and garlic to the fat in the pan, stir through and cook for a few seconds.

4 Stir in the saffron with its soaking water, tomatoes, chickpeas, potatoes, chorizo sausages and bay leaves.

5 Pour 450ml/¾ pint/scant 2 cups of the chickpea cooking liquid into the pan, add the water, and stir in salt and pepper to taste.

6 Bring to the boil, then reduce the heat and simmer for 45–50 minutes, stirring gently occasionally, until the potatoes are tender and the soup has thickened slightly.

7 Add the chopped parsley to the soup and adjust the seasoning. Ladle the soup into four large, warmed soup plates. Serve with crusty bread.

Serves four

115g/4oz/⅔ cup dried chickpeas, soaked overnight and drained
pinch of saffron strands
45ml/3 tbsp olive oil
225g/8oz uncooked mini chorizo sausages
5ml/1 tsp dried chilli flakes
6 garlic cloves, finely chopped
450g/1lb tomatoes, roughly chopped
350g/12oz new potatoes, quartered
2 bay leaves
450ml/¾ pint/scant 2 cups water
60ml/4 tbsp chopped fresh parsley
salt and ground black pepper
crusty bread, to serve

1 Place the chickpeas in a large pan. Cover with fresh water and bring to the boil, skimming off any scum as it forms. Cover and simmer for about 1½ hours, until tender. Add more water, if necessary, to keep the chick-peas covered during cooking. Drain, reserving the cooking liquid. Soak the saffron strands in a little warm water.

2 Heat the oil in a large, deep frying pan. Add the chorizo sausages and fry over a medium heat for 5 minutes, until a lot of oil has seeped out of the sausages and they are pale golden brown. Drain and set aside.

Energy 642kcal/2674kJ; Protein 21.7g; Carbohydrate 42.3g, of which sugars 8.1g; Fat 44g, of which saturates 12.5g; Cholesterol 68mg; Calcium 174mg; Fibre 6.1g; Sodium 997mg.

Scotch broth

Sustaining and warming, Scotch broth is custom-made for damp, chilly weather, and makes a delicious winter soup anywhere. This version has added pearl barley for extra slow-release carbohydrate, and it is added at the end so it tastes nutty and wholesome.

Serves six to eight

1kg/2¼lb lean neck (US shoulder or breast) of
    lamb, cut into large, even chunks
1.75 litres/3 pints/7½ cups cold water
1 large onion, chopped
175g/6oz/¾ cup pearl barley
bouquet garni
1 large carrot, chopped
1 turnip, chopped
3 leeks, chopped
1 small white cabbage, finely shredded
salt and ground black pepper
chopped fresh parsley, to garnish

1 Put the lamb and water in a large pan over a medium heat and gently bring to the boil. Skim off the scum with a spoon. Add the onion, half the barley and bouquet garni, and mix thoroughly.

2 Bring the soup back to the boil, then reduce the heat, partly cover the pan and simmer for a further 1 hour. Make sure that it does not boil too furiously.

3 Add the remaining vegetables and barley to the pan and season with salt and ground black pepper. Bring to the boil, partly cover again and simmer for about 35 minutes, until the vegetables are tender.

4 When the soup is cooked, remove the surplus fat that will have collected on the surface with a sheet of kitchen paper. Serve the soup hot, garnished with chopped parsley, with chunks of fresh bread.

Energy 290kcal/1214kJ; Protein 27.1g; Carbohydrate 13.3g, of which sugars 6.8g; Fat 14.6g, of which saturates 6.6g; Cholesterol 95mg; Calcium 65mg; Fibre 3.3g; Sodium 118mg.

Ribollita

With lots of vegetables and beans, this classic soup makes a healthy meal full of vitamins, slow-release carbohydrate and fibre. Vary the vegetables depending on what is available.

Serves four

115g/4oz/generous ½ cup dried cannellini
    beans, soaked overnight and drained
8 garlic cloves, unpeeled
30ml/2 tbsp olive oil
6 celery sticks, chopped
3 carrots, chopped
2 onions, chopped
400g/14oz can plum tomatoes, drained
30ml/2 tbsp chopped fresh flat leaf parsley
grated rind and juice of 1 lemon
800g/1¾lb cavolo nero cabbage, sliced
1 day-old ciabatta loaf
salt and ground black pepper
olive oil, to serve

1 Put the beans in a pan and cover with fresh water. Bring to the boil and boil for 10 minutes. Drain again. Cover generously with fresh cold water and add six garlic cloves. Bring to the boil, cover and simmer for 45–60 minutes, until the beans are tender. (The cooking time varies according to how old the beans are.) Set the beans aside in their cooking liquid.

2 Heat the oil in a pan. Peel and chop the remaining garlic and add it to the pan with the celery, carrots and onions. Cook gently for 10 minutes, until beginning to soften.

3 Stir in the tomatoes, parsley, lemon rind and juice. Cover and simmer for 25 minutes. Add the sliced cavolo nero cabbage and half the cannellini beans with enough of their cooking liquid to cover all of the ingredients. Simmer for 30 minutes.

4 Process the remaining beans with a little of their remaining cooking liquid in a food processor or blender until just smooth. Add to the pan and pour in boiling water to thin the mixture to the consistency of a thick soup.

5 Remove the crust from the ciabatta and tear the bread into rough pieces, then stir them into the soup. Season well. This soup should be very thick, but you may need to add a little more boiling water. Ladle the soup into bowls and drizzle over a little olive oil.

Energy 104kcal/436kJ; Protein 5.7g; Carbohydrate 14.5g, of which sugars 6.9g; Fat 3g, of which saturates 0.5g; Cholesterol 0mg; Calcium 78mg; Fibre 5.9g; Sodium 218mg.

Bean and pistou soup

This hearty soup makes an excellent vegetarian meal, with a good mix of carbohydrate and protein. Round off the food value by having fresh fruit to follow.

Serves four to six

150g/5oz/scant 1 cup dried haricot (navy)
   beans, soaked overnight in cold water
150g/5oz/scant 1 cup dried flageolet or
   cannellini beans, soaked overnight in
   cold water
1 onion, chopped
1.2 litres/2 pints/5 cups hot vegetable stock
2 carrots, roughly chopped
225g/8oz Savoy cabbage, shredded
1 large potato, about 225g/8oz,
   roughly chopped
225g/8oz French (green) beans, chopped
salt and ground black pepper
basil leaves, to garnish

For the pistou
4 garlic cloves
8 large sprigs basil leaves
90ml/6 tbsp olive oil
60ml/4 tbsp freshly grated Parmesan cheese

1 Drain the soaked haricot and flageolet or cannellini beans and place in a casserole pot. Add the chopped onion and pour over sufficient cold water to come 5cm/2in above the beans. Cover and place the pot in an unheated oven. Set the oven to 200°C/400°F/Gas 6 and cook for about 1½ hours, or until the beans are tender.

2 Drain the beans and onions. Place half the beans and onions in a food processor or blender and process to a paste. Return the drained beans and the bean paste to the casserole pot. Add the hot vegetable stock.

3 Add the chopped carrots, shredded cabbage, chopped potato and French beans to the pot. Season with salt and pepper, cover and return the pot to the oven. Reduce the oven temperature to 180°C/350°F/Gas 4 and cook for about 1 hour, or until all the vegetables are cooked right through.

4 Meanwhile, place the garlic and basil in a mortar and pound with a pestle, then gradually beat in the oil. Stir in the grated Parmesan. Stir half the pistou into the soup and then ladle into warmed soup bowls. Top each bowl of soup with a spoonful of the remaining pistou and serve garnished with basil.

Energy 332kcal/1392kJ; Protein 17.1g; Carbohydrate 33.3g, of which sugars 6.2g; Fat 15.4g, of which saturates 3.8g; Cholesterol 10mg; Calcium 211mg; Fibre 10.4g; Sodium 129mg.

American red bean soup with salsa

This Tex-Mex style soup is served with a cooling avocado and lime salsa to make a healthy vegetarian meal with plenty of slow-release carbohydrate.

3 Bring the tomato and bean mixture to the boil and simmer for 15–20 minutes. Cool the soup slightly, then purée it in a food processor or blender until smooth. Return to the rinsed-out pan and add seasoning to taste.

4 To make the guacamole salsa, halve, stone (pit) and peel the avocados, then dice them finely. Place in a small bowl and gently, but thoroughly, mix with the finely chopped red onion and chilli, and the coriander and lime juice.

5 Reheat the soup and ladle into bowls. Spoon a little guacamole salsa into the middle of each and serve, offering Tabasco sauce for those who want to spice up their soup.

Serves six

30ml/2 tbsp olive oil
2 onions, chopped
2 garlic cloves, chopped
10ml/2 tsp ground cumin
1.5ml/¼ tsp cayenne pepper
15ml/1 tbsp paprika
15ml/1 tbsp tomato purée (paste)
2.5ml/½ tsp dried oregano
400g/14oz can chopped tomatoes
2 x 400g/14oz cans red kidney beans,
    drained and rinsed
900ml/1½ pints/3¾ cups water
salt and ground black pepper
Tabasco sauce, to serve

For the guacamole salsa
2 avocados
1 small red onion, finely chopped
1 green chilli, seeded and finely chopped
15ml/1 tbsp chopped fresh coriander (cilantro)
juice of 1 lime

1 Heat the oil in a large, heavy-based pan and add the onions and garlic. Cook for about 4–5 minutes, until softened. Add the cumin, cayenne and paprika, and cook for 1 minute, stirring continuously.

2 Stir in the tomato purée and cook for a few seconds, then stir in the oregano. Add the chopped tomatoes, kidney beans and water.

EAT WELL
This is the sort of soup to make in a big batch and freeze in small portions ready to thaw in the microwave for an instant lunch or supper. Instead of salsa, the reheated soup can be topped with a poached egg and strips of quickly sautéed red pepper.

Energy 254kcal/1064kJ; Protein 10.8g; Carbohydrate 29.2g, of which sugars 9.1g; Fat 11.2g, of which saturates 2.1g; Cholesterol 0mg; Calcium 111mg; Fibre 10.6g; Sodium 535mg.

Cod, broad bean and spinach chowder

Fresh cod and vegetables are abundant in this hearty soup, which would make a well-balanced lunch. The soup is finished with crisp Granary croûtons for crunchy texture.

Serves six

1 litre/2 pints/4 cups milk
675g/1¼lb cod fillet, skinned and boned
30ml/2 tbsp olive oil
1 onion, sliced
2 garlic cloves, finely chopped
750g/1½lb potatoes, thickly sliced
450g/1lb fresh broad (fava) beans, podded
450g/1lb baby spinach leaves
pinch of grated nutmeg
30ml/2 tbsp snipped fresh chives
salt and ground black pepper
fresh chives, to garnish

For the Granary croûtons
60ml/4 tbsp olive oil
6 slices Granary (whole-wheat) bread, crusts
    removed and cut into large cubes

1 Pour the milk into a large pan and bring to the boil. Add the cod and simmer gently for 2 minutes, then remove from the heat and leave to stand for about 6 minutes, until the fish is just cooked. Use a slotted spoon to remove the fish from the cooking liquid.

2 Using a fork, flake the cooked cod into chunky pieces, removing bones or skin, then cover and set aside.

3 Heat the olive oil in a large pan and add the onion and garlic. Cook for about 5 minutes, until softened, stirring occasionally. Add the potatoes, stir in the milk and bring to the boil. Reduce the heat and cover the pan. Cook for 10 minutes. Add the broad beans; cook for 10 minutes more or until the beans are tender and the potatoes just begin to break up.

Tips and twists
When broad (fava) beans are out of season, frozen beans are a good alternative: cook them for 5 minutes.

4 Meanwhile, to make the croûtons, heat the oil in a frying pan and add the bread cubes. Cook over a medium heat, stirring often, until golden all over. Remove using a draining spoon and leave to drain on kitchen paper.

5 Add the pieces of cod to the soup and heat through gently.

6 Just before serving, add the spinach and stir for 1–2 minutes, until wilted. Season the soup well and stir in the nutmeg and chives.

7 Ladle the soup into six warmed soup bowls and scatter some croûtons on top of each. Garnish with fresh chives and serve at once.

Energy 502kcal/2110kJ; Protein 39.3g; Carbohydrate 51.6g, of which sugars 12.9g; Fat 16.7g, of which saturates 3.9g; Cholesterol 62mg; Calcium 452mg; Fibre 8.8g; Sodium 427mg.

Leek and oatmeal soup

This is a traditional Irish soup that combines two ingredients that have been staple foods in Ireland for centuries. The leeks and oatmeal make it a great slow-release carbohydrate meal.

Serves four to six

about 1.2 litres/2 pints/5 cups chicken stock
 and milk, mixed
30ml/2 tbsp medium pinhead oatmeal
6 large leeks, sliced into 2cm/¾in pieces
25g/1oz/2 tbsp butter
sea salt and ground black pepper
pinch of ground mace
30ml/2 tbsp chopped fresh parsley
single (light) cream and chopped fresh parsley
 leaves or chives, to garnish

Tips and twists

For an extra boost of minerals use this recipe to make nettle soup in the spring, when the nettle tops are young and tender. Strip about 10oz/275g nettle tops from the stems, chop them and add to the leeks. Continue as above.

1 Bring the stock and milk to the boil over a medium heat and sprinkle in the oatmeal. Stir well to prevent lumps forming, and then simmer gently.

2 Wash the leeks in a bowl. Melt the butter in a separate pan and cook the leeks over a gentle heat until softened slightly, then add them to the stock mixture. Simmer for a further 15–20 minutes, or until the oatmeal is cooked. Extra stock or milk can be added if the soup is too thick.

3 Season the soup with a little salt, ground black pepper and mace, stir in the parsley and serve in warmed bowls. Decorate with a swirl of cream and some chopped fresh parsley or chives, if you like.

EAT WELL

Add one or two heads of broccoli, chopped in small pieces, to the soup with the leeks.

Energy 73kcal/305kJ; Protein 2.3g; Carbohydrate 6.6g, of which sugars 2.2g; Fat 4.4g, of which saturates 2.3g; Cholesterol 9mg; Calcium 28mg; Fibre 2.5g; Sodium 29mg.

Italian pea and basil soup

This is a lovely, simple soup from Italy that makes the most of peas when they are in season. Frozen peas can be used instead, however, so the soup can be enjoyed at any time of the year.

Serves four

30ml/2 tbsp olive oil
2 large onions, chopped
1 celery stick, chopped
1 carrot, chopped
1 garlic clove, finely chopped
400g/14oz/3½ cups frozen petit pois
900ml/1½ pints/3¾ cups vegetable stock
25g/1oz/1 cup fresh basil leaves, roughly
   torn, plus extra to garnish
salt and freshly ground black pepper
freshly grated Parmesan cheese and natural
   (plain) yogurt, to serve

EAT WELL
Frozen peas are easy and delicious in this low GI soup. Make a big batch and freeze it for everyday vegetable goodness.

1 Heat the oil in a large saucepan and add the onions, celery, carrot and garlic. Cover the pan and cook over a low heat for 45 minutes or until the vegetables are soft, stirring occasionally to prevent the vegetables sticking.

2 Add the peas and stock to the pan and bring to the boil. Reduce the heat, add the basil and seasoning, then simmer for 10 minutes.

3 Spoon the soup into a food processor or blender and process until the soup is smooth. Ladle into warm bowls, add a swirl of yogurt, grated Parmesan and garnish with basil.

Tips and twists
Use fresh mint or a mixture of fresh parsley, mint and chives in place of the basil.

Energy 261kcal/1078kJ; Protein 8.7g; Carbohydrate 22.9g, of which sugars 10.9g; Fat 15.7g, of which saturates 2.3g; Cholesterol 0mg; Calcium 73mg; Fibre 7.3g; Sodium 16mg.

Caribbean salt cod soup with yam

Inspired by the ingredients of the Caribbean, this colourful chunky soup is served in deep bowls around a chive-flavoured sweet yam mash.

3 Stir in the tomatoes, wine and bay leaves and bring to the boil. Pour in the water, bring to the boil, reduce the heat and simmer for 10 minutes.

4 Meanwhile, trim the stalk ends off the okra and cut the pods into chunks. Add to the soup and cook for 10 minutes. Stir in the callaloo or spinach and cook for 5 minutes, until the okra is tender.

5 Meanwhile, prepare the creamed yam. Peel the yam and cut it into large dice, then place in a pan with the lemon juice and add cold water to cover. Bring to the boil and cook for 15–20 minutes, until tender.

6 Drain the yam, then return to the pan and dry it over the heat for a few seconds. Mash with the oil and yogurt, and season well. Stir in the chives.

7 Season the soup and stir in the chopped parsley. Spoon portions of creamed yam into the centres of six soup bowls and ladle the soup around it. Serve immediately.

Serves six

200g/7oz salt cod, soaked for 24 hours
15ml/1 tbsp olive oil
1 garlic clove, chopped
1 onion, chopped
1 green chilli, seeded and chopped
6 plum tomatoes, peeled and chopped
250ml/8fl oz/1 cup white wine
2 bay leaves
900ml/1½ pints/3¾ cups water
225g/8oz okra
225g/8oz callaloo or spinach
30ml/2 tbsp chopped fresh parsley
salt and ground black pepper

For the creamed yam
675g/1½lb yam
juice of 1 lemon
30ml/2 tbsp olive oil
30ml/2 tbsp low-fat Greek (US strained plain) yogurt
15ml/1 tbsp snipped fresh chives

1 While the cod is soaking you will need to change the water several times. Drain and skin the salt cod, then rinse it under cold running water. Cut into bitesize pieces, removing any bones, and set aside.

2 Heat the oil in a heavy pan. Add the garlic, onion and chilli, and cook for 4–5 minutes until softened. Add the salt cod and cook for 3–4 minutes, until it begins to colour.

EAT WELL

Mashing yam speeds up the rate at which it is digested (just like potatoes) but eating it as part of a meal (with protein from fish) slows down the process. Low-fat Greek yogurt gives a creamy texture, and olive oil adds flavour.

Energy 322kcal/1352kJ; Protein 10.7g; Carbohydrate 36.7g, of which sugars 5.3g; Fat 12.8g, of which saturates 6.6g; Cholesterol 40mg; Calcium 159mg; Fibre 4.6g; Sodium 137mg.

Moroccan chicken soup

Inspired by the ingredients of North Africa, this spiced soup is served with a rich and pungent lemon buttter. For a lower-fat alternative, brown fresh breadcrumbs in a little olive oil instead.

Serves six

50g/2oz/¼ cup butter
450g/1lb skinless boneless chicken breasts, cut into strips
1 onion, chopped
2 garlic cloves, crushed
7.5ml/1½ tsp plain (all-purpose) flour
15ml/1 tbsp harissa
1 litre/1¾ pints/4 cups chicken stock
400g/14oz can chopped tomatoes
400g/14oz can chickpeas, drained and rinsed
salt and ground black pepper
lemon wedges, to serve

For the charmoula
50g/2oz/¼ cup slightly salted butter, at room temperature
30ml/2 tbsp chopped fresh coriander (cilantro)
2 garlic cloves, crushed
5ml/1 tsp ground cumin
1 red chilli, seeded and chopped
pinch of saffron strands
finely grated rind of ½ lemon
5ml/1 tsp paprika
25g/1oz/1 cup dried breadcrumbs

3 Stir in the flour and cook for 3–4 minutes, stirring, until beginning to brown. Stir in the harissa and cook for a further 1 minute.

4 Gradually pour in the stock and cook for 2–3 minutes, until slightly thickened. Stir in the tomatoes.

5 Return the chicken to the soup and add the chickpeas. Cover and cook over a low heat for 20 minutes. Season well.

6 Meanwhile, to make the charmoula, put the butter into a bowl and beat in the coriander, garlic, cumin, chilli, saffron strands, lemon rind and paprika. When the mixture is well combined, stir in the coarse breadcrumbs.

7 Ladle the soup into warmed bowls. Spoon a little of the charmoula into the centre of each and leave for a few seconds to allow the butter to melt into the soup before serving with lemon wedges.

1 Melt the butter in a large, heavy pan. Add the chicken strips and cook for 5–6 minutes, until beginning to brown.

2 Use a slotted spoon to remove it from the pan and set aside. Add the onion and garlic and cook over a gentle heat for 4–5 minutes, until softened.

Energy 313kcal/1312kJ; Protein 25g; Carbohydrate 18.3g, of which sugars 3.3g; Fat 16.1g, of which saturates 9g; Cholesterol 88mg; Calcium 53mg; Fibre 3.6g; Sodium 207mg.

Miso broth with tofu

This flavoursome broth is simple and highly nutritious. In Japan, it is traditionally eaten for breakfast, but it also makes a good appetizer or light lunch.

Serves four

1 bunch of spring onions (scallions) or
    5 baby leeks
15g/½oz fresh coriander (cilantro)
3 thin slices fresh root ginger
2 star anise
1 small dried red chilli
1.2 litres/2 pints/5 cups dashi or
    vegetable stock
225g/8oz pak choi (bok choy) or other Asian
    greens, thickly sliced
200g/7oz firm tofu, cut into 2.5cm/1in cubes
60ml/4 tbsp red miso
30–45ml/2–3 tbsp Japanese soy sauce
1 fresh red chilli, seeded and
    shredded (optional)

1 Cut the coarse green tops off the spring onions or baby leeks and slice the rest of the spring onions or leeks finely on the diagonal. Place the green tops in a large pan with the stalks from the coriander, the ginger, star anise, dried chilli and stock.

2 Heat the mixture over a low heat until boiling, then lower the heat and simmer for about 10 minutes. Strain the broth, return it to the pan and reheat until simmering. Add the green portion of the sliced spring onions or leeks to the soup with the pak choi or Asian greens and tofu. Cook for 2 minutes.

3 In a small bowl, combine the miso with a little soup, then stir the mixture into the pan. Add soy sauce to taste.

4 Coarsely chop the coriander leaves and stir most of them into the soup with the white part of the spring onions or leeks. Cook for 1 minute, then ladle the soup into warmed bowls. Sprinkle with the remaining chopped coriander and the shredded fresh red chilli, if using, and serve immediately.

EAT WELL
Some rice cakes make a good accompaniment for the soup but for a more substantial snack, add noodles and simmer for the time suggested on the packet.

Energy 71kcal/297kJ; Protein 7.2g; Carbohydrate 4.2g, of which sugars 3.5g; Fat 2.9g, of which saturates 0.4g; Cholesterol 0mg; Calcium 372mg; Fibre 2.6g; Sodium 884mg.

Shiitake mushroom and red onion laksa

Wholemeal pitta bread is an unconventional accompaniment to this soup. Alternatively, use buckwheat noodles for slow-release carbohydrate in place of rice noodles.

Serves six

150g/5oz/2½ cups dried shiitake mushrooms
1.2 litres/2 pints/5 cups boiling
    vegetable stock
10ml/2 tsp tamarind paste
250ml/8fl oz/1 cup hot water
6 large dried red chillies, stems removed
    and seeded
2 lemon grass stalks, finely sliced
5ml/1 tsp ground turmeric
15ml/1 tbsp grated fresh galangal
1 onion, chopped
5ml/1 tsp dried shrimp paste
30ml/2 tbsp oil
175g/6oz rice vermicelli
1 red onion, very finely sliced
1 small cucumber, seeded and cut into strips
handful of fresh mint leaves, to garnish

1 Place the mushrooms in a bowl and pour in enough boiling stock to cover them, then leave to soak for about 30 minutes. Put the tamarind paste into a bowl and pour in the hot water.

2 Mash the paste with a fork against the side of the bowl to extract as much flavour as possible, then strain and reserve the liquid, discarding the pulp.

3 Soak the chillies in enough hot water to cover for 5 minutes, then drain, reserving the soaking liquid.

4 Process the lemon grass, turmeric, galangal, onion, soaked chillies and shrimp paste in a food processor or blender, adding a little soaking water from the chillies to form a paste.

5 Heat the oil in a large, heavy pan and cook the paste over a low heat for 4–5 minutes until fragrant.

6 Add the tamarind liquid and bring to the boil, then simmer for 5 minutes. Remove from the heat. Drain the mushrooms and reserve the stock.

7 Discard the stems of the mushrooms, then halve or quarter them, if large. Add the mushrooms to the pan together with their soaking liquid, the remaining stock and the palm sugar. Simmer for 25–30 minutes or until the mushrooms are tender.

8 Put the rice vermicelli into a large bowl and cover with boiling water, then leave to soak for 4 minutes or according to the packet instructions.

9 Drain well, then divide among six bowls. Top with onion and cucumber, then ladle in the boiling shiitaki soup. Add a small bunch of mint leaves to each bowl and serve immediately.

Energy 146kcal/611kJ; Protein 4.4g; Carbohydrate 27.1g, of which sugars 3.7g; Fat 2.3g, of which saturates 0.3g; Cholesterol 4mg; Calcium 27mg; Fibre 1g; Sodium 54mg.

Vegetarian Main Courses

Meals without meat, fish or poultry can still be
packed with valuable vegetable protein, and
including them as a regular feature of your diet
promotes healthy eating. There are lots of classic
and contemporary international dishes that are
favourite meal choices, and they just happen to be
vegetarian — try them and sample others for
all-important variety and balance.

Lentil and nut loaf

It is good to eat vegetarian meals regularly and this classic choice provides a valuable mix of protein and other nutrients. The loaf can be frozen after cooking, whole or cut in slices. Lemon, garlic and parsley are fresh flavouring ingredients for the lentils and nuts.

Serves six

115g/4oz/½ cup red lentils
115g/4oz/1 cup hazelnuts
115g/4oz/1 cup walnuts
1 large carrot
2 celery sticks
1 large onion
115g/4oz/1½ cups mushrooms
45ml/3 tbsp olive oil
1 garlic clove, crushed
pinch of ground mace
30ml/2 tbsp tomato purée (paste)
grated rind of 1 lemon
1 egg, beaten
90ml/6 tbsp chopped fresh parsley
150ml/¼ pint/⅔ cup water
salt and ground black pepper
pinch of ground mace

1 Cover the lentils with cold water and soak for 1 hour. Grind the nuts in a food processor, then place them in a large bowl.

2 Coarsely chop the carrot, celery, onion and mushrooms, add to the food processor and process until all the vegetables are finely chopped.

3 Heat the olive oil in a large pan or frying pan. Add the garlic and the processed vegetable mixture and fry gently over a low heat, stirring occasionally, for 5 minutes.

4 Stir in the mace and cook for 1 minute more. Remove the pan from the heat and set aside to cool.

5 Drain the lentils and stir them into the ground nuts. Add the vegetables, tomato purée, lemon rind, egg, chopped parsley and water. Season with salt and pepper.

6 Preheat the oven to 190°C/375°F/ Gas 5. Grease a 1kg/2¼lb loaf tin (pan) and line with baking parchment or foil. Press the mixture into the tin.

7 Bake for 1–1¼ hours, until just firm, covering the top with foil if it starts to burn. Leave to stand for 15 minutes, turn out and peel off the paper.

> **EAT WELL**
> Update this traditional vegetarian favourite by serving it with a punchy vegetable salad of roasted (bell) peppers tossed with spring onions (scallions), in a dressing flavoured with mustard and dill. Serve it all on a bed of mixed leaves, and add some boiled salad potatoes for a complete meal.

Energy 422kcal/1750kJ; Protein 12.2g; Carbohydrate 19g, of which sugars 7.1g; Fat 33.6g, of which saturates 6.7g; Cholesterol 49mg; Calcium 89mg; Fibre 4.1g; Sodium 225mg.

Baked peppers with egg and puy lentils

These oven-baked, stuffed peppers make a great main course, served with some leafy greens, but if you omit the egg, they also make a hearty appetizer or an excellent vegetarian light meal, as well as a tasty side dish for grilled fish, pork or lamb.

Serves four

75g/3oz/½ cup Puy lentils
2.5ml/½ tsp ground turmeric
2.5ml/½ tsp ground coriander
2.5ml/½ tsp paprika
450ml/¾ pint/1¾ cups vegetable stock
2 large (bell) peppers, halved and seeded
a little olive oil
15ml/1 tbsp chopped fresh mint
4 eggs
salt and ground black pepper
sprigs of coriander (cilantro), to garnish

EAT WELL
For a main meal, double the quantities and serve the (bell) peppers accompanied by basmati rice mixed with peas and parsley.

1 Put the Puy lentils in a large pan with the turmeric, coriander, paprika and vegetable stock.

2 Bring to the boil, stirring occasionally. Reduce the heat, part-cover the pan and simmer for 30–40 minutes. If the lentils start to dry out, add some more stock or a little water during cooking.

3 Brush the peppers lightly with a little olive oil and place them close together on a large non-stick baking tray, skin side down.

4 Preheat the oven to 190°C/375°F/ Gas 5. Stir the chopped fresh mint into the lentils, then fill the halved peppers with the lentil mixture.

5 Crack the eggs, one at a time, into a small jug (pitcher) and pour into the middle of each stuffed pepper. Stir edges of the egg white into the lentils with a fork, and sprinkle with salt and ground black pepper.

6 Bake the stuffed peppers for about 10 minutes or until the egg white is just set. Garnish with sprigs of coriander and serve immediately.

Energy 188kcal/788kJ; Protein 11.8g; Carbohydrate 16.3g, of which sugars 5.9g; Fat 9g, of which saturates 2.1g; Cholesterol 190mg; Calcium 58mg; Fibre 2.6g; Sodium 82mg.

Halloumi with beans

This salad can be grilled successfully on the stove, but if you are planning to get the barbecue going for another dish, use it for this recipe, too, and take advantage of the initial hot blast of cooking heat to slightly char and seal the cheese.

5 Pop each broad bean out of its skin to reveal the bright green inner bean. Discard the outer shells. Place the beans in a bowl, cover and set aside.

6 Place the halloumi and the potatoes in a wide dish. Whisk the garlic and oil together with a generous grinding of black pepper. Add to the dish and toss with the halloumi and potato skewers.

7 Place the cheese and potato skewers on a griddle over a medium heat and cook for 2 minutes on each side.

8 Add the cider vinegar to the oil and garlic remaining in the dish and whisk to mix. Toss in the beans, herbs and spring onions, with the cooked halloumi. Serve, with the potato skewers laid alongside.

Serves four

20 small new potatoes, total weight about
　　300g/11oz
200g/7oz extra-fine green beans, trimmed
675g/1½lb broad (fava) beans, shelled
　　(about 225g/8oz shelled weight)
200g/7oz halloumi cheese, cut into
　　5mm/¼in slices
1 garlic clove, crushed to a paste with a large
　　pinch of salt
45ml/3 tbsp olive oil
5ml/1 tsp cider vinegar or white wine vinegar
15g/½ oz/½ cup fresh basil leaves, shredded
45ml/3 tbsp chopped fresh savory
2 spring onions (scallions), finely sliced
salt and ground black pepper
a few sprigs of fresh savory, to garnish

1 Divide the potatoes among the four skewers, and thread them on.

2 Heat salted water in a pan large enough to take the skewers and, once boiling, add them. Boil for about 7 minutes, or until almost tender.

3 Add the prepared green beans and cook for 3 minutes more. Tip in the broad (fava) beans and cook for just 2 further minutes.

4 Drain all the vegetables in a large colander. Remove the potatoes, still on their skewers, and set to one side. Refresh the cooked broad beans under plenty of cold running water.

Energy 482kcal/2014kJ; Protein 25.2g; Carbohydrate 33.8g, of which sugars 4.7g; Fat 28.3g, of which saturates 9.5g; Cholesterol 29mg; Calcium 317mg; Fibre 13.3g; Sodium 223mg.

Mixed bean and tomato chilli

Canned chopped tomatoes are excellent for making quick tomato sauces, with minimum preparation. All canned beans and pulses are good in a diet designed to level out blood glucose levels as they help to slow down the digestion and absorption of carbohydrates.

Serves four

1 fresh red chilli
30ml/2 tbsp olive oil
1 celery stick, finely chopped
2 garlic cloves, crushed
2 bay leaves
2 onions, finely chopped
2 x 400g/14oz cans chopped tomatoes
2 x 400g/14oz cans mixed beans, drained
   and rinsed
a large handful of fresh coriander (cilantro)
120ml/4fl oz/½ cup natural (plain) yogurt

1 Seed and thinly slice the chilli, then put it into a pan. Add the olive oil, celery, garlic, bay leaves and onions. Cook, stirring occasionally, for about 15 minutes.

2 Pour the tomatoes into a pan. Add the mixed beans, bring to the boil. Cover and simmer for 30 minutes. Finely chop the fresh coriander. Set some aside for the garnish and add the remainder to the tomato and bean mixture. Stir the contents of the pan for a few seconds to mix all the ingredients together.

3 Bring the mixture to the boil, then quickly reduce the heat, cover and simmer gently for 10 minutes. Stir the mixture occasionally and add a dash of water if the sauce starts to dry out.

Tips and twists
This chilli is great just as it is, served with chunks of bread, but you may want to dress it up a bit occasionally. Try serving it over a mixture of long grain and wild rice, piling it into split pitta breads or using it as a filling for baked potatoes. Serve with sour cream or crème fraîche instead of yogurt.

4 Ladle the chilli into warmed individual bowls and top with yogurt. Sprinkle with coriander and serve.

Energy 309kcal/1302kJ; Protein 16.7g; Carbohydrate 43.7g, of which sugars 14.1g; Fat 8.7g, of which saturates 4.2g; Cholesterol 18mg; Calcium 193mg; Fibre 12.4g; Sodium 1202mg.

Vegetable moussaka

This is a full-flavoured main course dish that is great for meat-free meals. It can be served with warm fresh bread and a salad for a hearty meal, full of ingredients to balance blood glucose levels.

Serves six

450g/1lb aubergines (eggplants), sliced
115g/4oz/½ cup whole green lentils
600ml/1 pint/2½ cups vegetable stock
1 bay leaf
45ml/3 tbsp olive oil
1 onion, sliced
1 garlic clove, crushed
225g/8oz/3¼ cups mushrooms, cleaned and
  thickly sliced
400g/14oz can chickpeas, rinsed and drained
400g/14oz can chopped tomatoes
30ml/2 tbsp tomato purée (paste)
10ml/2 tsp dried herbes de Provence
300ml/½ pint/1¼ cups natural (plain) yogurt
3 eggs
50g/2oz/½ cup grated mature Cheddar
  cheese
salt and ground black pepper
sprigs of fresh flat leaf parsley, to garnish

1 Prepare the aubergines well in advance. Cut into thin to medium slices and arrange them in a colander. You will probably find it necessary to overlap the slices or place one on top of another. Sprinkle each layer liberally with salt. Cover and place a weight or a plate on top. Leave for at least 30 minutes, to allow the bitter juices to be extracted.

EAT WELL
Mature cheeses may have more fat than some of the lightly flavoured types, but a little goes a long way, so the overall result has less fat.

2 Meanwhile, place the lentils, stock and bay leaf in a pan, cover, bring to the boil and simmer for about 20 minutes, or until the lentils are just tender but not mushy. Drain thoroughly and keep warm.

3 Heat 15ml/1 tbsp of the oil in a large pan, add the onion and garlic and cook for 5 minutes, stirring. Stir in the lentils, sliced mushrooms, chickpeas, chopped tomatoes, tomato purée, herbs and 45ml/3 tbsp water. Bring to the boil, cover and simmer gently for 10 minutes.

4 Preheat the oven to 180°C/350°F/ Gas 4. Rinse the aubergine slices, drain and pat dry. Heat the remaining oil in a frying pan and fry the slices in batches.

5 Season the lentil mixture. Layer the aubergine slices and lentil mixture alternately in a shallow ovenproof dish, starting with the aubergines. Continue the layers until all the aubergine slices and lentil mixture are used up.

6 Beat the yogurt and eggs together well, and add a little salt and plenty of ground black pepper.

7 Pour the mixture over the aubergines and lentils. Sprinkle generously with the grated Cheddar cheese and bake for about 45 minutes, or until the topping is golden brown and bubbling.

8 Serve immediately, garnished with the flat leaf parsley and accompanied by a fresh green or mixed salad, if you like.

Tips and twists
Sliced courgettes (zucchini) or potatoes can be used instead of the aubergines in this dish. Simply slice them thinly and sauté them, taking care not to break the slices.

Energy 768kcal/3255kJ; Protein 60.2g; Carbohydrate 109.6g, of which sugars 10.3g; Fat 13.1g, of which saturates 2.9g; Cholesterol 99mg; Calcium 357mg; Fibre 21.8g; Sodium 320mg.

Braised beans and lentils

This delicious dish is wonderfully easy to make, but it is vital that you start soaking the pulses and wheat a day ahead. Use canned mixed beans, and non-soak lentils if you don't have time for soaking. Serve the braised beans with plenty of mixed salad and warm crusty bread. This makes a great vegetarian lunch or supper, full of protein and carbohydrate.

Serves four

200g/7oz/generous 1 cup mixed beans
    and lentils
25g/1oz/2 tbsp whole wheat grains
45ml/3 tbsp extra virgin olive oil
1 large onion, finely chopped
2 garlic cloves, crushed
5 or 6 large fresh sage leaves, chopped
juice of 1 lemon
6 spring onions (scallions), thinly sliced
60–75ml/4–5 tbsp chopped fresh dill
salt and ground black pepper

1 Put the beans, lentils and wheat in a large bowl and cover with cold water. Leave to soak overnight. Next day, drain the bean mixture.

2 Rinse the beans in cold water and drain again. Put in a large pan. Cover with plenty of cold water, bring to the boil, and cook for about 1½ hours, by which time all the beans will be soft and tender. Strain, reserving 475ml/16fl oz/ 2 cups of the cooking liquid. Return the bean mixture to the clean pan.

3 Heat the oil in a frying pan and fry the onion until light golden. Add the garlic and sage. As soon as the garlic becomes aromatic, add the mixture to the beans. Stir in the reserved liquid, add seasoning and simmer for about 15 minutes. Add the lemon juice. Serve topped with spring onions and dill.

Energy 286kcal/1204kJ; Protein 14.8g; Carbohydrate 38.2g, of which sugars 6.1g; Fat 9.3g, of which saturates 1.3g; Cholesterol 0mg; Calcium 75mg; Fibre 4.6g; Sodium 27mg.

Butter beans with tomatoes

This bean dish is warming, delicious and simple. The sort of food that goes down well with everyone, from childhood to dotage, and it is full of vegetable goodness, fibre and slow-release carbohydrate. Serve it with lots or warm bread and a bowl or grated cucumber in yogurt, flavoured with garlic and mint, for a feast of a meal.

Serves four

400g/14oz/1¾ cups butter (wax) beans
30ml/2 tbsp extra virgin olive oil
2 or 3 onions, total weight about 300g/11oz, chopped
1 celery stick, thinly sliced
2 carrots, peeled and cubed
3 garlic cloves, thinly sliced
5ml/1 tsp each dried oregano and thyme
400g/14oz can chopped tomatoes
30ml/2 tbsp tomato purée (paste) diluted in 300ml/½ pint/1¼ cups hot water
45ml/3 tbsp finely chopped flat leaf parsley
salt and ground black pepper

1 Place the beans in a large bowl, cover with plenty of cold water, then leave to soak overnight. The next day, drain the beans, then rinse them under cold water and drain again.

2 Tip the beans into a large pan, pour in plenty of cold water to cover, then bring to the boil. Cover the pan and cook the beans until they are almost tender. They should not be allowed to disintegrate through overcooking.

3 Preheat the oven to 180°C/350°F/ Gas 4. Heat the olive oil in the clean pan, add the chopped onions and sauté until light golden.

4 Add the celery, carrots, garlic and dried herbs and stir until the garlic becomes aromatic.

5 When the beans are cooked, tip them into a colander to drain, discarding the cooking liquid. Set aside.

6 Stir the tomatoes into the onions, cover and cook for 10 minutes. Pour in the diluted tomato purée, then add the beans to the pan.

7 Stir in the parsley, with a little salt and plenty of black pepper.

8 Tip the bean mixture into a baking dish and bake for 30 minutes, checking the beans once or twice and adding a little more hot water if they look too dry. The surface should be slightly scorched and caramelized.

Tips and twists
Never add salt to dried beans or pulses of any kind before they are cooked, as it will make their skins leathery and tough.

Energy 250kcal/1058kJ; Protein 16.2g; Carbohydrate 37.4g, of which sugars 8.4g; Fat 5.1g, of which saturates 0.7g; Cholesterol 0mg; Calcium 105mg; Fibre 12.7g; Sodium 29mg.

Spicy chickpea and aubergine stew

This makes a delicious, nutritious meat-free meal – just the sort of dish to include on a regular basis for long-term blood glucose balance.

EAT WELL
• Make a mixed raita to serve with the stew: stir lots of diced cucumber, carrot, spring onion and shredded spinach with chopped fresh mint and a little chopped fresh chilli (if you like) into yogurt.
• Instead of onion, top with toasted flaked (sliced) almonds.

3 Drain the chickpeas and put them in a large pan with enough water to cover them. Bring to the boil over a medium heat, then reduce the heat and simmer for 30 minutes, or until tender. Drain them thoroughly.

4 Heat the oil in a large pan. Add the garlic and chopped onion and cook gently until soft. Add the spices and cook, stirring, for a few seconds.

5 Add the aubergine cubes and stir to coat with the spices and onion. Cook for 5 minutes. Add the tomatoes and chickpeas. Cover and simmer for 20 minutes.

Serves four

3 large aubergines (eggplants), cubed
200g/7oz/generous 1 cup chickpeas, soaked
  overnight in cold water
30ml/2 tbsp olive oil
3 garlic cloves, finely chopped
2 large onions, chopped
2.5ml/½ tsp ground cumin
2.5ml/½ tsp ground cinnamon
2.5ml/½ tsp ground coriander
3 x 400g/14oz cans chopped tomatoes
salt and ground black pepper
cooked basmati rice, to serve

For the garnish
30ml/2 tbsp extra virgin olive oil
1 onion, sliced
1 garlic clove, sliced
a few sprigs of fresh coriander (cilantro)

1 Place the diced aubergines in a colander and sprinkle them with plenty of salt. Sit the colander in a bowl and leave to stand for at least 30 minutes, to allow the bitter juices to seep out of the flesh.

2 Rinse the aubergine cubes thoroughly with cold running water and pat dry on kitchen paper.

6 To make the garnish, heat the olive oil in a frying pan and, when very hot, add the sliced onion and garlic. Fry until golden and crisp.

7 Serve the thick stew with rice, topped with the crispy fried onion and garlic, and garnished with a sprig of fresh coriander.

Energy 303kcal/1281kJ; Protein 15.3g; Carbohydrate 45.3g, of which sugars 19.2g; Fat 8.2g, of which saturates 1.3g; Cholesterol 0mg; Calcium 141mg; Fibre 12.8g; Sodium 53mg.

Spinach filo pie

This is the healthy alternative to those rich little triangular pies that are traditionally deep-fried.
This makes a brilliant meal when served with a lentil salad.

Serves six

1kg/2¼lb fresh spinach, thoroughly washed
4 spring onions (scallions), chopped
300g/11oz feta cheese, crumbled or coarsely
    grated
2 large eggs, beaten
30ml/2 tbsp chopped fresh flat leaf parsley
15ml/1 tbsp chopped fresh dill, plus a few
    sprigs to garnish
45ml/3 tbsp currants (optional)
about 8 sheets of filo pastry, each measuring
    30 x 18cm/12 x 7in, thawed if frozen
extra virgin olive oil
ground black pepper

Tips and twists

Any crumbly hard cheese will also
work well in this pie. Try English
Lancashire or Vermont Cheddar for
a change.

1 Ensure the spinach is cleaned
throughly by rinsing in cold water and
draining at least 3 times. Then dry
thoroughly with kitchen paper.

2 Break off any thick stalks from the
spinach, then blanch the leaves in a
very small amount of boiling water for
1–2 minutes, or until just wilted.

3 Drain the spinach and refresh under
cold water, then drain again, squeeze
dry and chop it roughly. Place in a bowl
together with the spring onions and the
crumbled feta cheese.

4 Add the beaten eggs to the spinach
and cheese and stir them in thoroughly.
Mix in the fresh herbs and currants, if
using. Season the mixture with lots of
ground black pepper.

5 Preheat the oven to 190°C/375°F/
Gas 5. Brush a sheet of filo pastry with
oil and fit it into a 23cm/9in pie dish,
allowing it to hang over the edges. Add
three to four more sheets, placing them
at different angles and brushing each
very sparsley with olive oil.

6 Spoon the filling into the pastry case,
then top with all but one of the
remaining filo sheets, brushing each
with olive oil. Fold the overhanging filo
over the top to seal. Oil the reserved filo
and scrunch it over the top of the pie.

7 Brush the pie with olive oil. Sprinkle
with a little water to stop the filo edges
from curling, then place on a baking
sheet. Bake for about 40 minutes, or
until golden and crisp. Allow the pie to
cool for 15 minutes before serving.

Energy 396kcal/1640kJ; Protein 16.8g; Carbohydrate 13.8g, of which sugars 4g; Fat 30.7g, of which saturates 10.1g; Cholesterol 111mg; Calcium 528mg; Fibre 4.8g; Sodium 988mg.

Wild mushroom and fontina tarts

If you use cultivated mushrooms instead of dried ones, sauté them first in a little olive oil so that their moisture is removed. Serve these tarts warm with rocket leaves.

Serves four

25g/1oz/½ cup dried wild mushrooms
30ml/2 tbsp olive oil
1 red onion, chopped
2 garlic cloves, chopped
30ml/2 tbsp medium-dry sherry
1 egg
120ml/4fl oz/½ cup single (light) cream
25g/1oz Fontina cheese, thinly sliced
salt and ground black pepper
rocket (arugula) leaves, to serve

For the pastry
115g/4oz/1 cup wholemeal (whole-wheat)
    flour
50g/2oz/4 tbsp unsalted butter
25g/1oz/¼ cup walnuts, roasted and ground
1 egg, lightly beaten

1 To make the pastry, rub the flour and butter together until the mixture resembles fine breadcrumbs, then stir in the walnuts.

2 Add the egg and mix to a soft dough. Form the dough into a ball, then wrap in clear film (plastic wrap) and chill for about 30 minutes.

3 Meanwhile, soak the mushrooms in 300ml/½ pint/1¼ cups boiling water for 30 minutes. Drain and reserve the liquid. Heat the oil in a frying pan, and add the onion and fry for 5 minutes, then add the garlic and fry for 2 minutes, stirring.

4 Add the soaked mushrooms and cook for 7 minutes over a high heat until the edges become crisp. Add the sherry and the reserved liquid.

5 Cook over a high heat for about 10 minutes until the liquid evaporates. Season and set aside to cool.

6 Preheat the oven to 200°C/400°F/ Gas 6. Lightly grease four 10cm/4in tartlet tins (pans). Roll out the pastry on a lightly floured work surface and line the tins. Prick the pastry, line with greaseproof (waxed) paper and baking beans and bake blind for 10 minutes. Remove the paper and beans.

7 Whisk the egg and cream to mix, add to the mushroom mixture, then season to taste. Spoon into the pastry cases, top with cheese slices and bake for 18 minutes until the filling is set. Serve warm with rocket.

EAT WELL
The wholemeal (whole-wheat) flour and walnuts in this recipe help to slow down carbohydrate digestion – especially useful for special meals with a dessert.

Tips and twists
You can prepare the pastry cases in advance. Bake them blind for 10 minutes, then store in an airtight container for up to 2 days.

Energy 409kcal/1701kJ; Protein 10.2g; Carbohydrate 21.9g, of which sugars 2.3g; Fat 31g, of which saturates 13.4g; Cholesterol 143mg; Calcium 121mg; Fibre 2.3g; Sodium 199mg.

Mediterranean one-crust pie

This free-form crust is the easiest way to make a pie. It encases a rich tomato, aubergine and kidney bean filling in a wholemeal cheese pastry.

Serves four

500g/1¼lb aubergine (eggplant), cubed
1 red (bell) pepper
30ml/2 tbsp olive oil
1 large onion, finely chopped
1 courgette (zucchini), sliced
2 garlic cloves, crushed
15ml/1 tbsp fresh oregano or 5ml/1 tsp
   dried, plus fresh oregano leaves to garnish
200g/7oz/1½ cups canned red kidney beans,
   drained and rinsed
115g/4oz/1 cup pitted black olives, rinsed
375g/13oz/⅔ cup passata (bottled, strained
   tomatoes)
1 egg, beaten, or a little milk
30ml/2 tbsp semolina
salt and ground black pepper

For the pastry
75g/3oz/⅔ cup plain (all-purpose) flour
75g/3oz/⅔ cup wholemeal (whole-wheat)
   flour
75g/3oz/6 tbsp butter
25g/1oz/⅓ cup grated Parmesan cheese

1 Preheat the oven to 220°C/425°F/ Gas 7. To make the pastry, sift the plain and wholemeal flours into a large bowl. Rub in the butter until the mixture resembles fine breadcrumbs, then stir in the grated Parmesan. Mix in enough cold water to form a firm dough.

2 Turn out the dough on to a lightly floured work surface and form into a smooth ball. Wrap the dough in clear film (plastic wrap) or a plastic bag and chill for about 30 minutes.

3 To make the filling, place the aubergine in a colander and sprinkle with salt, then leave for about 30 minutes. Rinse them, drain, and pat dry with kitchen paper.

4 Meanwhile, place the pepper on a baking tray and roast in the oven for 20 minutes, until the skin is slightly charred and the flesh is soft. Put the pepper in a plastic bag and leave until cool enough to handle. Peel and seed, then dice the flesh. Set aside.

5 Heat the oil in a large heavy frying pan. Fry the onions for 5 minutes until softened. Add the aubergine and fry for 5 minutes. Add the courgettes, garlic and oregano, and cook for a further 5 minutes, stirring frequently. Add the beans and olives, stir, then add the passata and pepper. Cook until heated through, and set aside to cool.

6 Roll out the pastry on a lightly floured board to form a rough 30cm/12in round. Place on a lightly oiled baking sheet. Brush with beaten egg, sprinkle on the semolina, leaving a 4cm/1½in border, then spoon in the filling.

7 Gather up the edges of the pastry to partly cover the filling – it should be open in the middle. Brush with the remaining egg or milk and bake for 30–35 minutes until golden. Garnish with oregano.

Energy 554kcal/2318kJ; Protein 17.7g; Carbohydrate 56.6g, of which sugars 15.7g; Fat 30.2g, of which saturates 4.2g; Cholesterol 13mg; Calcium 295mg; Fibre 11.6g; Sodium 1353mg.

Grilled vegetable pizza

Anyone with a gluten allergy will find all the ingredients for this pizza dough available as gluten-free versions. Home-made pizza is far healthier than bought, with the topping of vegetables, and a base that provides a source of slow-release carbohydrate. Use low-fat cheese, if you like.

Serves six

1 courgette (zucchini), sliced
1 small aubergine (eggplant), sliced
30ml/2 tbsp olive oil
1 yellow (bell) pepper, seeded and sliced
115g/4oz/1 cup cornmeal
50g/2oz/½ cup potato flour
50g/2oz/½ cup soya flour
5ml/1 tsp baking powder
2.5ml/½ tsp salt
50g/2oz/4 tbsp butter
105ml/7 tbsp semi-skimmed (low-fat) milk
4 plum tomatoes, skinned and chopped
30ml/2 tbsp chopped fresh basil
115g/4oz mozzarella cheese, sliced
salt and ground black pepper
fresh basil sprigs, to garnish

1 Preheat the grill. Brush the courgette and aubergine slices with a little oil and place on a grill rack with the pepper slices. Cook under the grill until lightly browned, turning once.

2 Meanwhile, preheat the oven to 200°C/400°F/Gas 6. Place the cornmeal, potato flour, soya flour, baking powder and salt in a mixing bowl and stir to mix.

3 Lightly rub in the butter until the mixture resembles coarse breadcrumbs. This can also be done in the food processor. Then gradually stir in enough of the milk to make a soft, but not sticky, dough.

4 Place the dough on a sheet of baking parchment on a baking sheet and roll or press it out to form a 25cm/10in round, making the edges slightly thicker than the centre.

5 Brush the pizza dough with any remaining oil, then spread the chopped tomatoes over the dough.

6 Sprinkle the chopped plum tomato with the chopped basil and season with salt and pepper. Arrange the grilled vegetables over the herbs and top with the cheese.

7 Bake for 25–30 minutes until crisp and golden brown. Garnish the pizza with fresh basil sprigs and serve immediately, cut into slices.

Tips and twists
Instead of cornmeal, potato and soya flours, use 225g/8oz/2 cups of half plain (all-purpose) and half wholemeal (whole-wheat) flours.

Energy 400kcal/1666kJ; Protein 11.9g; Carbohydrate 34.6g, of which sugars 9.6g; Fat 23.9g, of which saturates 5.3g; Cholesterol 18mg; Calcium 166mg; Fibre 4.4g; Sodium 240mg.

Vegetable pancakes with tomato salsa

Spinach is packed full of vitamins and minerals, and this recipe uses a great pile of it. The pancakes make a great appetizer or serve them with a new potato salad for a main course. This dish relies on the natural flavour of the vegetables, so find the ripest tomatoes possible.

Makes ten

225g/8oz spinach
1 small leek
a few sprigs of fresh coriander (cilantro)
   or parsley
3 large (US extra large) eggs
50g/2oz/½ cup plain (all-purpose)
   flour, sifted
oil, for frying
25g/1oz/⅓ cup freshly grated Parmesan
   cheese
salt, ground black pepper and freshly
   grated nutmeg

For the salsa
2 tomatoes, peeled and chopped
¼ fresh red chilli, finely chopped
2 pieces sun-dried tomato in oil, drained
   and chopped
1 small red onion, chopped
1 garlic clove, crushed
60ml/4 tbsp olive oil
30ml/2 tbsp sherry
2.5ml/½ tsp soft light brown sugar

1 Prepare the tomato salsa: place all the ingredients in a bowl and toss together to combine. Cover and leave to stand in a cool place for 2–3 hours.

2 To make the pancakes, finely shred or chop the spinach, leek and coriander or parsley. If you prefer, chop them roughly in a food processor.

3 Place the chopped vegetables in a bowl and beat in the eggs and seasoning. Blend in the flour and 30–45ml/2–3 tbsp water and leave to stand for 20 minutes.

4 To cook the pancakes, drop spoonfuls of the batter into a lightly oiled frying pan and cook until golden underneath. Using a fish slice, or metal spatula, turn the pancakes over and cook briefly on the other side.

5 Carefully lift the pancakes out of the pan, drain on kitchen paper and keep warm while you cook the remaining mixture in the same way. Sprinkle the pancakes with grated Parmesan cheese and serve with the salsa.

EAT WELL
Adding vegetables to pancake batter is a great way of pumping up their food value – for example, spinach is a good source of vitamins and folic acid. Chopped lightly cooked broccoli is another good alternative.

Energy 153kcal/634kJ; Protein 4.6g; Carbohydrate 6.2g, of which sugars 2.1g; Fat 11.8g, of which saturates 2.2g; Cholesterol 63mg; Calcium 92mg; Fibre 1.3g; Sodium 84mg.

Tofu and pepper kebabs

A simple coating of ground, dry-roasted peanuts pressed on to cubed tofu provides plenty of additional flavour along with the peppers. Use metal or bamboo skewers, soaking the bamboo type in water for 30 minutes to prevent them from burning.

Serves four

250g/9oz firm tofu
50g/2oz/½ cup dry-roasted peanuts
2 red and 2 green (bell) peppers
60ml/4 tbsp sweet chilli dipping sauce

EAT WELL
Tofu is a good source of valuable soya protein. Serve with rice and a salad of cauliflower florets with spring onions and cherry tomatoes.

1 Pat the tofu dry on kitchen paper and cut it into small cubes. Grind the nuts in a blender and spread on a plate.

2 Turn the tofu cubes in the ground nuts to coat thoroughly on all sides.

3 Preheat the grill (broiler) to medium. Using a sharp knife, halve and seed the red and green peppers, and cut them into large chunks.

4 Thread the chunks of pepper on to skewers with the tofu cubes and place on a foil-lined grill (broiling) rack. Grill (broil) the kebabs, turning frequently, for 10–12 minutes, until the peppers and peanuts are beginning to brown. Serve immediately with the dipping sauce.

Energy 187kcal/778kJ; Protein 10.2g; Carbohydrate 16.8g, of which sugars 15.1g; Fat 9.1g, of which saturates 1.6g; Cholesterol 0mg; Calcium 342mg; Fibre 3.7g; Sodium 214mg.

Pan-fried tofu with caramelized sauce

Tofu is often used as a meat substitute for vegetarians, and is good way of adding protein to your diet. This traditional dish was created by Chinese Buddhist monks, who invented many delicious tofu and other soya bean products. Omit the butter for a lower-fat version.

Serves four

2 x 285g/10¼oz packets tofu blocks
4 garlic cloves
30ml/2 tbsp vegetable oil
4 knobs of butter (optional)
watercress or rocket (arugula), to garnish

For the marinade
4 spring onions (scallions)
60ml/4 tbsp sake
60ml/4 tbsp shoyu or soy sauce
60ml/4 tbsp mirin (sweet cooking sake)

1 Unpack the tofu blocks and discard the liquid, then wrap in three layers of kitchen paper.

2 Put a large plate or a wooden chopping board on top as a weight and leave for 30 minutes to allow time for the excess liquid to be absorbed by the paper. This process makes the tofu firmer and, when cooked, it will be crisp on the outside.

3 To make the marinade, chop the spring onions finely. Mix with the other ingredients in a wide, shallow bowl.

4 Unwrap the tofu from the kitchen paper. Slice one block horizontally in half, then cut each half into four pieces. Repeat with the other block of tofu, so you end up with 16 pieces. Place the tofu in the marinade for 15 minutes.

5 Take the tofu out of the marinade and wipe off the excess with kitchen paper. Reserve the marinade.

6 Slice the garlic very thinly. Heat half the oil in a frying pan and fry the garlic for a few moments until golden. Turn the garlic pieces frequently to prevent them from sticking and burning. Scoop them out on to kitchen paper. Reserve the oil in the pan.

7 Add more oil to the frying pan and reheat. When the oil starts sizzling, reduce the heat to medium and add the pieces of tofu one by one. Cover the pan and cook until the edge of the tofu is browned and quite firm, this will take approximately 5–8 minutes each side.

8 Pour the marinade into the pan. Cook for 2 minutes, or until the spring onions are soft. Remove the tofu and arrange four pieces on each plate. Pour over the marinade and spring onion mixture and top with a piece of butter, if using. Sprinkle with the garlic chips and garnish with watercress or rocket.

Energy 271kcal/1127kJ; Protein 12.7g; Carbohydrate 11.5g, of which sugars 10g; Fat 17.9g, of which saturates 7.4g; Cholesterol 27mg; Calcium 742mg; Fibre 0.4g; Sodium 1152mg.

Stir-fried seeds and vegetables

The contrast between the crunchy seeds and vegetables and the rich, savoury sauce is what makes this dish so delicious. Super-speedy when tossed together in the wok, serve this with buckwheat noodles for some useful slow-release carbohydrate.

Serves four

30ml/2 tbsp vegetable oil
30ml/2 tbsp sesame seeds
30ml/2 tbsp sunflower seeds
30ml/2 tbsp pumpkin seeds
2 garlic cloves, finely chopped
2.5cm/1in piece fresh root ginger, peeled and
    finely chopped
2 large carrots, cut into batons
2 large courgettes (zucchini), cut into batons
90g/3½oz/1½ cups oyster mushrooms,
    broken in pieces
150g/5oz watercress or spinach leaves,
    coarsely chopped
small bunch fresh mint or coriander (cilantro),
    leaves and stems chopped
60ml/4 tbsp black bean sauce
30ml/2 tbsp light soy sauce
15ml/1 tbsp rice vinegar

1 Heat the oil in a wok. Add the seeds. Toss over a medium heat for 1 minute, then add the garlic and ginger and continue to stir-fry until the ginger is aromatic and the garlic is golden.

2 Add the carrot and courgette batons and mushroom pieces to the wok and stir-fry over a medium heat for a further 5 minutes, or until all the vegetables are crisp-tender and golden at the edges.

3 Add the watercress or spinach with the fresh herbs. Toss over the heat for 1 minute, then stir in the black bean sauce, soy sauce and vinegar. Stir-fry for 1–2 minutes, until combined and hot. Serve immediately.

EAT WELL

When trying to keep weight under control, main dishes based on lots of light, but satisfying, vegetables are good choices. Include enough slow-release carbohydrate to keep fat storage down and blood glucose stable.

Tips and twists

Oyster mushrooms are delicate, so it is usually better to tear them into pieces along the lines of the gills, rather than slice them with a knife.

Energy 205kcal/849kJ; Protein 6.9g; Carbohydrate 9.7g, of which sugars 7.7g; Fat 15.6g, of which saturates 2g; Cholesterol 0mg; Calcium 159mg; Fibre 3.4g; Sodium 294mg.

Cashew and yellow vegetable curry

Cashew nuts ground to a paste with yogurt are a creamy alternative to coconut milk in curries, replacing the saturated fat in coconut with good fat. The curry paste will keep in the fridge for a week. Serve Thai fragrant rice with this colourful curry.

Serves four

100g/4oz unsalted, unroasted cashew nuts
200ml/7fl oz/scant 1 cup natural (plain) yogurt
30ml/2 tbsp sunflower oil
150ml/¼ pint/⅔ cup vegetable stock
200g/7oz snake beans, cut into 2cm/¾in
   lengths
200g/7oz baby corn
4 baby courgettes (zucchini), sliced
1 small aubergine (eggplant), cubed or sliced
fresh coriander (cilantro) leaves, to garnish
noodles or rice, to serve

For the curry paste
10ml/2 tsp hot chilli powder
10ml/2 tsp ground coriander
10ml/2 tsp ground cumin
5ml/1 tsp ground turmeric
15ml/1 tbsp chopped fresh galangal
10ml/2 tsp finely grated garlic
30ml/2 tbsp finely chopped lemon grass
4 red Asian shallots, finely chopped
5ml/1 tsp finely chopped lime rind

1 Make the curry paste. Place the spices, galangal, garlic, lemon grass, shallots and lime rind in a small food processor and blend with 30–45ml/2–3 tbsp of cold water to make a smooth paste. Add a little more water if the paste seems too dry.

2 Grind the cashew nuts in a food processor or blender. Then add the yogurt in two batches, blending well to make a smooth paste. Blend in 150ml/¼pint/⅔ cup water.

3 Heat a large wok or frying pan over a medium heat and add the sunflower oil. When hot add 30–45ml/2–3 tbsp of the curry paste and stir-fry for 1–2 minutes.

4 Add the cashew milk to the wok. Cook gently for 8–10 minutes, or until the mixture starts to separate.

5 Add the stock and vegetables and cook gently for 8–10 minutes, until the vegetables are just tender. Garnish with coriander leaves and serve with noodles or rice.

Tips and twists
You will need a good food processor or blender to make the curry paste, preferably one with an attachment for processing smaller quantities. You can use a mortar and pestle, but it will be hard work.
   Vary the vegetables in the curry, adding green beans, peppers and mushrooms and new potatoes.

Energy 279kcal/1161kJ; Protein 9.8g; Carbohydrate 17.4g, of which sugars 13.3g; Fat 19.4g, of which saturates 3.6g; Cholesterol 5mg; Calcium 99mg; Fibre 3.3g; Sodium 824mg.

Fish and Shellfish

Full-of-goodness fish and shellfish are excellent in all sorts of dishes, for different occasions, from light salads and grills to irresistible, everyday pies and stir-fries. With lots of vegetables and a wide range of carbohydrate accompaniments, these fish meals are low in bad fat and a good source of fats that are valuable for healthy eating. Discover and enjoy!

Roast monkfish with garlic

The combination of monkfish and garlic is superb and a good low-fat alternative to traditional meat for a special meal. Serve with vibrant greens or canned flageolet beans.

Serves four

1kg/2¼ lb monkfish tail, skinned
14 fat garlic cloves
5ml/1 tsp fresh thyme leaves
30ml/2 tbsp olive oil
juice of 1 lemon
2 bay leaves
salt and ground black pepper

1 Preheat the oven to 220°C/425°F/ Gas 7. Remove any membrane from the fish and cut out the central bone.

2 Peel two garlic cloves and cut them into thin slivers. Scatter a quarter of the garlic slices and half of the thyme leaves over the cut side of the fish, then close it up and use fine kitchen string to tie it into a neat shape, like a boned, rolled piece of meat. Pat the fish dry with kitchen paper.

3 Make incisions on either side of the fish and push in the remaining garlic slivers. Heat half the olive oil in a frying pan which can safely be transferred to the oven. When the oil is very hot, put the monkfish into the pan and brown it all over for about 5 minutes, until it is evenly coloured.

4 Season the fish with salt and pepper, sprinkle with lemon juice and scatter over the remaining thyme.

5 Tuck the bay leaves under the monkfish, arrange the unpeeled garlic cloves around it and drizzle the remaining olive oil over. Transfer the frying pan to the oven and roast for 20–25 minutes, until cooked through.

6 Place on a warmed serving dish with the garlic and some green beans. To serve, remove the string and cut the monkfish into thick slices.

EAT WELL

For a special occasion, par-boil small new potatoes until half cooked, then drain and toss with 1–2 tbsp olive oil on a roasting pan. Roast in the oven until crisp and well browned. They are good as an alternative to chips (fries).

Energy 173kcal/727kJ; Protein 30.5g; Carbohydrate 2.7g, of which sugars 0.3g; Fat 4.4g, of which saturates 0.7g; Cholesterol 27mg; Calcium 18mg; Fibre 0.7g; Sodium 34mg.

Cod with pancetta and butter beans

Cod steaks wrapped in pancetta and roasted are superb with butter beans and juicy cherry tomatoes – a combination of low GI butter beans and low-fat fish for a balanced meal.

Serves four

200g/7oz/1 cup butter (wax) beans, soaked
  overnight in cold water to cover
2 leeks, thinly sliced
2 garlic cloves, chopped
8 fresh sage leaves
45ml/3 tbsp fruity olive oil
8 thin slices of pancetta
4 thick cod steaks, skinned
12 cherry tomatoes
salt and ground black pepper

1 Drain the beans, tip into a pan and cover with cold water. Bring to the boil and skim off the foam on the surface. Lower the heat, then stir in the leeks, garlic and four sage leaves. Simmer for 1–1½ hours until the beans are tender, adding more water if necessary. Drain, return to the pan, season, stir in 15ml/ 1 tbsp olive oil and keep warm.

2 Preheat the oven to 200°C/400°F/ Gas 6. Wrap two slices of pancetta around the edge of each cod steak, tying it on with kitchen string or securing it with a wooden cocktail stick (toothpick). Insert a sage leaf between the pancetta and the cod. Season the fish with salt and pepper.

Tips and twists
Use cannellini beans in place of butter (wax) beans, and streaky bacon instead of pancetta. Use haddock or salmon instead of cod.

3 Heat a heavy frying pan, add 15ml/ 1 tbsp of the remaining oil and seal the cod steaks two at a time for 1 minute on each side. Transfer the steaks to an ovenproof dish and roast in the oven for 5 minutes.

4 Add the tomatoes to the dish and drizzle over the remaining olive oil. Roast for 5 minutes more, until the cod steaks are cooked but still juicy. Serve them on a bed of butter beans with the roasted tomatoes. Garnish with parsley.

EAT WELL
To add valuable vegetable content to this dish, serve it with a big pile of freshly cooked green beans tossed with lemon juice and topped with snipped chives and black pepper.

Energy 449kcal/1883kJ; Protein 44.5g; Carbohydrate 25.3g, of which sugars 3.9g; Fat 19.5g, of which saturates 3g; Cholesterol 84mg; Calcium 85mg; Fibre 9.8g; Sodium 403mg.

Filo fish pies

Filo is a useful alternative to fatty puff pastry, or even shortcrust, and it makes a fabulous case for light-textured fish. Serve with roasted new potatoes for some slow-release carbohydrate.

Serves six

400g/14oz spinach, trimmed
1 egg, lightly beaten
2 garlic cloves, crushed
450g/1lb white fish fillet
juice of 1 lemon
olive oil
8–12 filo pastry sheets, thawed if frozen,
   quartered
15ml/1 tbsp finely snipped fresh chives
200ml/7fl oz/scant 1 cup half-fat
   crème fraîche
15ml/1 tbsp chopped fresh dill
salt and ground black pepper

Tips and twists

If you prefer to make one large pie, use a 20cm/8in tin (pan) and bake for around 45 minutes.

1 Preheat the oven to 190°C/375°F/ Gas 5. Wash the spinach, then cook in a lidded pan with just the water that clings to the leaves. When wilted, drain, squeeze as dry as possible and chop.

2 Put the spinach in a bowl, add the egg and garlic, season with salt and pepper and set aside. Cut the fish into small pieces and place in a bowl. Stir in the lemon juice. Season with salt and pepper and toss lightly.

3 Brush the inside of six 13cm/5in tartlet tins (muffin pans) with a little olive oil. Fit a piece of filo pastry into the tins, draping it so it hangs over the sides. Brush with a little olive oil, then add another sheet at right angles to the first. Continue to line the tins in this way.

4 Spread the spinach evenly over the pastry. Add the diced fish and season well. Stir the chives into the crème fraîche and spread the mixture over the top of the fish. Scatter the dill over.

5 Draw the overhanging pieces of pastry together and scrunch lightly to make a lid. Brush sparsely with oil. Bake for about 15–20 minutes, until golden brown.

Energy 233kcal/972kJ; Protein 18.4g; Carbohydrate 9.1g, of which sugars 2.2g; Fat 14g, of which saturates 8.2g; Cholesterol 84mg; Calcium 170mg; Fibre 1.7g; Sodium 213mg.

Warm swordfish and rocket salad

Swordfish is robust enough to take the sharp flavours of rocket and Pecorino cheese. If you can't find Pecorino, use a good Parmesan instead.

Serves four

4 swordfish steaks, about 175g/6oz each
75ml/5 tbsp extra virgin olive oil, plus extra
  for serving
juice of 1 lemon
30ml/2 tbsp finely chopped fresh parsley
115g/4oz rocket leaves (arugula)
115g/4oz Pecorino cheese
salt and ground black pepper

1 Lay the swordfish in a shallow dish. Mix 60ml/4 tbsp of the olive oil with the lemon juice. Pour over the fish. Season, sprinkle on the parsley and turn the fish to coat, cover with clear film (plastic wrap) and marinate for 10 minutes.

2 Heat a griddle until very hot. Take the fish out of the marinade and pat it dry with kitchen paper. Grill for 2–3 minutes on each side until the swordfish is just cooked through, but still juicy.

Tips and twists
Tuna or shark steaks would be equally good in this recipe.

3 Meanwhile, put the rocket leaves in a bowl and season with a little salt and plenty of pepper. Add the remaining 15ml/1 tbsp olive oil and toss well. Shave the Pecorino over the top of the tossed rocket salad.

4 Place the swordfish steaks on four individual plates and arrange a little pile of salad on each steak.

Energy 452kcal/1880kJ; Protein 43.6g; Carbohydrate 0.5g, of which sugars 0.4g; Fat 30.6g, of which saturates 9.5g; Cholesterol 101mg; Calcium 401mg; Fibre 0.6g; Sodium 581mg.

Baked sea bass with fennel

Now that sea bass is farmed, it is much easier to get hold of, but you can use any large firm-fleshed fish for this recipe. A whole salmon is also delicious cooked this way.

Serves four

4 fennel bulbs, washed, with tops and
    bottoms trimmed
4 tomatoes, peeled and diced
8 drained canned anchovy fillets,
    halved lengthways
a large pinch of saffron threads, soaked in
    30ml/2 tbsp hot water
150ml/¼ pint/⅔ cup chicken or
    fish stock
2 red or yellow (bell) peppers, seeded and
    each cut into 12 strips
4 garlic cloves, chopped
15ml/1 tbsp chopped fresh marjoram
45ml/3 tbsp olive oil
1 sea bass, about 1.75kg/4–4½ lb, scaled
    and cleaned
salt and ground black pepper
chopped parsley, to garnish

1 Preheat the oven to 200°C/400°F/ Gas 6. Quarter the fennel bulbs lengthwise. Cook in lightly salted boiling water for 5 minutes, until barely tender. Drain and arrange in a shallow ovenproof dish. Season with pepper, then set aside.

2 Spoon the diced tomatoes and anchovy strips on top of the fennel. Stir the saffron and water into the stock and pour the mixture over the tomatoes.

3 Lay the strips of pepper on top of the fennel and sprinkle with the choped garlic and marjoram. Drizzle 30ml/2 tbsp of the olive oil over the peppers and season with a little salt and plenty of black pepper. Bake the vegetables in the oven for 15 minutes.

4 Season the prepared sea bass inside and out and lay it on top of the fennel and pepper mixture. Drizzle the remaining olive oil over the fish.

5 Return to the oven and bake for 30–40 minutes more, until the sea bass flesh comes away easily from the bone when tested with the point of a sharp knife. Serve, garnished with parsley.

Moroccan-spiced mackerel

Mackerel is extremely good for you. The Moroccan spices in this dish counteract the richness of the fish. Trout can also be used for this recipe.

Serves four

30ml/2 tbsp sunflower oil
15ml/1 tbsp paprika
5–10ml/1–2 tsp harissa or chilli powder
10ml/2 tsp ground cumin
10ml/2 tsp ground coriander
2 garlic cloves, crushed
juice of 2 lemons
30ml/2 tbsp chopped fresh mint leaves
30ml/2 tbsp chopped fresh coriander (cilantro)
4 mackerel, cleaned
salt and ground black pepper
lemon wedges, to serve
mint sprigs, to garnish

1 To make the marinade, whisk together the oil, spices, garlic and lemon juice in a bowl. Season with a little salt and black pepper, then stir in the chopped mint and coriander.

2 Make two or three diagonal slashes on either side of each mackerel so that they can absorb the marinade. Rub the marinade all over the fish and place in a flat-bottomed dish.

3 Cover the dish with clear film (plastic wrap) and place it in the refrigerator for at least 3 hours or more if you wish. Don't leave the fish any longer than 7 hours, however.

4 When you are ready to cook the mackerel, preheat the grill to medium-high. Transfer the fish to a rack set over a grilling (broiling) pan and grill (broil) for 5–7 minutes on each side until cooked, turning the fish once and basting them several times with the marinade. Serve hot or cold with lemon wedges, garnished with mint.

EAT WELL
Serve a refreshing orange and almond couscous salad with either of these fish dishes. Mix orange segments with toasted flaked (sliced) almonds and green beans. Serve on couscous tossed with spring onions (scallions) and grated orange rind.

Energy 296kcal/1241kJ; Protein 38.7g; Carbohydrate 12.3g, of which sugars 11.9g; Fat 10.5g, of which saturates 1.6g; Cholesterol 144mg; Calcium 308mg; Fibre 7.2g; Sodium 391mg.
Energy 422kcal/1753kJ; Protein 31.8g; Carbohydrate 1.9g, of which sugars 0.1g; Fat 31.9g, of which saturates 6g; Cholesterol 86mg; Calcium 51mg; Fibre 1.3g; Sodium 117mg.

Trout with tamarind and chilli

Take trout out of its traditional box by cooking it in a spicy, tangy sauce. Serve with lots of stir-fried vegetables and buckwheat noodles for a low GI meal.

4 Put the tamarind pulp in a small bowl and pour on the boiling water. Mash with a fork until soft. Tip into a food processor or blender, add the shallots, fresh chilli, ginger and *nam pla* and whizz to a coarse pulp.

5 Heat the stir-fry oil in a large frying pan and fry the trout, for about 5 minutes on each side, until the skin is crisp and browned and the flesh cooked. Put on warmed plates and spoon over some sauce. Sprinkle with the coriander and serve with the sauce.

Serves four

4 trout, about 350g/12oz each, cleaned
6 spring onions (scallions), sliced
60ml/4 tbsp soy sauce
15ml/1 tbsp stir-fry oil
30ml/2 tbsp chopped fresh coriander (cilantro)

For the sauce
50g/2oz tamarind pulp
105ml/7 tbsp boiling water
2 shallots, roughly chopped
1 fresh red chilli, seeded and chopped
1cm/½ in piece fresh root ginger, peeled
   and chopped
45ml/3 tbsp *nam pla* (Thai fish sauce)

1 Slash the trout diagonally four or five times on each side with a sharp knife.

2 Put the fish into a flat-bottomed dish. Fill the cavities of the fish with some of the sliced spring onions and douse each fish with the soy sauce. Carefully turn the fish over to coat both sides with the sauce.

3 Sprinkle any remaining spring onions over the fish and set aside.

Energy 316kcal/1326kJ; Protein 45.9g; Carbohydrate 5.9g, of which sugars 5g; Fat 12.2g, of which saturates 2.4g; Cholesterol 184mg; Calcium 88mg; Fibre 0.7g; Sodium 1504mg.

Mackerel with black beans

Addling lots of flavour is important when establishing new eating habits: shiitake mushrooms, zesty fresh ginger and pungent salted black beans are perfect for this robust mackerel dish.

Serves four

8 x 115g/4oz mackerel fillets
20 dried shiitake mushrooms
15ml/1 tbsp finely julienned fresh root ginger
3 star anise
45ml/3 tbsp dark soy sauce
15ml/1 tbs Chinese rice wine
15ml/1 tbsp salted black beans
6 spring onions (scallions), finely shredded
30ml/2 tbsp sunflower oil
5ml/1 tsp sesame oil
4 garlic cloves, very thinly sliced
sliced cucumber and steamed basmati rice,
   to serve

1 Divide the mackerel fillets between two lightly oiled heatproof plates, with the skin-side up. Using a small, sharp knife, make three to four diagonal slits in each one, then set aside.

2 Place the dried shiitake mushrooms in a large bowl and pour over enough boiling water to cover. Leave to soak for 20–25 minutes. Drain, reserving the soaking liquid, discard the stems and slice the caps thinly.

3 Place a trivet or a steamer rack in a large wok and pour in 5cm/2in of the mushroom liquid (top up with water if necessary). You can also use a large pan, or roasting tin. Add half the ginger and the star anise.

4 Push the remaining ginger strips into the slits in the fish and scatter the sliced mushrooms over the top. Bring the liquid in the wok to a boil and lower one of the prepared plates on to the trivet. Cover the wok, reduce the heat and steam for 10–12 minutes, or until the mackerel is cooked.

5 Remove the plate and repeat with the second plate of fish, adding liquid to the wok if necessary.

6 Transfer the steamed fish to a serving platter and keep warm. Ladle 105ml/ 7 tbsp of the steaming liquid into a clean wok with the soy sauce, wine and black beans, place over a gentle heaet and bring to a simmer. Spoon over the fish and sprinkle over the spring onions.

7 Wipe out the wok with a piece of kitchen paper and place over a medium heat. Add the oils and garlic and stir-fry for a few minutes until lightly golden. Pour over the fish and serve with sliced cucumber and steamed basmati rice.

> **EAT WELL**
> • Mackerel is a good source of healthy fish oils and it is bursting with flavour, which can be more satisfying than sheer bulk.
> • A salad of cucumber, watercress and mustard or rocket (arugula) is good with this dish, with Thai rice.
> • Eating some protein with high–GI rice reduces the overall GI value of the meal.

Energy 693kcal/2872kJ; Protein 45.5g; Carbohydrate 1.9g, of which sugars 0.5g; Fat 55.9g, of which saturates 10.4g; Cholesterol 128mg; Calcium 35mg; Fibre 0.6g; Sodium 152mg.

Fish pie

Fish pie can be varied to suit your eating preferences: for example, use olive oil in the mashed potatoes for a delicious, healthy alternative to butter, and omit the cheese.

Serves four

450g/1lb cod or haddock fillets
225g/8oz smoked cod fillets
300ml/½ pint/1¼ cups milk
½ lemon, sliced
1 bay leaf
1 fresh thyme sprig
4–5 black peppercorns
50g/2oz/¼ cup butter
25g/1oz/¼ cup plain (all-purpose) flour
30ml/2 tbsp chopped fresh parsley
5ml/1 tsp anchovy essence (extract)
150g/5oz/2 cups shiitake or chestnut
  mushrooms, sliced
salt, ground black pepper and cayenne pepper

For the topping
450g/1lb potatoes, cooked and mashed
  with milk
30ml/2 tbsp olive oil
2 tomatoes, sliced
25g/1oz/¼ cup grated Cheddar cheese
  (optional)

1 Put the fish skin side down in a shallow pan. Add the milk, lemon slices, bay leaf, thyme and peppercorns.

2 Bring to the boil, then lower the heat and poach gently for about 5 minutes, until just cooked. Strain off and reserve the milk. Remove the fish skin and flake the flesh, discarding any bones.

3 Melt half the butter in a small pan, stir in the flour and cook gently for 1 minute. Add the milk and boil, whisking, until smooth and creamy.

4 Stir the parsley and anchovy essence into the sauce, season to taste.

5 Heat the remaining butter in a frying pan, add the sliced mushrooms and sauté until tender. Season and add to the flaked fish. Mix the sauce into the fish and stir gently to combine. Transfer the mixture to an ovenproof casserole.

6 Preheat the oven to 200°C/400°F/ Gas 6. Beat the mashed potato with the olive oil until very creamy. Season, then spread the topping evenly over the fish. Fork up the surface and arrange the sliced tomatoes around the edge. Sprinkle with grated cheese, if using.

7 Bake for 20–25 minutes, until the topping is browned. If you prefer, finish the browning under a hot grill (broiler).

> **EAT WELL**
> Add finely chopped barely cooked broccoli and spring onions (scallions) to mashed potato for a healthy, full-flavoured pie top.

Energy 458kcal/1921kJ; Protein 29.5g; Carbohydrate 32.8g, of which sugars 5.8g; Fat 25g, of which saturates 3.7g; Cholesterol 74mg; Calcium 216mg; Fibre 1g; Sodium 867mg.

Cod caramba

This colourful Mexican dish, with its contrasting crunchy topping and tender fish filling, provides lots of vegetable food value, and is good accompanied by rice and red kidney beans.

Serves four

450g/1lb cod fillets
225g/8oz smoked cod fillets
300ml/½ pint/1¼ cups fish stock
30ml/2 tbsp olive oil
1 onion, sliced
2 garlic cloves, crushed
1 green and 1 red (bell) pepper, diced
2 courgettes (zucchini), diced
115g/4oz/⅔ cup drained canned or thawed
    frozen corn kernels
2 tomatoes, peeled and chopped
juice of 1 lime
Tabasco sauce
salt, ground black pepper and
    cayenne pepper

For the topping
75g/3oz tortilla chips
50g/2oz/½ cup grated Cheddar cheese
coriander (cilantro) sprigs, to garnish
lime wedges, to serve

1 Lay the fish in a shallow pan and pour over the fish stock. Bring to the boil, lower the heat, cover and poach for about 8 minutes, until the flesh flakes easily when tested with the tip of a sharp knife. Leave to cool slightly, then remove the skin and separate the flesh into large flakes. Keep hot.

2 Heat the olive oil in a pan, add the onion and garlic and cook over a low heat until soft. Add the peppers, stir and cook for 2 minutes. Stir in the courgettes and cook for 3 minutes more, until all the vegetables are tender.

3 Stir in the corn and tomatoes, then add lime juice and Tabasco to taste. Season with a little salt, black pepper and cayenne.

4 Cook for a couple of minutes to heat the corn and tomatoes, then stir in the fish and transfer to a dish that can safely be used under the grill (broiler).

5 Preheat the grill. Make the topping by crushing the tortilla chips, then mixing in the grated cheese. Add cayenne pepper and sprinkle over the fish.

6 Place the dish under the grill until the topping is crisp and brown. Serve, garnished with coriander sprigs and lime wedges.

Energy 293kcal/1223kJ; Protein 26.6g; Carbohydrate 15.8g, of which sugars 7.5g; Fat 13.9g, of which saturates 6.9g; Cholesterol 78mg; Calcium 123mg; Fibre 3.2g; Sodium 927mg.

Grilled mackerel with spicy dhal

Red lentils have a low GI value and they are good spiced as an accompaniment to healthy mackerel. Flat bread gives additional carbohydrate. Chopped fresh tomatoes and onion salad bring vegetable goodness, which you could augment with steamed broccoli or cabbage.

Serves four

250g/9oz/1 cup red lentils, or yellow split
  peas (soaked overnight)
1 litre/1¾ pints/4 cups water
15ml/1 tbsp sunflower oil
2.5ml/½ tsp each mustard seeds, cumin
  seeds, fennel seeds, and fenugreek or
  cardamom seeds
5ml/1 tsp ground turmeric
3–4 dried red chillies, crumbled
30ml/2 tbsp tamarind paste
5ml/1 tsp soft brown sugar
30ml/2 tbsp chopped fresh coriander (cilantro)
4 mackerel or 8 large sardines
salt and ground black pepper
fresh red chilli slices and finely chopped
  coriander, to garnish
flat bread and chopped tomatoes, to serve

1 Rinse the lentils or split peas, drain them thoroughly and put them in a pan. Pour in the water and bring to the boil. Lower the heat, partially cover the pan and simmer the pulses for 30–40 minutes, stirring occasionally, until they are tender and mushy.

2 Heat the oil in a wok or shallow pan. Add the mustard seeds, then cover and cook for a few seconds, until they pop. Remove the lid, add the rest of the seeds, with the turmeric and chillies and fry for a few more seconds.

3 Stir in the pulses, with salt to taste. Mix well; stir in the tamarind paste and sugar. Bring to the boil, then simmer for 10 minutes, until thick. Stir in the chopped fresh coriander.

4 Clean the fish then heat a ridged griddle pan or the grill (broiler) until very hot. Make slashes on both sides of each fish and remove the head.

5 Season the fish, then grill (broil) for 5–7 minutes on each side, until the skin is crisp. Garnish with red chilli and chopped coriander, and serve with the dhal, flat bread and tomatoes.

Energy 637kcal/2665kJ; Protein 48.3g; Carbohydrate 36.2g, of which sugars 2.6g; Fat 34.1g, of which saturates 6.6g; Cholesterol 93mg; Calcium 52mg; Fibre 3.1g; Sodium 124mg.

Smoked haddock with cabbage

Smoked fish and robust cabbage are a deliciously healthy combination, and full of flavour when cooked with tomatoes and flavoured with mustard. Use haddock that has not been dyed in the smoking process, as this is free from additives. Serve with new potatoes or couscous.

Serves four

1 Savoy or pointu cabbage
675g/1½lb undyed smoked haddock fillet
300ml/½ pint/1¼ cups milk
½ onion, peeled and sliced into rings
2 bay leaves
½ lemon, sliced
4 white peppercorns
4 ripe tomatoes
30ml/2 tbsp olive oil
30ml/2 tbsp wholegrain mustard
juice of 1 lemon
salt and ground black pepper
30ml/2 tbsp chopped fresh parsley, to garnish

1 Cut the cabbage in half, remove the central core and thick ribs, then shred the cabbage. Cook in a pan of lightly salted boiling water, for about 8 minutes, until just tender. Leave in the pan until required.

2 Meanwhile, put the haddock in a large shallow pan with the milk, onion and bay leaves. Add the lemon slices and peppercorns. Bring to simmering point, cover and poach until the fish flakes easily when tested with the tip of a sharp knife. This will take 8–10 minutes, depending on the thickness of the fillets. Set aside until needed.

3 Cut the tomatoes in half horizontally, season them with salt and pepper and grill (broil) until lightly browned. Drain the cabbage, refresh under cold water and drain again.

4 Melt the butter in a shallow pan or wok, add the cabbage and toss over the heat for 2 minutes. Mix in the mustard and season to taste. Tip the cabbage into a warmed serving dish.

5 Drain the haddock. Skin and cut the fish into four pieces.

6 Place the fish on top of the cabbage, add some onion rings and grilled (broiled) tomato. Pour on the lemon juice, sprinkle with parsley and serve.

Energy 319kcal/1340kJ; Protein 36.1g; Carbohydrate 14.2g, of which sugars 13.7g; Fat 13.1g, of which saturates 7.3g; Cholesterol 90mg; Calcium 146mg; Fibre 4.2g; Sodium 1512mg.

Crab cakes

These crab cakes are bound with egg and yogurt and grilled instead of fried, making them a lower-fat alternative to fish cakes. The onion relish can be also be used in sandwiches.

Serves four

For the onion relish
2 red onions, finely diced
1 clove garlic, crushed
apple juice
balsamic vinegar

450g/1lb mixed brown and white crab meat
30ml/2 tbsp tartare sauce
2.5–5ml/½–1 tsp mustard powder
1 egg, lightly beaten
Tabasco sauce
45ml/3 tbsp chopped fresh parsley
4 spring onions (scallions), finely chopped
50–75g/2–3oz/½–¾ cup breadcrumbs,
sunflower oil, for brushing
salt, ground black pepper and cayenne pepper

1 Make the onion relish. Fry the onions and garlic in a little olive oil. Add a splash of apple juice and balsamic vinegar. Cook on a high heat, stirring, until the liquid disappears. Set aside.

2 Put the crab meat in a bowl and stir in the tartare sauce, with the mustard and egg. Season with Tabasco, salt, pepper and cayenne.

3 Stir the chopped parsley and spring onions, and 50g/2oz/½ cup of the breadcrumbs into the crab mixture.

4 Mix thoroughly. The mixture should be just firm enough to hold together; depending on how much brown crab meat there is, you may need to add some more breadcrumbs.

5 Divide the mixture into 8 portions, roll each into a ball and flatten slightly to make a thick flat disc. Spread out the crab cakes on a platter and put in the refrigerator for 30 minutes.

6 Preheat the grill (broiler). Brush the cakes with a little sunflower oil and place on a grill (broiling) rack. Cook the crab cakes until golden brown on both sides, turning once.

7 Serve with a spring onion garnish and a spoonful of the red onion relish.

Energy 285kcal/1187kJ; Protein 23.9g; Carbohydrate 10.3g, of which sugars 0.9g; Fat 16.7g, of which saturates 2.4g; Cholesterol 134mg; Calcium 178mg; Fibre 0.8g; Sodium 768mg.

Chilli-herb seared scallops

Tender, succulent scallops taste superb when marinated in fresh chilli, fragrant mint and aromatic basil, then quickly seared in a piping hot wok.

Serves four

20–24 king scallops, cleaned
60ml/4 tbsp olive oil
finely grated rind and juice of 1 lemon
30ml/2 tbsp finely chopped mixed fresh mint
    and basil
1 fresh red chilli, seeded and finely chopped
salt and ground black pepper
500g/1½lb pak choi (bok choy)

1 Place the scallops in a shallow, non-metallic bowl in a single layer. In a clean bowl, mix together half the oil, the lemon rind and juice, chopped herbs and chilli and spoon over the scallops. Season well with salt and black pepper, cover and set aside.

2 Using a sharp knife, cut each pak choi lengthways into four pieces.

3 Heat a wok over a high heat. When hot, drain the scallops (reserving the marinade) and add to the wok.

4 Cook the scallops for 1 minute on each side, or until cooked to your liking. Pour the marinade over the scallops.

5 When the marinade has sizzled for a moment, remove the wok from the heat. Transfer the scallops and juices to a platter and keep warm. Wipe out the wok with a piece of kitchen paper.

6 Place the wok over a high heat. When all traces of moisture have evaporated, add the remaining oil. When the oil is hot add the pak choi and stir-fry over a high heat for 2–3 minutes, until the leaves wilt.

7 Divide the greens among four warmed serving plates, then top with the reserved scallops and their juices and serve immediately.

Tips and twists
If you can't find pak choi (bok choy) use Chinese broccoli, purple sprouting broccoli or any other leafy green vegetable instead.

Energy 410kcal/1714kJ; Protein 44.5g; Carbohydrate 8.3g, of which sugars 2.1g; Fat 22.3g, of which saturates 3.5g; Cholesterol 82mg; Calcium 286mg; Fibre 3.2g; Sodium 494mg.

Fragrant tiger prawns with dill

This elegant dish is fresh and light and equally good as a simple supper or for a dinner party.
The delicate fresh prawns go really well with the slightly cooked cucumber and fragrant dill, and
all you need is rice or noodles for carbohydrate.

Serves four to six

500g/1¼lb raw tiger prawns (jumbo shrimp),
   heads and shells removed but tails left on
500g/1¼lb cucumber
30ml/2 tbsp olive oil
15ml/1 tbsp finely chopped garlic
45ml/3 tbsp chopped fresh dill
juice of 1 lemon
salt and ground black pepper
steamed rice or noodles, to serve

1 Using a small, sharp knife, carefully
make a shallow slit along the back of
each prawn and use the point of the
knife to remove the black vein.

2 Peel the cucumber and slice in half
lengthways. Using a small teaspoon,
gently scoop out all the seeds and
discard. Cut the cucumber into
4 x 1cm/1½ x ½in sticks. Heat a wok
over a high heat, then add the oil.

3 When the oil is hot, add the
cucumber and garlic and fry over a
high heat for 2–3 minutes, stirring
continuously.

4 Add the prepared prawns to the wok
and continue to stir-fry over a high heat
for 3–4 minutes, or until the prawns
turn pink and are just cooked through,
then remove from the heat.

5 Add the fresh dill and lemon juice to
the wok and toss to combine. Season
well with salt and ground black pepper
and serve immediately with steamed
rice or noodles.

Energy 165kcal/691kJ; Protein 15.7g; Carbohydrate 10.5g, of which sugars 10.1g; Fat 7g, of which saturates 0.9g; Cholesterol 171mg; Calcium 78mg; Fibre 0.3g; Sodium 167mg.

Asparagus and langoustine salad

For a really extravagant treat, you could make this attractive salad with medallions of lobster. For a cheaper version, use large prawns, allowing six per serving. Be careful not to overcook the langoustines, which are usually sold partially cooked already.

Serves four

16 langoustines
16 fresh asparagus spears, trimmed
2 carrots
30ml/2 tbsp olive oil
1 garlic clove, peeled
15ml/1 tbsp chopped fresh tarragon
4 fresh tarragon sprigs and some chopped, to garnish

For the dressing
30ml/2 tbsp tarragon vinegar
120ml/4fl oz/½ cup olive oil
salt and ground black pepper

1 Shell the langoustines and keep the discarded parts for stock. Set aside.

2 Steam the asparagus over boiling salted water until just tender, but still a little crisp. Refresh under cold water, drain and place in a shallow dish.

3 Peel the carrots and cut into fine julienne shreds. Cook in a pan of lightly salted boiling water for about 3 minutes, until tender but still crunchy. Drain, refresh under cold water, drain again. Place in the dish with the asparagus.

4 Make the dressing. In a jug (pitcher), whisk the tarragon vinegar with the oil. Season to taste. Pour over the asparagus and carrots and leave to marinate for about 30 minutes or up to 2 hours at the most.

5 Heat the oil with the garlic in a pan until very hot. Add the langoustines and sauté quickly until just heated through. Discard the garlic.

6 Cut the asparagus spears in half and arrange on four individual plates with the carrots. Drizzle over the dressing left in the dish and top each portion with four langoustine tails.

7 Top with the tarragon sprigs and scatter the chopped tarragon on top. Serve immediately.

Energy 320kcal/1323kJ; Protein 16.3g; Carbohydrate 4g, of which sugars 3.8g; Fat 26.6g, of which saturates 3.9g; Cholesterol 146mg; Calcium 93mg; Fibre 2.3g; Sodium 150mg.

Meat, Poultry and Game

This chapter is packed with heart-warming classics — casseroles, roasts and grills that are perfect for special meals or prepared to fit perfectly into healthy everyday eating. International seasonings and sauces bring important variety, demanding different types of carbohydrate accompaniments and tasting fabulous with all sorts of vegetables and salads.

Black bean chilli con carne

Fresh green and dried red chillies add plenty of fire to this classic Tex-Mex dish of tender beef cooked in a spicy tomato sauce. Serve with rice or baked potatoes for a low GI meal.

Serves six

225g/8oz/1¼ cups dried black beans
500g/1¼lb braising steak
30ml/2 tbsp vegetable oil
2 onions, chopped
1 garlic clove, crushed
1 fresh green chilli, seeded and
   finely chopped
15ml/1 tbsp paprika
10ml/2 tsp ground cumin
10ml/2 tsp ground coriander
400g/14oz can chopped tomatoes
300ml/½ pint/1¼ cups beef stock
1 dried red chilli, crumbled
5ml/1 tsp hot pepper sauce
1 fresh red (bell) pepper, seeded and chopped
salt
fresh coriander (cilantro), to garnish
boiled rice, to serve

1 Put the beans in a large pan. Add enough cold water to cover them, bring to the boil and boil vigorously for about 10 minutes. Drain, transfer to a clean bowl, cover with cold water and leave to soak for about 8 hours or overnight.

2 Preheat the oven to 150°C/300°F/ Gas 2. Cut the braising steak into small dice. Heat the vegetable oil in a large, flameproof casserole. Add the chopped onion, crushed garlic and chopped green chilli and cook them gently for 5 minutes until soft, using a slotted spoon to transfer the mixture to a plate.

3 Increase the heat to high, add the meat to the casserole and brown on all sides, then stir in the paprika, ground cumin and ground coriander.

4 Add the tomatoes, beef stock, dried chilli and hot pepper sauce. Drain the beans and add them to the casserole, with enough water to cover.

5 Bring the casserole to simmering point, cover and cook in the oven for 2 hours. Stir occasionally and add extra water, if necessary.

6 Season the casserole with salt and add the chopped red pepper. Replace the lid, return the casserole to the oven and cook for 30 minutes more, or until the meat and beans are tender. Sprinkle over the fresh coriander and serve with rice.

EAT WELL
This is also good made with chopped chicken or turkey breast fillet, without skin, for a low-fat main course.

Tips and twists
Red kidney beans are traditionally used in chilli con carne, but in this recipe black beans are used instead. They are the same shape and size as red kidney beans but have a shiny black skin. They are also known as Mexican or Spanish black beans.
   Use minced (ground) beef in place of the braising steak.

Energy 289kcal/1216kJ; Protein 27.3g; Carbohydrate 24.7g, of which sugars 7.9g; Fat 9.7g, of which saturates 2.8g; Cholesterol 45mg; Calcium 61mg; Fibre 7.8g; Sodium 65mg.

Fried rice with beef

A little meat goes a long way in stir-fry dishes. Tossed with rice and broccoli, this dish has enough beef for ample flavour and it slows down the rate at which the rice is digested.

Serves four

200g/7oz lean beef steak, chilled
15ml/1 tbsp vegetable oil
2 garlic cloves, finely chopped
1 egg
250g/9oz/2¼ cups cooked jasmine rice
2 heads broccoli, coarsely chopped
30ml/2 tbsp dark soy sauce
15ml/1 tbsp light soy sauce
15ml/1 tbsp Thai fish sauce
ground black pepper
chilli sauce, to serve

1 Trim the steak and cut it, across the grain of the meat, into very thin strips with a sharp knife.

2 Heat the oil in a wok or frying pan and cook the garlic over a low to medium heat until golden. Do not let it burn. Increase the heat to high, add the steak and stir-fry for 2 minutes.

3 Move the pieces of beef to the edges of the wok or pan and break the egg into the centre. When the egg starts to set, stir-fry it with the meat.

4 Add the rice and toss all the contents of the wok together, scraping up any residue on the base, then add the broccoli, soy sauces, sugar and fish sauce and stir-fry for 2 minutes more.

5 Season to taste with pepper and serve immediately with chilli sauce.

EAT WELL
Be generous with vegetables and mean with meat in stir-fries. Add crisp mangetout (snow) peas or sticks of carrot and red (bell) pepper for a good mix of nutrients.

Tips and twists
Soy sauce is made from fermented soya beans. The first extraction is sold as light soy sauce and has a delicate fragrance. Dark soy has been allowed to mature for longer.

Energy 385kcal/1606kJ; Protein 20.7g; Carbohydrate 52.7g, of which sugars 2.5g; Fat 9.8g, of which saturates 2.8g; Cholesterol 81mg; Calcium 59mg; Fibre 1.6g; Sodium 590mg.

Chunky burgers with spicy relish

These home-made burgers are a much healthier alternative to high-fat commercial types. Wholemeal breadcrumbs add bulk to the lean beef, and serving with tomato relish adds vitamins.

Serves four

350g/12oz lean minced (ground) beef
1 onion, chopped
30ml/2 tbsp chopped fresh flat leaf parsley
30ml/2 tbsp tomato purée (paste)
100g/4oz fresh wholemeal (whole-wheat)
  breadcrumbs
1 egg, beaten
salt and ground black pepper
4 burger buns
1 little gem lettuce heart, separated into leaves

For the spicy relish
15ml/1 tbsp olive oil
1 shallot, chopped
1 garlic clove, crushed
1 small green chilli, seeded and finely chopped
8 very ripe tomatoes, skinned and chopped

1 In a large bowl, place the minced beef, onion, parsley, tomato purée, breadcrumbs, egg and seasoning, then use your hands to mix until it is thoroughly combined.

2 Divide the mixture into quarters and shape into chunky burgers, pressing them firmly between your hands.

3 To make the relish, heat the olive oil in a pan and cook the shallot, garlic and chilli for a few minutes, stirring, until softened. Stir in the chopped fresh tomatoes and simmer for 10 minutes.

4 Meanwhile, preheat the grill (broiler), a griddle or frying pan. Grill (broil) or fry the burgers for about 5 minutes on each side, or until cooked through. Keep warm.

5 Split and lightly toast the buns on the inside. Arrange a few lettuce leaves on the bases, then top with the burgers. Add a dollop of warm spicy relish. Replace the bun tops and serve, offering the remaining relish and extra lettuce leaves separately.

Italian meatballs

Bound with oats and dressed with a good portion of red peppers, serve these meatballs on a generous portion of pasta for a healthy balance.

Serves four

10ml/2 tsp sunflower oil
1 large onion, chopped
2 garlic cloves, finely chopped
15ml/1 tbsp fresh thyme leaves
450g/1lb lean minced (ground) beef
100g/4oz rolled oats
1 large egg
salt and ground black pepper
fresh thyme leaves, to garnish

For the sauce
4 red (bell) peppers, halved and seeded
1 onion, quartered
400g/14oz can chopped tomatoes

1 Heat the oil in a frying pan and cook the onion and garlic for 5 minutes, or until softened. Remove the pan from the heat and add the thyme, then turn the mixture into a bowl.

2 Add the minced beef, rolled oats, egg and seasoning to the onion mixture. Mix until all the ingredients are thoroughly combined.

3 Use your hands to shape the mixture into 20 small meatballs, then chill them until the sauce is ready.

4 To make the sauce, preheat the grill (broiler). Arrange the peppers on a rack with the pieces of onion. Grill (broil) for 12–15 minutes, turning frequently, or until the pepper skins are blackened.

5 Remove the grill from the heat, cover the peppers with a dish towel and leave to cool. Peel the peppers and place them in a blender or food processor with the grilled (broiled) onion and the tomatoes. Process until smooth, then add seasoning to taste.

6 Cook the meatballs in a large, non-stick frying pan for about 10–15 minutes, gently rolling them around to brown them evenly all over.

7 Add the puréed pepper and tomato mixture and bring to the boil, then reduce the heat and simmer for 10 minutes, turning the balls to coat once or twice during cooking. Transfer to a dish and scatter with thyme leaves to garnish, then serve at once.

Energy 484kcal/2021kJ; Protein 27.9g; Carbohydrate 30.2g, of which sugars 7.7g; Fat 28.8g, of which saturates 9.3g; Cholesterol 68mg; Calcium 120mg; Fibre 2.2g; Sodium 473mg.
Energy 341kcal/1427kJ; Protein 33g; Carbohydrate 18.3g, of which sugars 12.9g; Fat 15.5g, of which saturates 5.6g; Cholesterol 120mg; Calcium 44mg; Fibre 3.7g; Sodium 160mg.

Beef and guinness casserole

Stout and beef are natural partners. This vegetable-rich and meat-modest version of a popular casserole is a healthy choice for any occasion, including informal entertaining. Serve with mashed potatoes and green vegetables: the protein helps to slow down carbohydrate digestion.

Serves four

30ml/2 tbsp olive oil
450g/1lb stewing beef (such as rib steak or
   shoulder), cut into thin slices
2 onions, chopped
3 leeks, sliced
3 carrots, sliced
4 celery sticks, sliced
2 garlic cloves, finely chopped
300ml/½ pint/1¼ cups well-reduced
   beef stock
150ml/¼ pint/⅔ cup Guinness
50g/2oz/¼ cup butter
75g/3oz streaky (fatty) bacon, trimmed
   and diced
200g/7oz wild or cultivated mushrooms,
   quartered or sliced
50g/2oz shallots or small onions, left whole
25g/1oz/¼ cup plain (all-purpose) flour
salt and ground black pepper

1 Heat the oil in a pan and brown the meat. Transfer to a casserole. Sauté the vegetables for 5 minutes in the pan, then add to the meat, with the garlic, stock, Guinness and seasoning. Cover and bring to the boil, then reduce the heat and simmer for about 1½ hours.

2 Remove the meat from the casserole and strain the cooking liquid and reserve. Discard the vegetables.

3 Clean the casserole and sauté the bacon, mushrooms and shallots or onions in the butter for 5–10 minutes, stirring continuously. Sprinkle in the flour, and cook, stirring, over a low heat for 2–3 minutes. Slowly blend in the cooking liquid and bring to a simmer.

4 Return the meat to the casserole, and simmer until the meat is heated through. Serve with mashed potatoes.

Energy 367kcal/1529kJ; Protein 35.3g; Carbohydrate 6.9g, of which sugars 5.7g; Fat 19.6g, of which saturates 6.4g; Cholesterol 87mg; Calcium 32mg; Fibre 1.2g; Sodium 119mg.

Beef casserole

Adding a good amount of mushrooms to this dish bulks out a modest portion of meat, keeping the dish full flavoured and balancing protein and vegetables. The traditional accompaniment is creamy mashed potato, but a healthier choice would be leafy greens and brown rice.

Serves four

450g/1lb lean stewing beef
25g/1oz/¼ cup plain (all-purpose) flour
2.5ml/½ tsp paprika
45ml/3 tbsp sunflower oil
2 large onions, peeled and chopped
350g/12oz button (white) mushrooms, quartered
2 garlic cloves, crushed with a little salt
grated rind of 1 orange
300ml/½ pint/1¼ cups red wine
150ml/¼ pint/⅔ cup beef stock
salt and ground black pepper

1 Preheat the oven to 180°C/350°F/ Gas 4. Cut the meat into cubes.

2 Mix the flour with salt, pepper and paprika, spread on a tray or large plate, and coat the meat.

3 Heat a large pan, add 30ml/2 tbsp of the oil and brown the meat. Do this in batches if your pan is small.

4 Transfer the meat to a casserole. Brown the onions in the fat in the pan. Add the onions to the casserole. Keeping the pan hot, add the rest of the oil and brown the mushrooms. Add to the casserole.

5 Add the rest of the ingredients to the casserole and bring to the boil, stirring to combine the orange rind and evenly distribute the meat and mushrooms.

6 Cover the casserole and place in the preheated oven for about 3 hours, until the meat is tender. Serve with mashed potato or brown rice and lots of steamed leafy green vegetables.

Energy 457kcal/1905kJ; Protein 36.8g; Carbohydrate 12.2g, of which sugars 4.7g; Fat 20g, of which saturates 6.5g; Cholesterol 87mg; Calcium 78mg; Fibre 2.3g; Sodium 169mg.

Braised lamb with pearl barley

In this slow-cooked stew the pearl barley absorbs all the rich juices and stock to become full-flavoured and nutty. Pearl barley is a good source of low GI carbohydrate.

Serves four

a little plain (all-purpose) flour
450g/1lb boned shoulder of lamb, cut
    into cubes
60ml/4 tbsp olive oil
1 large onion, chopped
2 garlic cloves, chopped
4 celery sticks, sliced
900ml–1 litre/1½–1¾ pints/3¾–4 cups
    lamb stock
175g/6oz/1cup pearl barley
225g/8oz baby carrots
225g/8oz baby turnips
salt and ground black pepper
30ml/2 tbsp chopped fresh marjoram,
    to garnish

1 Season the flour and toss the cubed lamb in it, until well coated. Set aside.

2 Heat 45ml/3 tbsp of the oil in a flameproof casserole. Cook the onion and garlic until softened, add the celery, then cook until browned. Remove the vegetables from the casserole.

3 Add the remaining oil to the casserole. Brown the lamb in batches. When all the meat is browned, return it to the casserole with the onion mixture.

4 Stir in 900ml/1½ pints/3¾ cups of the stock. Add the pearl barley. Cover, then bring to the boil, reduce the heat and simmer for 1 hour. Add some of the remaining stock, if necessary.

5 Add the carrots and turnips to the casserole for a final 15 minutes of cooking. Stir in seasoning to taste, and serve garnished with marjoram.

Energy 560kcal/2342kJ; Protein 37g; Carbohydrate 36g, of which sugars 10.2g; Fat 30.9g, of which saturates 10.4g; Cholesterol 128mg; Calcium 82mg; Fibre 3.7g; Sodium 179mg.

Roast lamb with beans

Roasting the lamb slowly on a bed of beans results in a dish that combines meltingly tender meat with low GI carbohydrate all in one pot. Serve with seasonal vegetables.

Serves six

8–10 garlic cloves, peeled
1.8–2kg/4–4½lb leg of lamb
30ml/2 tbsp olive oil
450g/1lb spinach leaves
2 x 400g/14oz cans flageolet, cannellini or
    haricot (navy) beans, drained
400g/14oz can butter (lima) beans, drained
2 large, fresh rosemary sprigs, plus extra
    to garnish
15–30ml/1–2 tbsp drained, bottled
    green peppercorns

1 Preheat the oven to 150°C/300°F/ Gas 2. Set four garlic cloves aside and slice the rest lengthways into three or four pieces. Make shallow slits in the skin of the lamb and insert a piece of garlic into each.

2 Heat the olive oil in a heavy, shallow flameproof casserole or a roasting pan that is large enough to hold the leg of lamb. Add the reserved garlic cloves and the fresh spinach leaves to the casserole or pan.

3 Cook over a medium heat, stirring occasionally, for 4–5 minutes, or until the spinach is wilted.

4 Add the beans and tuck the rosemary sprigs and peppercorns among them. Place the lamb on top, then cover the casserole or pan with foil or a lid.

5 Roast the lamb for 3–4 hours until it is cooked to your taste. Slice the lamb and serve it hot with the beans, garnished with the remaining fresh rosemary sprigs.

Energy 705kcal/2945kJ; Protein 74.3g; Carbohydrate 22.2g, of which sugars 4.2g; Fat 35.9g, of which saturates 15.4g; Cholesterol 246mg; Calcium 186mg; Fibre 8.7g; Sodium 775mg.

Griddled loin of lamb with barley risotto

A loin of lamb is taken from the back or the saddle, and it should be completely clear of visible fat or gristle for relatively lean meat. Barley makes fabulous risotto – delicious and a lower GI carbohydrate than the usual rice.

3 Add half of the remaining stock and stir until absorbed. Finally add the rest of the stock, stirring all the time. You will create a thick, creamy mixture, with the barley still having a little "bite" to it.

4 Grate the cheese and add to the barley when it has absorbed all the stock. Stir in well, season with salt and ground black pepper, and keep warm.

5 Brushing a griddle or pan with olive oil. Heat until very hot. Brush the lamb with the remaining olive oil and season with salt and pepper. Sear all over, then reduce the heat and cook for a further 8 minutes, turning from time to time. Leave to rest for 5 minutes.

6 Carve each loin, at an angle, into three slices. Place a mound of risotto on each warmed plate, prop the slices of lamb on it. drizzle with a little virgin olive oil, if using.

Serves four

750ml/1¼ pints/3 cups chicken stock
30ml/2 tbsp olive oil
1 onion, finely chopped
225g/8oz/1 cup barley
50g/2oz mature cheese, such as Parmesan, Cheddar or double Gloucester
3 loins of lamb
salt and ground black pepper
virgin olive oil, to serve (optional)

1 Bring the stock to the boil. Heat half the olive oil in a pan, and sweat the onion until translucent.

2 Add the barley to the pan and mix with the onion until evenly coated with oil. Add one-third of the stock, and bring to the boil. Reduce the heat and stir until the liquid is absorbed.

Energy 827kcal/3460kJ; Protein 49.8g; Carbohydrate 53.2g, of which sugars 2.2g; Fat 47.7g, of which saturates 25.2g; Cholesterol 223mg; Calcium 55mg; Fibre 0.5g; Sodium 348mg.

Stir-fried pork with dried shrimp

Stir-fries are great for getting protein into perspective. Lots of flavour and vegetables bulk out a modest amount of meat. Serve with a good portion of jasmine rice and a beansprout and spring onion salad on the side.

Serves four

250g/9oz pork fillet (tenderloin), sliced
30ml/2 tbsp vegetable oil
2 garlic cloves, finely chopped
45ml/3 tbsp dried shrimps
10ml/2 tsp dried shrimp paste
30ml/2 tbsp soy sauce
juice of 1 lime
1 small fresh red or green chilli, seeded and
    finely chopped
450g/1lb spring greens (collards) or
    4 pak choi (bok choy), shredded

1 Put the pork in the freezer for about 30 minutes, then cut it into thin slices. Heat the oil in a wok or frying pan and cook the garlic until golden brown.

2 Add the pork to the wok and stir-fry for about 4 minutes, until just cooked through. Add the shrimp, stir in the shrimp paste, soy sauce and lime juice.

3 Add the chilli and pak choi or spring greens and toss over the heat until the vegetables are just wilted.

4 Transfer the stir-fry to warmed individual bowls and serve immediately.

Energy 200kcal/833kJ; Protein 23.1g; Carbohydrate 6.3g, of which sugars 6.2g; Fat 9.2g, of which saturates 1.7g; Cholesterol 96mg; Calcium 334mg; Fibre 2.4g; Sodium 1223mg.

Pork tenderloin with puy lentils

Pork has become one of the leanest meats and the tenderloin is free from visible fat. Puy lentils are a good source of low GI carbohydrate and delicious in this spicy sauce.

Serves four

500g/1¼lb pork tenderloin
15ml/1 tbsp sunflower oil
8–12 large spinach leaves
1 onion, chopped
1 garlic clove, finely chopped
2.5cm/1in piece fresh root ginger,
    finely grated
1 red chilli, finely chopped (optional)
250g/9oz/generous 1 cup Puy lentils
750ml/1¼ pints/3 cups chicken or
    vegetable stock
200ml/7fl oz/scant 1 cup milk
salt and ground black pepper

2 Preheat the oven to 180°C/350°F/ Gas 4. Heat the oil in a frying pan, add the pork and brown over a high heat on all sides. Remove the meat from the pan and set aside.

5 Add the onion to the oil in the frying pan and cook for about 5 minutes, stirring occasionally, until softened. Add the chopped garlic, grated ginger and finely chopped chilli, if using, and fry for a further 1 minute.

1 Cut the pork tenderloin widthways into two equal pieces. Season the pork well with salt and ground black pepper.

3 Meanwhile, place the spinach leaves one by one, so they stay separate, into a large pan of boiling water and cook for 1 minute, or until just wilted. Drain immediately in a colander and refresh under cold running water. Drain well.

6 Add the lentils to the onion mixture in the frying pan and then stir in the chicken or vegetable stock. Bring to the boil, then boil rapidly for 10 minutes. Remove the pan from the heat and stir in the milk. Transfer the onion and lentil mixture to a casserole and arrange the pork tenderloins on top.

7 Cover the casserole and place it in the oven. Cook for 45 minutes, or until the lentils are cooked.

8 To serve, remove the spinach-wrapped pork tenderloins from the casserole using a slotted spoon or tongs and cut the pork into thick slices.

EAT WELL
Serve the pork with a stir-fry of red onion, red (bell) peppers, beetroot (beet) (cooked and cut into sticks), red cabbage (shredded) and carrots. The protein and lentils help to slow down the digestion of the carbohydrate from high–GI ingredients such as carrots.

4 Lay the cooked, cooled spinach leaves on the work surface, overlapping them slightly to form a rectangle. Place the pork tenderloin on top and wrap the leaves around the pork to enclose it completely.

9 Stir the lentils and spoon them, with some of the cooking juices, on to warmed, individual plates and top each portion with a few of the pork slices.

Tips and twists
Wrap the pork in slices of prosciutto, instead of the spinach leaves, and secure with wooden cocktail sticks (toothpicks).

Energy 399kcal/1683kJ; Protein 42.3g; Carbohydrate 39.1g, of which sugars 5g; Fat 9.2g, of which saturates 4g; Cholesterol 87mg; Calcium 81mg; Fibre 3.5g; Sodium 206mg.

Bacon with cabbage and parsley sauce

A whole piece of bacon or gammon is delicious boiled with simple cabbage and a classic parsley sauce. Serve modest portions of meat with lots of vegetables and use any left-over meat to flavour a pasta and vegetable salad or a mixed vegetable stir-fry.

Serves six

1.3kg/3lb bacon or gammon
1 carrot, chopped
2 celery sticks, chopped
2 leeks, chopped
5ml/1 tsp peppercorns
15ml/1 tbsp oven-dried breadcrumbs
15ml/1 tbsp English mustard
7.5ml/1½ tsp light muscovado (brown) sugar
25g/1oz/2 tbsp butter
900g/2lb green cabbage, sliced

For the parsley sauce
25g/1oz/2 tbsp butter
25g/1oz/¼cup plain (all-purpose) flour
300ml/½ pint/1¼ cups half cooking liquid and
  half milk
bunch of parsley, leaves chopped
ground black pepper

1 Place the bacon joint in a large pan. Add the vegetables to the pan, with the peppercorns. Cover with cold water and bring to the boil. Simmer gently for about 20 minutes per 450g/1lb. Preheat the oven to 200°C/400°F/Gas 6.

EAT WELL
Boiled new potatoes and mashed carrot and swede (rutabaga) are great with bacon or ham. Instead of using butter when mashing, add plenty of black pepper and drizzle in a little olive oil. Served with meat, the high GI value of carrots and swede is balanced and they may not swing blood glucose as drastically as they can do.

---

2 Remove the joint from the pan, reserving the cooking liquid. Cut off the rind, and score the fat. Place in a roasting pan. Mix the breadcrumbs, mustard, sugar and 15g/½oz/1 tbsp butter; spread over the joint. Place in the oven for 15–20 minutes.

3 To make the parsley sauce, melt the butter in a pan, add the flour and cook for 1–2 minutes, stirring constantly. Gradually whisk in the cooking liquid and milk. Bring to the boil and simmer for 3–4 minutes, then stir in the parsley. Season to taste with pepper.

4 In a large pan cook the cabbage with a little of the cooking liquid from the bacon. Drain well, season to taste and toss in the remaining butter.

5 To serve, slice the bacon and serve on a bed of cabbage, with a little of the parsley sauce.

Energy 689kcal/2857kJ; Protein 40.4g; Carbohydrate 16.3g, of which sugars 10.6g; Fat 51.5g, of which saturates 23.1g; Cholesterol 155mg; Calcium 139mg; Fibre 5g; Sodium 3461mg.

Ostrich casserole with chickpeas

Lean and firm, ostrich meat is full-flavoured and delicious with the soft-textured sweet potatoes and chickpeas in this quick and easy, yet rich, stew. If you cannot find ostrich meat, substitute any lean red meat, such as venison or beef, in this recipe.

Serves four

45ml/3 tbsp olive oil
1 large onion, chopped
2 garlic cloves, finely chopped
450g/1lb ostrich fillet, cut into short strips
450g/1lb sweet potatoes, peeled and diced
2 x 400g/14oz cans chopped tomatoes
400g/14oz can chickpeas, drained
salt and ground black pepper
fresh oregano, to garnish

EAT WELL
Couscous is a quick and easy carbohydrate accompaniment. For a rounded meal, serve a good mixed fruit salad to follow.

1 Heat half the oil in a flameproof casserole. Add the chopped onion and garlic, and cook for about 5 minutes until softened but not coloured.

2 Remove the onions and garlic from the casserole using a slotted spoon and set aside. Add the remaining oil to the casserole and heat.

3 Brown the meat in batches over a high heat. When the last batch is cooked, replace all the meat and the onions in the casserole, with the potatoes, tomatoes and chickpeas.

4 Bring to the boil, reduce the heat and simmer for 25 minutes. Season and serve garnished with the fresh oregano.

Energy 639kcal/2682kJ; Protein 49g; Carbohydrate 51.2g, of which sugars 16.5g; Fat 27.9g, of which saturates 8.2g; Cholesterol 98mg; Calcium 108mg; Fibre 9.7g; Sodium 393mg.

Chicken with chickpeas and almonds

The almonds in this Moroccan-style recipe are cooked until soft, adding an interesting texture.

Serves 4

75g/3oz/½ cup blanched almonds
75g/3oz/½ cup chickpeas, soaked overnight
and drained
4 part-boned chicken breast portions, skinned
30ml/2 tbsp olive oil
2.5ml/½ tsp saffron threads
2 Spanish onions, finely sliced
900ml/1½ pints/3¾ cups chicken stock
1 small cinnamon stick
60ml/4 tbsp chopped fresh flat leaf parsley,
plus extra to garnish
lemon juice, to taste
salt and ground black pepper

1 Place the almonds and chickpeas in a casserole of water and bring to the boil. Boil for 10 minutes, then reduce the heat. Simmer for 1½ hours until the chickpeas are soft. Drain and set aside.

2 Place the skinned chicken pieces in the casserole, together with the olive oil, half of the saffron, and salt and plenty of black pepper. Heat gently to start cooking the chicken.

3 Add the onions and stock, bring to the boil. Add the reserved almonds, chickpeas and cinnamon stick. Cover and cook very gently for 45–60 minutes until the chicken is completely tender.

4 Transfer the cooked chicken to a serving plate and keep warm. Bring the sauce to the boil and cook over a high heat until it is well reduced, stirring frequently with a wooden spoon.

5 Add the chopped parsley and remaining saffron to the casserole and cook for a further 2–3 minutes. Add a little lemon juice, then pour over the chicken, garnish with extra parsley.

Chicken with cinnamon

A thick tomato and almond sauce coats chicken pieces in this subtly spiced dish.

Serves four

30ml/2 tbsp sunflower oil
4 chicken quarters
1 onion, grated or very finely chopped
1 garlic clove, crushed
5ml/1 tsp ground cinnamon
good pinch of ground ginger
1.3–1.6kg/3–3½lb very ripe, sweet tomatoes,
peeled, cored and roughly chopped
50g/2oz/⅓ cup blanched almonds
15ml/1 tbsp sesame seeds
salt and ground black pepper
chopped flat leaf parsley, to garnish

1 Heat the oil in a large, flameproof casserole. Add the chicken and cook over a medium heat for about 3 minutes until it is lightly browned. Add the grated or chopped onion, garlic, cinnamon and ginger.

2 Add the tomatoes to the casserole with seasoning to taste, and heat gently until the tomatoes bubble.

3 Lower the heat and then cover the casserole. Simmer very gently for about 1 hour, stirring and turning the chicken occasionally, or until it is completely cooked through (pierce the thigh area to check that the meat juices are clear). Lift out the chicken pieces and transfer them to a plate.

4 Increase the heat and cook the tomato sauce until it is reduced to a thick purée, stirring frequently. Return the chicken pieces to the pan and cook for 2–3 minutes to heat through.

5 Transfer the chicken and sauce to a warmed serving dish and sprinkle with the blanched almonds and sesame seeds. Serve garnished with parsley.

> **EAT WELL**
> Cinnamon enriches the sauce in this Moroccan-style dish that would traditionally be sweetened with honey, but is equally delicious without. Use chicken breasts for a lower fat version. Chickpeas and rice (mixed) and a green bean and green (bell) pepper salad go well.

Energy 431kcal/1803kJ; Protein 44.4g; Carbohydrate 11g, of which sugars 1.7g; Fat 23.6g, of which saturates 7.9g; Cholesterol 132mg; Calcium 110mg; Fibre 4g; Sodium 180mg.
Energy 325kcal/1362kJ; Protein 27.6g; Carbohydrate 12.2g, of which sugars 11.5g; Fat 18.9g, of which saturates 2.9g; Cholesterol 43mg; Calcium 92mg; Fibre 4.7g; Sodium 104mg.

Roast chicken and vegetables

This is a delicious, vegetable-rich alternative to traditional roast chicken. The recipe also works very well with guinea fowl. Root vegetables can also be used instead of Mediterranean varieties.

4 Arrange the potatoes around the chicken and roll them in the cooking juices until they are thoroughly coated. Return the pan to the hot oven to continue roasting.

5 After 30 minutes, add the aubergine, red pepper, fennel and garlic cloves to the pan. Drizzle the vegetables with the remaining oil, and season to taste with salt and pepper.

6 Add the remaining sprigs of thyme to the pan, tucking the sprigs in among the vegetables. Return the chicken and vegetables to the oven and cook for 30–50 minutes more, basting and turning the vegetables occasionally during cooking.

7 To find out if the chicken is cooked, push the tip of a small sharp knife between the thigh and breast – if the juices run clear, rather than pink, it is done. The vegetables should be tender and beginning to brown. Let the chicken stand for 20 minutes, keeping the vegetables warm, before carving. Serve with a green vegetable.

Serves 4

1.8–2.25kg/4–5lb roasting chicken
30ml/2 tbsp extra virgin olive oil
½ lemon
a few sprigs of fresh thyme
675g/1½lb small new potatoes
1 aubergine (eggplant), cut into 2.5cm/
 1in cubes
2 red or yellow (bell) pepper, seeded
 and quartered
2 fennel bulbs, trimmed and quartered
8 large garlic cloves, unpeeled
coarse salt and ground black pepper

1 Preheat the oven to 200°C/400°F/ Gas 6. Rub the chicken all over with olive oil and season with pepper. Place the lemon half inside the bird, with a sprig or two of thyme.

2 Put the chicken breast side down in a large roasting pan. Place in the oven and roast for about 30 minutes.

3 Remove the chicken from the oven and season with salt. Turn the chicken right side up, and baste with the juices from the pan.

Energy 798kcal/3310kJ; Protein 43.3g; Carbohydrate 23.7g, of which sugars 6.1g; Fat 59.3g, of which saturates 13.6g; Cholesterol 208mg; Calcium 45mg; Fibre 4.2g; Sodium 183mg.

Hunter's chicken

This is a good simple chicken dish, for everyday eating. You may prefer to use skinless chicken for a lower fat meal. Either way it is delicious with pasta and a mixed pepper salad.

Serves four

30ml/2 tbsp olive oil
4 chicken portions, on the bone
1 large onion, thinly sliced
400g/14oz can chopped tomatoes
150ml/¼ pint/⅔ cup red wine
150ml/¼ pint/⅔ cup stock
1 garlic clove, crushed
1 rosemary sprig, finely chopped, plus extra
    whole sprigs to garnish
115g/4oz fresh field (portobello) mushrooms,
    thinly sliced
salt and ground black pepper

1 Heat the oil in a large, flameproof casserole until foaming. Add the chicken portions and fry for 5 minutes. Remove the chicken pieces and drain on kitchen paper.

2 Add the sliced onion and cook gently, stirring frequently, for about 3 minutes then stir in the tomatoes, red wine and stock. Add the crushed garlic and chopped rosemary and season. Bring to the boil, stirring continuously.

3 Return the chicken to the casserole and turn to coat with the sauce. Cover and simmer gently for 30 minutes.

4 Add the fresh mushrooms to the casserole and stir well to mix into the sauce. Continue simmering gently, uncovered, for 10 minutes, until the sauce has reduced. Taste and add more ground black pepper if necessary.

5 Garnish with the fresh rosemary sprigs, and serve immediately.

EAT WELL

In some instances, eating mashed potatoes can push up blood glucose levels too sharply; instead, try tossing boiled salad or new potatoes with a little olive oil and black pepper, then lightly crush them with a vegetable masher.

Energy 386kcal/1622kJ; Protein 53.6g; Carbohydrate 4.5g, of which sugars 4.1g; Fat 14.5g, of which saturates 4.5g; Cholesterol 155mg; Calcium 28mg; Fibre 1.5g; Sodium 141mg.

Chicken with summer vegetables

This is an all-in-the-pot dish, with the chicken providing the stock for the rest of the cooking and the sauce. Summer vegetables are wonderfully packed with flavour, and it is up to you to pick the selection you prefer: add canned beans for low GI carbohydrate and fibre.

Serves six

1.8kg/4lb boiling fowl (stewing chicken)
1 onion, peeled, studded with 6 cloves
1 bay leaf
a sprig each of thyme and parsley
10 black peppercorns
12 small potatoes, washed
8 small shallots, peeled
vegetables of your choice, including
   sugarsnap peas, carrots, courgettes
   (zucchini), broad (fava) beans and peas
2 x 400g/15oz cans flageolet beans
25g/1oz/2 tbsp butter
30ml/2 tbsp plain (all-purpose) flour
60ml/4 tbsp chopped fresh tarragon

1 Place the chicken in a large pan with the onion, bay leaf, thyme, parsley and peppercorns, with water to cover. Bring to the boil. Reduce the heat and simmer gently for 1½ hours. Skim off the froth, and add water if necessary.

2 Meanwhile prepare all the vegetables and place them in rows on a tray in order of cooking time, from the longest to the shortest.

3 Once cooked, remove the chicken from the pan and keep warm. Remove all the seasonings, either with a slotted spoon or by straining the mixture, then bring the cooking liquid back to the boil, skimming off any fat that may have appeared on the top.

4 Start to cook the vegetables in the liquid, putting the potatoes in first, then adding the shallots and carrots, if using, and finally the green vegetables that take no time at all – sugarsnap peas, for example, should go in when the potatoes are cooked. Add the flageolet beans for the final 5 minutes.

5 When the vegetables are cooked, place the chicken on a serving dish and surround with all the vegetables.

6 In a small pan melt the butter, add the flour and stir to create a roux. Slowly add some liquid from the large pan until a sauce is created – about 600ml/1 pint/2½ cups – and allow to simmer for a few minutes to reduce down and strengthen the flavour.

7 At the last moment stir in the chopped tarragon then ladle the sauce over the chicken and vegetables. Bring to the table and serve immediately.

Energy 713kcal/2973kJ; Protein 51.2g; Carbohydrate 39.3g, of which sugars 13g; Fat 40g, of which saturates 12.9g; Cholesterol 261mg; Calcium 103mg; Fibre 5.4g; Sodium 250mg.

Pheasant with oatmeal herb stuffing

Game is a good source of low-fat protein. Pheasant is delicate and delicious with the richly flavoured herb stuffing. The traditional accompaniment is game chips and redcurrant sauce, but mashed potatoes and lots of barely cooked courgettes are just as good.

Serves four to six
2 oven-ready pheasants
6 unsmoked bacon rashers (strips)
30ml/2 tbsp olive oil
15g/½oz/2 tbsp seasoned flour
450ml/¾ pint/scant 2 cups
    chicken stock
salt and ground black pepper
watercress or rocket (arugula), to garnish

For the stuffing
1 small onion, finely chopped
225g/8oz chicken or pheasant livers, trimmed
    and finely chopped
115g/4oz/1 cup pinhead oatmeal
about 120ml/4fl oz/½ cup milk

1 To prepare the stuffing, put the onion and the pheasant livers into a mixing bowl with the oatmeal. Mix thoroughly and season with salt and pepper. Add enough milk to moisten slightly.

2 Preheat the oven to 200°C/400°F/ Gas 6. Wipe the birds inside and out and divide the stuffing between the two birds, spooning it in loosely to allow space for the oatmeal to expand.

3 Use cotton string to truss the pheasants for cooking, and lay the bacon rashers over the breasts.

4 Lay the birds in a roasting pan and drizzle the oil over them. Place in the oven and cook for 45–50 minutes, basting often.

5 Ten minutes before the end of the cooking time, remove the bacon rashers and set aside. Baste the birds and then dredge them with seasoned flour. Baste again and return to the oven to brown.

6 When cooked, remove the trussing strings and put the pheasants on to a heated serving dish. Keep warm, uncovered, while you make the gravy. Pour all but 30ml/2 tbsp of the fat out of the roasting pan.

7 Sprinkle the remaining flour into the roasting pan, stirring to blend and dislodge any sediment on the bottom.

8 Gradually blend in the stock, season and bring to the boil. Simmer for a few minutes, stirring, then pour into a heated sauceboat.

9 To serve, garnish the pheasant breasts with the bacon pieces and watercress or rocket. Hand the gravy round separately.

Energy 846kcal/3529kJ; Protein 69.7g; Carbohydrate 25.2g, of which sugars 1.1g; Fat 52.5g, of which saturates 23.1g; Cholesterol 598mg; Calcium 92mg; Fibre 2.3g; Sodium 697mg.

Venison pie

This is a super-healthy version of shepherd's pie using rich yet lean venison. The mixed vegetable mash has a relatively high GI value but including it with protein slows down digestion. Have lots of green vegetables, such as kale or cabbage, and green beans, on the side.

Serves six

30ml/2 tbsp olive oil
3 leeks, washed, trimmed and chopped
1kg/2¼lb minced (ground) venison
30ml/2 tbsp chopped fresh parsley
300ml/½ pint/1¼ cups game consommé
salt and ground black pepper

For the topping
1.4kg/3¼lb mixed root vegetables, such as potatoes, sweet potatoes, parsnips and swede (rutabaga), coarsely chopped
15ml/1 tbsp horseradish sauce
30ml/2 tbsp olive oil

1 Heat the oil in a pan over a medium heat. Add the leeks and cook for about 8 minutes, or until they are softened and beginning to brown.

2 Add the minced venison to the pan and cook over a medium heat, stirring constantly, for about 10 minutes or until the venison is browned all over.

Tips and twists

This pie can be made with other minced (ground) meats, such as beef, lamb or pork, or a mixture of pork and beef. You may need to adapt the cooking times for these, but the basic recipe remains the same. You can also use other types of game, such as finely chopped or minced rabbit or hare.

3 Add the fresh parsley and stir it in thoroughly, then add the consommé and salt and ground black pepper. Stir well. Bring the mixture to the boil over a medium heat, then reduce the heat to low, cover and simmer for about 20 minutes, stirring occasionally.

4 Meanwhile, preheat the oven to 200°C/400°F/Gas 6 and prepare the pie topping. Cook the chopped root vegetables in boiling salted water to cover for 15–20 minutes.

5 Drain the vegetables and put them in a bowl. Mash them together with the horseradish sauce, olive oil and plenty of ground black pepper.

6 Spoon the venison mixture into a large ovenproof dish and cover the top evenly with the mashed vegetables.

7 Bake in the preheated oven for 20 minutes, or until piping hot and beginning to brown. Serve immediately, with steamed green vegetables.

EAT WELL

For a carbohydrate-packed mash that is not digested too speedily, combine crushed cooked lentils, chickpeas or butter (lima) beans with the vegetables. Red lentils are good with carrots, swedes (rutabaga) and sweet potatoes; try chickpeas or butter beans with potatoes. Olive oil is delicious with chives or parsley in mash.

Energy 307kcal/1291kJ; Protein 39.8g; Carbohydrate 13.2g, of which sugars 12.5g; Fat 12g, of which saturates 4.1g; Cholesterol 93mg; Calcium 154mg; Fibre 5.8g; Sodium 176mg.

Guinea fowl with beans and curly kale

Guinea fowl is delicious cooked with colourful herb-flavoured beans and vegetables, providing a balanced one-pot meal. If you don't have a clay pot, use a large, ovenproof casserole instead. A leafy side salad with mangetout makes a palate-refreshing accompaniment.

2 Place the remaining oil in a frying pan, add the shallots, garlic and celery and sauté for 4–5 minutes. Remove the shallots, garlic and celery with a slotted spoon and place in the pot. Stir in the tomatoes and beans. Tuck in the thyme and bay leaves.

3 Put the guinea fowl in the frying pan and brown on all sides, then pour in the wine and stock and bring to the boil. Lift the bird out of the pan, place it on top of the vegetables, and then pour the liquid over the top.

4 Cover and place in the oven. For a clay pot, set the oven to 200°C/400°F/Gas 6 when you put the pot in. Cook for 1 hour.

5 Add the curly kale to the pot or casserole, nestling it among the beans. Cover and cook for a further 10–15 minutes, or until the guinea fowl is tender. Season the bean mixture and serve immediately.

Serves four

1.3kg/3lb guinea fowl
45ml/3 tbsp olive oil
4 shallots or 2 onions, chopped
1 garlic clove, crushed
4 celery sticks, sliced
400g/14oz can chopped tomatoes
2 x 400g/14oz cans mixed beans, drained
5 fresh thyme sprigs
2 bay leaves
150ml/¼ pint/⅔ cup dry white wine
300ml/½ pint/1¼ cups well-flavoured chicken stock
450g/1lb curly kale
salt and ground black pepper

1 If using a clay pot, soak it in cold water for 20 minutes, then drain. If using an ovenproof casserole: preheat the oven to 180°C/350°F/Gas 4. Rub the guinea fowl with 15ml/1 tbsp of the olive oil and season.

EAT WELL
Guinea fowl is a farmed bird with a good flavour similar, but superior, to chicken. Shredded red cabbage is a good alternative to kale, and it can be added at the beginning of cooking, with the beans as a base for cooking the bird.

Energy 617kcal/2585kJ; Protein 53.1g; Carbohydrate 32.9g, of which sugars 8.7g; Fat 28.6g, of which saturates 1.5g; Cholesterol 0mg; Calcium 98mg; Fibre 11.6g; Sodium 1017mg.

Partridge with lentils and sausage

Grey partridge is a game bird indigenous to Scotland, although it is often called the English partridge, and is slightly smaller than the European red-legged variety. Its wonderful rich flavour is complemented by lovely earthy Puy lentils and lean venison sausages.

Serves four

450g/1lb/2 cups Puy lentils
30ml/2 tbsp olive oil
4 grey partridges
2 venison sausages
1 garlic clove, peeled but left whole
250ml/8fl oz/1 cup stock
salt and ground black pepper

1 Preheat the oven to 180°C/350°F/ Gas 4. Wash the lentils then simmer them in water for about 10 minutes to soften slightly. Drain then set aside.

2 Heat the oil in a large ovenproof frying pan and place the partridges, breast side down, in the pan. Brown both breasts lightly.

3 Set the partridges on their backs, season lightly with salt and ground black pepper and cook in the preheated oven for 15 minutes. When cooked, remove the partridges from the oven, allow to cool slightly, then remove the legs and keep the rest warm.

4 Put the large frying pan back on the hob and brown the two sausages. Add the Puy lentils and garlic and stir to coat in the juices from the partridges and the sausages. Then add the stock and simmer for a few minutes.

5 Place the partridge legs on top of the lentil mixture and return to the oven for a further 15 minutes.

6 Remove the pan from the oven and set aside the partridge legs and sausages. Discard the garlic. Season the lentils with salt and ground black pepper, and if there is still a lot of liquid remaining, boil over a low heat to evaporate a little of the excess moisture. Then, off the heat, gradually swirl in the remaining oil.

7 Remove the breasts from the carcasses and set aside. Cut the sausages into pieces and stir into the lentil mixture.

8 To serve, place a leg on individual warmed plates, put the lentils on top and then the breast, sliced lengthwise, on top of the lentils.

Energy 1309kcal/5495kJ; Protein 152.1g; Carbohydrate 59.4g, of which sugars 2.1g; Fat 53g, of which saturates 20.1g; Cholesterol 55mg; Calcium 255mg; Fibre 10.2g; Sodium 761mg.

Salads and Vegetable Dishes

Eating would be dull without vegetables. They look lively, taste exciting and make you feel fantastic. Raw or cooked, as a starter, for a light meal or to complement a main dish — vegetables bring flavour, colour, texture and essential nutrients to a healthy diet. From simple to sophisticated, enjoy vegetables every day and salads throughout the week.

Watermelon and feta salad

The combination of sweet watermelon with salty feta cheese is refreshing and flavoursome. Eating protein and fat from the feta with the watermelon helps to balance its high GI characteristics; so do the olives and seeds. This salad makes an excellent accompaniment to warm pearl barley or bulgur wheat tossed with lots of chives and tarragon.

Serves four

4 slices watermelon, chilled
130g/4½oz feta cheese, cubed
handful of mixed seeds, such as pumpkin
   seeds and sunflower seeds, lightly toasted
10–15 black olives

Tips and twists
The best choice of olives for this recipe are plump black ones, such as kalamata, other shiny, brined varieties or dry-cured black olives.

1 Cut the rind off the watermelon and remove as many seeds as possible. The sweetest and juiciest part is right in the core, and you may want to cut off any whiter flesh just under the skin.

2 Cut the flesh into triangular chunks. Mix the watermelon, feta cheese, mixed seeds and black olives. Cover and chill the salad for 30 minutes in the refrigerator before serving.

Energy 256kcal/1066kJ; Protein 7.7g; Carbohydrate 12.9g, of which sugars 11.6g; Fat 19.7g, of which saturates 6.2g; Cholesterol 23mg; Calcium 165mg; Fibre 1.4g; Sodium 616mg.

Quail's egg salad

Eating a healthy diet does not mean missing out on good things but moderating them instead. Bishop Kennedy is a full-fat soft cheese, with its rind washed in malt whisky to produce a distinctive orange-red crust and a strong creamy taste. A little goes a long way in this salad. If you can't find Bishop Kennedy, use a blue cheese, such as Gorgonzola or Stilton instead.

Serves four

8 quail's eggs
vinegar, for poaching
½ red onion, finely chopped
½ leek, cut into fine strips and blanched
75g/3oz Bishop Kennedy cheese, finely diced
½ red cabbage, shredded
mixed salad leaves, including Little Gem
  (Bibb) lettuce and lollo bionda
10ml/2 tsp pine nuts
salad dressing

1 Poach the quail's eggs. You need a shallow pan of simmering water with a dash of vinegar added, an eggcup, a slotted spoon and a pan of iced water.

2 Using a thin knife, carefully break the shell of an egg and open it up into the eggcup. Gently lower the cup into the simmering water, allowing some water to cover and firm up the egg, then slide it into the water and cook for 1 minute.

4 When all the eggs are cooked, lift them out of the water and dry them on kitchen paper. This last bit can be done just before you assemble the salad since the quail's eggs will keep in cold water while the salad is prepared.

Tips and twists

If you can't find or don't want to use quail's eggs, use three regular eggs and poach them for 3 minutes. You could also replace the quail eggs with two hard boiled eggs and cut them into quarters.

3 Lift the egg out with a slotted spoon and put it straight into iced water.

5 Combine the salad ingredients, including the pine nuts (which can be lightly toasted, if you like). Toss with your chosen dressing. To serve, simply place the diced Bishop Kennedy and the quail's eggs on top of the salad.

Energy 256kcal/1067kJ; Protein 12.5g; Carbohydrate 19.3g, of which sugars 3.6g; Fat 14.9g, of which saturates 3.7g; Cholesterol 110mg; Calcium 100mg; Fibre 6.1g; Sodium 101mg.

Spiced aubergine salad

Aubergine, tomatoes and cucumber lightly spiced with cumin and coriander make a fresh-tasting salad when topped with yogurt. They are delicious with canned mixed beans tossed with chopped spring onion and grated lemon rind for a super-healthy meal.

Serves four

2 small aubergines (eggplants), sliced
45ml/3 tbsp extra virgin olive oil
15ml/1 tbsp red wine vinegar
2 garlic cloves, crushed
15ml/1 tbsp lemon juice
2.5ml/½ tsp ground cumin
2.5ml/½ tsp ground coriander
½ cucumber, thinly sliced
2 well-flavoured tomatoes, thinly sliced
30ml/2 tbsp natural (plain) yogurt
salt and ground black pepper
chopped fresh flat leaf parsley, to garnish

1 Preheat the grill (broiler) or a griddle. Lightly brush the aubergine slices with olive oil and cook on both sides.

2 When they are done, remove the aubergine slices to a chopping board and cut them into quarters.

3 Mix together the remaining oil, the vinegar, garlic, lemon juice, cumin and coriander. Season with salt and pepper and mix thoroughly.

4 Add the the warm aubergines to the dressing and stir well to coat. Chill for at least 2 hours. When ready to serve, add the cucumber and tomatoes.

5 Transfer to a serving dish and spoon the yogurt on top. Sprinkle with parsley and serve.

Energy 161kcal/669kJ; Protein 2.3g; Carbohydrate 5.8g, of which sugars 5.5g; Fat 14.6g, of which saturates 2.2g; Cholesterol 0mg; Calcium 37mg; Fibre 3.7g; Sodium 15mg.

Grilled leek and courgette salad

Served on crisp, sweet lettuce, this makes a delicious summery appetizer or main course. Feta cheese is a superb ingredient as it has loads of flavour so you don't need so much, a firm crumbly texture, and it is not as high in fat as matured cheeses.

Serves six

12 slender, baby leeks
6 small courgettes (zucchini)
45ml/3 tbsp extra virgin olive oil, plus extra
    for brushing
finely shredded rind and juice of ½ lemon
1–2 garlic cloves, finely chopped
½ fresh red chilli, seeded and diced
pinch of caster (superfine) sugar (optional)
50g/2oz/½ cup black olives, stoned (pitted)
    and roughly chopped
30ml/2 tbsp chopped fresh mint
150g/5oz feta cheese, sliced or crumbled
salt and ground black pepper
fresh mint leaves, to garnish

1 Bring a pan of water to the boil. Add the leeks and cook for 2–3 minutes.

2 Drain the leeks, refresh under cold water, then squeeze out any excess water and leave to drain.

3 Cut the courgettes in half lengthwise. Place in a colander, adding 5ml/1 tsp salt to the layers, and leave to drain for about 45 minutes. Rinse well under running water and pat dry thoroughly on a piece of kitchen paper.

4 Heat the grill (broiler). Brush the leeks and courgettes lightly with oil. Grill (broil) the leeks for 2–3 minutes each side and the courgettes for about 5 minutes on each side.

5 Place the grilled leeks in a shallow dish, together with the courgettes.

6 Place the remaining oil in a small bowl and whisk in the lemon rind, 15ml/1 tbsp lemon juice, the garlic, chilli and a pinch of sugar, if using. Season to taste with salt and ground black pepper.

7 Pour the dressing over the leeks and courgettes. Stir in the olives and mint, then set aside to marinate for a few hours, turning the vegetables once or twice. If the salad has been marinated in the refrigerator, remove it 30 minutes before serving and bring back to room temperature.

8 Add the crumbled feta cheese just before serving, and garnish with several fresh mint leaves.

Energy 197kcal/812kJ; Protein 6.2g; Carbohydrate 3.4g, of which sugars 2.9g; Fat 17.6g, of which saturates 5.3g; Cholesterol 18mg; Calcium 140mg; Fibre 2.6g; Sodium 552mg.

Warm bean salad with rocket

This is an easy dish, as black-eyed beans do not need to be soaked overnight. Adding spring onions and loads of dill elevates a carbohydrate and protein rich meal into something refreshing and aromatic. It can be served hot or at room temperature.

Serves four

275g/10oz/1½ cups black-eyed beans (peas)
6 spring onions (scallions), sliced
a large handful of fresh rocket (arugula)
  leaves, chopped if large
45–60ml/3–4 tbsp chopped fresh dill
30ml/2 tbsp extra virgin olive oil
juice of 1 lemon, or to taste
10–12 black olives
salt and ground black pepper
small cos or romaine lettuce leaves, to serve

Tips and twists
For a no-cook version, replace the black-eyed beans (peas) with canned chickpeas.

1 Thoroughly rinse the beans and drain them well. Transfer to a pan and pour in cold water to just about cover. Slowly bring to the boil over a low heat. As soon as the water is boiling, remove the pan from the heat and drain the water off immediately.

2 Put the beans back in the pan with fresh cold water to cover and add a pinch of salt – this will make their skins harder and stop them from disintegrating when they are cooked.

3 Bring the beans to the boil over a medium heat, then lower the heat and cook them until they are soft but not mushy. They will take 20–30 minutes only, so keep an eye on them.

4 Drain the beans, reserving 75–90ml/5–6 tbsp of the cooking liquid. Transfer the beans to a large salad bowl. Add the remaining ingredients immediately, including the reserved liquid, and mix.

5 Serve piled on the lettuce leaves, or leave to cool slightly and serve later.

Energy 238kcal/1007kJ; Protein 16.1g; Carbohydrate 31g, of which sugars 2.4g; Fat 6.4g, of which saturates 0.9g; Cholesterol 0mg; Calcium 114mg; Fibre 12.3g; Sodium 580mg.

Tomato and feta salad

This salad is a twist on a traditional Greek salad, with plenty of purslane or rocket added to the traditional combination of tomato, pepper, onion, cucumber, feta and olives. Wholemeal pitta breads are good with the salad, or serve on a bed of warm pearl barley for a main course.

Serves four

225g/8oz tomatoes
1 red onion, thinly sliced
1 green (bell) pepper, cored and sliced in
  thin ribbons
1 piece of cucumber, about 15cm/6in in
  length, peeled and sliced in rounds
150g/5oz feta cheese, cubed
a large handful of fresh purslane, trimmed of
  thick stalks
8–10 black olives
30ml/2 tbsp extra virgin olive oil
15ml/1 tbsp lemon juice
1.5ml/¼ tsp dried oregano
salt and ground black pepper

1 Cut the tomatoes into quarters and place them in a salad bowl. Add the onion, green pepper, cucumber, feta, purslane and olives.

2 Sprinkle the extra virgin olive oil, lemon juice and oregano on top. Add salt and ground black pepper to taste, then toss to coat everything in the olive oil and lemon, and to amalgamate the flavours of the ingredients.

3 If possible, let the salad stand for 10–15 minutes at room temperature before serving, but don't leave for too long or the cucumber will spoil.

Energy 369kcal/1528kJ; Protein 9.6g; Carbohydrate 7.7g, of which sugars 7.7g; Fat 33.5g, of which saturates 10.4g; Cholesterol 35mg; Calcium 211mg; Fibre 3g; Sodium 1303mg.

Bean salad with tuna and red onion

This class salad makes a great main meal, with slow-release carbohydrate, protein and vitamins. For a more substantial meal, add green or red peppers and serve with barley, rice or bread.

Serves four

250g/9oz/1½ cups dried haricot (navy) or
   cannellini beans, soaked overnight in
   cold water
1 bay leaf
200–250g/7–9oz fine green beans, trimmed
1 large red onion, very thinly sliced
45ml/3 tbsp chopped fresh flat leaf parsley
200–250g/7–9oz good-quality canned tuna in
   olive oil, drained
200g/7oz cherry tomatoes, halved
salt and ground black pepper
a few onion rings, to garnish

For the dressing
45ml/3 tbsp extra virgin olive oil
15ml/1 tbsp tarragon vinegar
5ml/1 tsp tarragon mustard
1 garlic clove, finely chopped
5ml/1 tsp grated lemon rind
a little lemon juice
pinch of caster (superfine) sugar (optional)

1 Drain the haricot or cannellini beans and bring them to the boil in a pan of fresh water with the bay leaf added. Boil rapidly for about 10 minutes, then reduce the heat and boil steadily for approximately 1–1½ hours, until tender, then drain and discard the bay leaf.

2 Place the dressing ingredients apart from the lemon juice and sugar in a jug (pitcher) or bowl and mix. Season with salt, pepper, lemon juice and a pinch of caster sugar, if you like. Leave to stand.

3 Blanch the green beans in boiling water for 3–4 minutes. Drain, refresh under cold water and drain again.

4 Place the beans in a bowl. Add half the dressing and toss. Stir in the onion and half the parsley, then season to taste. Flake the tuna and add to the beans with the tomatoes.

5 Arrange the salad on four plates. Drizzle the remaining dressing over the salad, garnish with parsley and a few onion rings and serve.

Energy 443kcal/1857kJ; Protein 29.1g; Carbohydrate 33.7g, of which sugars 6.4g; Fat 22.3g, of which saturates 3.3g; Cholesterol 25mg; Calcium 100mg; Fibre 11.9g; Sodium 162mg.

Anchovy and roasted pepper salad

Sweet peppers, salty anchovies and plenty of garlic make an intensely flavoured salad that is delicious with wholemeal pasta, rice, barley or couscous.

Serves four

2 red, 2 orange and 2 yellow (bell) peppers, halved and seeded
50g/2oz can anchovies in olive oil
2 garlic cloves
45ml/3 tbsp balsamic vinegar

Tips and twists

If you find anchovies too salty, remove them from the can, dab them dry with kitchen towel to remove most of the oil, and then place in a saucer of milk. Remove and dry again on kitchen towel once they have soaked for about 10–15 minutes, and you will find the saltiness has been reduced.

1 Preheat the oven to 200°C/400°F/ Gas 6. Place the peppers in a roasting pan and roast for 30–40 minutes. Transfer to a bowl and cover with clear film (plastic wrap).

2 When the peppers are cool, peel them and cut into strips. Drain the anchovies, reserving the oil. Halve the fillets lengthwise.

3 Slice the garlic cloves as thinly as possible and place them in a large bowl. Stir in the olive oil, balsamic vinegar and a little black pepper.

4 Add the sliced peppers and anchovy fillets and use a spoon or fork to fold the ingredients together. Cover the salad with clear film and chill until you are ready to serve.

Energy 108kcal/453kJ; Protein 6g; Carbohydrate 16.4g, of which sugars 15.5g; Fat 2.4g, of which saturates 0.5g; Cholesterol 8mg; Calcium 83mg; Fibre 4.6g; Sodium 506mg.

Sautéed herb salad with chilli and lemon

Firm-leafed fresh herbs, such as flat leaf parsley and mint tossed in a little olive oil, make a fabulous base for all sorts of meals. Preserved lemons can be found in good delicatessens.

Serves four

a large bunch each of flat leaf parsley, mint
    and fresh coriander (cilantro)
a bunch of rocket (arugula)
115g/4oz spinach leaves
30ml/2 tbsp olive oil
2 garlic cloves, finely chopped
1 red chilli, seeded and finely chopped
½ preserved lemon, finely chopped
salt and ground black pepper
45–60ml/3–4 tbsp Greek (US strained plain)
    yogurt, to serve

Tips and twists
Flavour the yogurt with a little crushed garlic, if you like.

1 Roughly chop the herbs and combine with the rocket and spinach. Heat the olive oil in a wide, heavy pan. Stir in the garlic and chilli, and fry until they begin to colour. Toss in the herbs and leaves and cook gently, until they begin to wilt.

2 Add the preserved lemon and season to taste. Serve warm with yogurt.

Energy 142kcal/585kJ; Protein 3.6g; Carbohydrate 3.1g, of which sugars 2.7g; Fat 12.9g, of which saturates 2.1g; Cholesterol 2mg; Calcium 216mg; Fibre 4.4g; Sodium 82mg.

Fresh tuna salad niçoise

Fresh tuna transforms this classic colourful salad into something really special. The good mix of protein, vegetables and ample potatoes makes a well-balanced main meal.

Serves four

4 tuna steaks, about 150g/5oz each
olive oil, for brushing
225g/8oz fine green beans, trimmed
1 small, crisp-leaved lettuce
12–16 new potatoes, boiled
4 ripe tomatoes, or 12 cherry tomatoes
2 red (bell) peppers, seeded and sliced
4 hard-boiled eggs, peeled and sliced
8 drained anchovy fillets in oil, halved
   lengthwise
16 large black olives
salt and ground black pepper
12 fresh basil leaves, to garnish

For the dressing
15ml/1 tbsp red wine vinegar
30ml/2 tbsp olive oil
1 fat garlic clove, crushed

1 Brush the tuna lightly on both sides with olive oil and season with salt and black pepper.

2 Heat a ridged griddle pan or the grill (broiler) until very hot, then grill (broil) the tuna steaks for 1–2 minutes on each side; the flesh should still be pink and juicy in the middle. Set aside.

3 Cook the beans in a pan of lightly salted boiling water for 4–5 minutes or until crisp-tender. Drain, refresh under cold water and drain again.

4 Separate the lettuce leaves and wash and dry them. Arrange them on four individual serving plates.

5 To make the dressing, whisk together the vinegar, olive oil and garlic and season to taste.

6 Slice the potatoes and tomatoes, if large (leave cherry tomatoes whole) and divide them among the plates. Arrange the fine green beans and red pepper strips over them.

7 Shell the hard-boiled eggs and cut them into thick slices. Place two half eggs on each plate with an anchovy fillet draped over. Scatter four olives on to each plate. Drizzle the dressing over the salads, arrange the tuna steaks on top, scatter over the basil and serve.

Energy 578kcal/2408kJ; Protein 46.4g; Carbohydrate 15g, of which sugars 10.6g; Fat 37.5g, of which saturates 7.1g; Cholesterol 235mg; Calcium 127mg; Fibre 4.7g; Sodium 585mg.

Braised red cabbage

Red cabbage is a hardy vegetable that is ideal for mixing with robust spices and flavourings. Lightly spiced with a sharp, sweet flavour, braised red cabbage is traditionally served as an accompaniment to roast pork, duck and game dishes, but it also goes well with fish dishes.

3 Layer the shredded cabbage in a large ovenproof dish with the onions, apples, spices, and salt and ground black pepper. Pour over the vinegar and walnut oil.

4 Cover the dish with a lid and cook in the preheated oven for about 1½ hours, stirring a couple of times, until the cabbage is very tender. Serve immediately, garnished with the parsley.

Serves four to six

1kg/2¼lb red cabbage
2 cooking apples
2 onions, chopped
1.5ml/¼ tsp freshly grated nutmeg
pinch of ground cloves
1.5ml/¼ tsp ground cinnamon
15ml/1 tbsp red wine vinegar
30ml/2 tbsp walnut oil
salt and ground black pepper
chopped flat leaf parsley, to garnish

1 Preheat the oven to 160ºC/325ºF/ Gas 3.

2 Cut away and discard the large white ribs from the outer cabbage leaves using a large, sharp knife, then finely shred the cabbage. Peel, core and coarsely grate the apples.

Energy 160kcal/668kJ; Protein 4.3g; Carbohydrate 23.8g, of which sugars 22.4g; Fat 5.8g, of which saturates 3.3g; Cholesterol 13mg; Calcium 140mg; Fibre 6.6g; Sodium 58mg.

Kale with mustard dressing

This is a winter dish from Ireland, where sea kale is used, its pale green fronds have a slightly nutty taste. Use curly kale or a dark green cabbage if you can't get sea kale, although you will need to boil it briefly for a few minutes before chilling and serving.

Serves four

250g/9oz sea kale or curly kale
45ml/3 tbsp light olive oil
5ml/1 tsp wholegrain mustard
15ml/1 tbsp white wine vinegar
pinch of caster (superfine) sugar
salt and ground black pepper

1 Wash the kale, drain, then trim it and tear in pieces. Cook briefly if needed.

2 Whisk the oil into the mustard in a bowl. When it is blended completely, whisk in the white wine vinegar. It should begin to thicken.

3 Season the mustard dressing to taste with sugar, a little salt and plenty of ground black pepper.

4 Toss the sea kale in the dressing and serve immediately.

Energy 99kcal/409kJ; Protein 2.1g; Carbohydrate 1.9g, of which sugars 1.9g; Fat 9.3g, of which saturates 1.3g; Cholesterol 0mg; Calcium 82mg; Fibre 1.9g; Sodium 27mg.

Broccoli with sesame seeds

Quick cooking is best for tender young purple-sprouting broccoli, so that the rich colour and crunchy texture is retained. A splash of soy sauce and some toasted sesame seeds complement the flavour of this supremely healthy vegetable.

Serves two

225g/8oz purple-sprouting broccoli
15ml/1 tbsp sesame seeds
15ml/1 tbsp olive oil
15ml/1 tbsp soy sauce
salt and ground black pepper

EAT WELL
When purple-sprouting broccoli is not available, remove the stalks from ordinary broccoli and dice them, then blanch them in boiling water for 2–3 minutes before stirring with the broccoli tops.
For a healthy lunch, make a double portion and serve it with couscous, topped with chopped walnuts or pine nuts.

1 Using a sharp knife, cut off and discard any thick stems from the broccoli and cut the broccoli into long, thin florets.

2 Spread out the sesame seeds in a small frying pan and dry-fry over a medium heat until toasted. Shake the pan occasionally and do not leave them unattended as the seeds will readily burn if left just a fraction too long.

3 Heat the olive oil in a wok or large frying pan and add the broccoli. Stir-fry for 3–4 minutes, or until tender, adding a splash of water if the pan becomes too dry.

4 Add the soy sauce to the broccoli, then season with salt and ground black pepper to taste. Add the toasted sesame seeds, toss to combine and serve immediately.

Energy 270kcal/1115kJ; Protein 13.1g; Carbohydrate 5.4g, of which sugars 4.6g; Fat 21.7g, of which saturates 3.3g; Cholesterol 0mg; Calcium 229mg; Fibre 7.1g; Sodium 1089mg.

Young vegetables with tarragon

This is almost a salad, but the vegetables here are just lightly cooked to bring out their different flavours. The tarragon adds a wonderful depth to this bright, fresh dish. Broccoli, cauliflower or Brussels sprouts are also good cooked this way.

Serves four

5 spring onions (scallions)
30ml/2 tbsp olive oil
1 garlic clove, crushed
115g/4oz asparagus tips
115g/4oz mangetouts (snow peas), trimmed
115g/4oz broad (fava) beans
2 Little Gem (Bibb) lettuces
5ml/1 tsp finely chopped fresh tarragon
salt and ground black pepper

Tips and twists

For a main meal, serve the vegetables with wholemeal (whole-wheat) pasta, topped with low-fat fromage frais and Parmesan shavings.

1 Cut the spring onions into quarters lengthways and fry them gently over a medium-low heat in the oil with the garlic.

2 Add the asparagus tips, mangetouts and broad beans to the frying pan. Mix in well with the oil, and add enough water to just cover the base of the pan.

3 Bring the vegetables to the boil, and then reduce the heat. Allow to simmer for 5–8 minutes, until the vegetables are starting to soften but not overcooked.

4 Cut the lettuce into quarters and add to the pan. Cook for 3 minutes then, off the heat, add the tarragon, and serve.

Energy 124kcal/515kJ; Protein 5.1g; Carbohydrate 6.8g, of which sugars 3.5g; Fat 8.7g, of which saturates 3.8g; Cholesterol 13mg; Calcium 62mg; Fibre 3.9g; Sodium 44mg.

Courgettes in tomato sauce

This rich-flavoured dish can be served hot or cold, as a base for grilled gammon or griddled tofu, or with plain roast chicken. Cut the courgettes into fairly thick slices, so that they retain their texture and stay slightly crunchy.

Serves four

15ml/1 tbsp olive oil
1 onion, chopped
1 garlic clove, chopped
4 courgettes (zucchini), thickly sliced
400g/14oz can chopped tomatoes
2 tomatoes, peeled, seeded and chopped
15ml/1 tbsp tomato purée (paste)
salt and ground black pepper

> **EAT WELL**
> Add two sliced, seeded red (bell) peppers with the courgettes in step 1 and serve in baked potatoes, with poached eggs.

1 Heat the olive oil in a heavy pan, add the chopped onion and garlic and sauté for about 5 minutes, or until the onion is softened, stirring occasionally.

2 Add the thickly sliced courgettes to the onion and garlic and cook for a further 5 minutes.

3 Add the canned and fresh tomatoes, and tomato purée to the pan, and stir together. Simmer for 10–15 minutes until the sauce is thickened and the courgettes are tender. If the sauce becomes too dry, add a little water. Season to taste and serve.

Baked fennel with a crumb crust

Baked fennel is tasty and versatile – good with classic roasts or all kinds of dishes, from pasta and risotto to pizza or tortilla. This crunchy breadcrumb topping complements it perfectly.

Serves four

4 fennel bulbs, cut lengthwise into quarters
1 garlic clove, chopped
75g/3oz/1½ cups day-old wholemeal
    (whole-wheat) breadcrumbs
45ml/3 tbsp chopped fresh flat leaf parsley
30ml/2 tbsp olive oil
salt and ground black pepper
a few fronds of fennel leaves, to garnish
    (optional)

> **EAT WELL**
> Vegetables with good flavour and texture, such as fennel, are excellent with tofu or bean curd. For a delicious main dish, cut a couple of packets of firm tofu into thick fingers and arrange them in the dish with the fennel.

1 Cook the fennel in a pan of boiling salted water for 10 minutes. Preheat the oven to 190°C/375°F/Gas 5. Drain the fennel and place in a large earthenware baking tray.

2 In a small bowl, mix together the chopped garlic, wholemeal breadcrumbs and chopped fresh flat leaf parsley, then stir half of the olive oil.

3 Brush the fennel with the rest of the olive oil. Sprinkle the breadcrumb mixture evenly over the top, then season well with salt and pepper. Place the dish in the hot oven.

4 Bake the fennel for about 30 minutes, or until it is tender and the breadcrumb topping is crisp and golden brown. Serve the baked fennel hot, garnished with a few fronds of fennel leaves, if you like.

Energy 89kcal/370kJ; Protein 4.3g; Carbohydrate 9.2g, of which sugars 8.6g; Fat 4.1g, of which saturates 0.7g; Cholesterol 0mg; Calcium 54mg; Fibre 3.2g; Sodium 235mg.
Energy 114kcal/477kJ; Protein 3g; Carbohydrate 12.6g, of which sugars 3.1g; Fat 6.1g, of which saturates 0.8g; Cholesterol 0mg; Calcium 67mg; Fibre 4.3g; Sodium 114mg.

Lentil dhal with roasted garlic and spices

This spicy lentil dhal makes a healthy meal when served with basmati rice or Indian breads, and any dry-spiced dish, particularly a cauliflower, spinach or green bean and potato dish. If you don't like hot chillies, leave out the dried red ones, but keep in the green for their flavour.

5 Stir the tomatoes in to the dahl and then adjust the seasoning, adding a little lemon juice to taste if necessary.

6 Add the roasted garlic purée, cumin and ground coriander, then season with salt and pepper to taste. Cook for 10–15 minutes, stirring frequently.

7 To finish the spicy garnish: melt the remaining oil in a frying pan. Add the cumin and mustard seeds and fry until the mustard seeds pop.

8 Pour the roasted seeds into the dhal, then stir in the chillies and curry leaves, swirling the mixture into the cooked dhal. Garnish with fresh coriander, and the spicy fried shallots and garlic mixture and serve hot.

Serves four

1 onion, chopped
2 green chillies, seeded and chopped
15ml/1 tbsp chopped fresh root ginger
225g/8oz/1 cup yellow or red lentils
900ml/1½ pints/3¾ cups water
45ml/3 tbsp puréed roasted garlic
5ml/1 tsp ground cumin
5ml/1 tsp ground coriander
200g/7oz tomatoes, peeled and diced
a little lemon juice
salt and ground black pepper
coriander (cilantro) sprigs, to garnish

For the spicy garnish
45ml/3 tbsp groundnut (peanut) oil
4–5 shallots, sliced
2 garlic cloves, thinly sliced
5ml/1 tsp cumin seeds
5ml/1 tsp mustard seeds
3–4 small dried red chillies
8–10 fresh curry leaves

1 First begin the spicy garnish. Heat 30ml/2 tbsp of the oil in a large, heavy pan. Add the shallots and fry them over a medium heat, stirring occasionally, until they are crisp and browned.

2 Add the garlic to the shallots and cook, stirring frequently, for a moment or two until the garlic colours slightly. Use a slotted spoon to remove the mixture from the pan and set aside.

3 To cook the dhal, add the onion, chillies and ginger to the pan and cook for 10 minutes, until golden.

4 Stir in the lentils and add the water, then bring to the boil, reduce the heat and part-cover the pan. Simmer, stirring occasionally, for 50–60 minutes, until the lentils have broken down and the dhal has a consistency similar to a very thick soup.

Energy 234kcal/979kJ; Protein 9.5g; Carbohydrate 23.8g, of which sugars 3.1g; Fat 11.8g, of which saturates 5.3g; Cholesterol 20mg; Calcium 28mg; Fibre 2.5g; Sodium 73mg.

Cabbage with bacon

You don't need much bacon, especially if it is smoked, to make all the difference to the flavour of this cabbage dish, turning it into a delicious vegetable accompaniment. Try serving it with pasta tossed with canned kidney beans for a well-balanced meal.

Serves four

30ml/2 tbsp oil
115g/4oz smoked bacon, finely chopped
1 onion, finely chopped
500g/1¼lb cabbage (red, white or Savoy)
ground black pepper

1 Heat the oil in a large pan or frying pan with a lid over a medium heat, add the bacon and cook for about 7 minutes, stirring occasionally, until crisp at the edges.

2 Add the chopped onion to the pan and cook until it becomes golden.

3 Shred the cabbage quite finely, discarding the core. Wash and drain.

4 Add the cabbage to the bacon and season with black pepper. Stir for a few minutes so that the cabbage is coated in the oil. Reduce the heat.

5 Continue to cook the cabbage, stirring frequently, for 8–10 minutes until it is tender but still crisp. If you prefer it softer, cover the pan for part of the cooking time. Serve immediately.

Tips and twists

This dish is equally delicious if you use spring greens (collards) or curly kale instead of cabbage.

To make a substantial dish to serve for lunch or supper, add button (white) mushrooms, chunks of salad potato and skinned, seeded and chopped tomatoes.

Energy 151kcal/623kJ; Protein 6.7g; Carbohydrate 7.4g, of which sugars 7g; Fat 10.5g, of which saturates 2.6g; Cholesterol 15mg; Calcium 67mg; Fibre 2.8g; Sodium 452mg.

Cauliflower with egg and lemon

Sautéeing the cauliflower slightly before briefly cooking in water means it is full of flavour in this piquant sauce. This dish is delicious served with plain-cooked fish or chicken.

Serves four

30ml/2 tbsp extra virgin olive oil
1 medium cauliflower, divided into
    large florets
2 eggs
juice of 1 lemon
5ml/1 tsp cornflour (cornstarch), mixed to a
    cream with a little cold water
30ml/2 tbsp chopped fresh flat leaf parsley
salt

1 Heat the olive oil in a large heavy pan, add the cauliflower florets and sauté over a medium to high heat until they start to brown slightly.

2 Pour in enough hot water to almost cover the cauliflower, then cover the pan and cook for 7–8 minutes until the florets are just soft. Remove the pan from the heat and leave to stand, covered, while you make the sauce.

3 Beat the eggs in a bowl, add the lemon juice and cornflour and beat until mixed. Beat in a few tablespoons of the hot liquid from the cauliflower.

4 Pour the egg mixture slowly over the cauliflower, then stir gently. Place the pan over a very gentle heat for 2 minutes to thicken the sauce, but do not allow to boil. Spoon into a serving bowl, sprinkle with parsley and serve.

EAT WELL
Think of this as the new, lighter cauliflower cheese! No need to abandon the latter, but this lively dish makes a light and delicious lunch for two (not four) with chunks of wholemeal (whole-wheat) toast.
• For a delicious twist on kedgeree, poach chunks of skinless smoked haddock fillet (discard bones) with the cauliflower and serve the finished dish with basmati rice tossed with grated lemon rind and chopped fresh coriander (cilantro).

Energy 201kcal/833kJ; Protein 7g; Carbohydrate 4.4g, of which sugars 2.7g; Fat 17.5g, of which saturates 3g; Cholesterol 95mg; Calcium 51mg; Fibre 2.2g; Sodium 47mg.

Masala beans with fenugreek

The secret of this super-fast dish is the spice mixture that coats the vegetables. Cooking is kept to the minimum so that individual flavours are still detectable.

Serves four

1 onion
5ml/1 tsp ground cumin
5ml/1 tsp ground coriander
5ml/1 tsp sesame seeds
5ml/1 tsp chilli powder
2.5ml/½ tsp crushed garlic
1.5ml/¼ tsp ground turmeric
5ml/1 tsp salt
30ml/2 tbsp olive oil
1 tomato, quartered
225g/8oz/1½ cups green beans, blanched
1 bunch fresh fenugreek leaves,
    stems discarded
60ml/4 tbsp chopped fresh coriander (cilantro)
15ml/1 tbsp lemon juice

1 Roughly chop the onion. Mix together the cumin and coriander, sesame seeds, chilli powder, garlic, turmeric and salt.

2 Put the chopped onion and spice mixture into a food processor or blender, and process for 30–45 seconds until you have a rough paste.

3 In a wok or large, heavy pan, heat the oil over a medium heat and fry the spice paste for about 5 minutes, stirring the mixture occasionally.

4 Add the tomato quarters, blanched green beans, fresh fenugreek and chopped coriander.

5 Stir-fry the contents of the pan for about 5 minutes, then sprinkle in the lemon juice and serve.

Tips and twists
Instead of fresh fenugreek, substitute 15ml/1 tbsp dried fenugreek, and a handful of finely shredded baby spinach leaves.

Energy 70kcal/289kJ; Protein 1.6g; Carbohydrate 2.7g, of which sugars 2.1g; Fat 6g, of which saturates 0.7g; Cholesterol 0mg; Calcium 47mg; Fibre 2g; Sodium 6mg.

Desserts

Think dessert: think fruit. That's a whole world of
flavours, textures and colours to use in as many
different cooking styles. Desserts can make a useful
contribution to good eating — dairy produce, nuts
and dried ingredients are important in a balanced
diet. Avoiding sweet stuff is not negative — discover
other irresistible desserts that are more exciting.

Baked ricotta cakes with red fruits

These vanilla-flavoured cheesecakes are lightly sweetened with honey for a special meal.
Select naturally sweet fruit as a base for the sauce to avoid adding additional sweetener.

Serves four

250g/9oz/generous 1 cup ricotta cheese
2 egg whites, lightly whisked
15ml/1 tbsp clear honey
5ml/1 tsp vanilla essence (extract)
450g/1lb/4 cups mixed fresh or frozen fruit,
    such as strawberries, cherries, blueberries,
    raspberries and blackberries
fresh mint leaves, to decorate (optional)

EAT WELL
The natural sweetness and flavour
of fruit perfectly complements
these ricotta-based baked
cheesecakes, which are meant to
be creamy rather than sweet.

---

1 Preheat the oven to 180°C/350°F/
Gas 4. Place the ricotta cheese in a
bowl and break it up with a wooden
spoon. Add the whisked egg whites,
honey and vanilla essence and mix
thoroughly until the mixture is smooth
and well combined.

2 Very lightly grease four ramekins with
sunflower oil. Spoon the ricotta mixture
into the ramekins and level the tops.
Bake for 20 minutes, or until the ricotta
cakes are risen and golden.

3 Meanwhile, make the fruit sauce.
Reserve about a quarter of the fruit for
decoration. Measure about 30ml/2 tbsp
water and pour into a heavy-bottomed
pan and place on a medium heat.

4 Add the rest of the fruit to the pan,
and heat gently until softened. Remove
the pan from the heat and set aside to
cool slightly.

5 Purée the fruit in a blender or food
processor or press it through a sieve
(strainer). Serve the sauce, warm or
cold, with the ricotta cakes. Decorate
with the reserved berries and a few
mint leaves, if using.

Tips and twists
If using frozen fruit for the sauce,
there is no need to add extra water
because there are usually plenty of
ice crystals clinging to the berries.
Adding extra water may make the
sauce too runny.

Energy 161kcal/674kJ; Protein 8.1g; Carbohydrate 11.5g, of which sugars 11.5g; Fat 9.6g, of which saturates 5.9g; Cholesterol 26mg; Calcium 23mg; Fibre 0.6g; Sodium 63mg.

Fruit-filled soufflé omelette

A light and fluffy soufflé omelette filled with fresh, juicy strawberries is a decadent and indulgent treat. Select naturally sweet fruit, such as strawberries, peaches or nectarines.

Serves three

75g/3oz/¾ cup strawberries, hulled
3 eggs, separated
15ml/1 tbsp caster (superfine) sugar
45ml/3 tbsp double (heavy) cream, whipped
a few drops of vanilla extract
15g/½oz/1 tbsp butter

1 Hull the strawberries and cut them in half. Set aside. In a bowl, beat the egg yolks and sugar until pale and fluffy, then fold in the cream and vanilla extract. Whisk the egg whites in a very large, grease-free bowl until stiff, then carefully fold into the yolks.

2 Melt the butter in an omelette pan. When sizzling, pour in the egg mixture and cook until set, shaking the pan occasionally. Spoon on the strawberries and, tilting the pan, slide the omelette so that it folds over.

3 Carefully slide the omelette on to a warm serving plate. Cut the omelette into three pieces, then transfer to two other warmed plates and serve immediately.

EAT WELL
Use a non-stick pan for cooking with minimum fat. Forget superior non-stick frying pans (the coating still deteriorates when cooking over high heat), instead replace less-expensive more frequently.

Tips and twists
Use any type of soft fruit in place of the strawberries. Slices of peach, fresh berries or a combination of several fruits will all work well.

Energy 289kcal/1201kJ; Protein 6.8g; Carbohydrate 12.3g, of which sugars 12.3g; Fat 20.5g, of which saturates 10.9g; Cholesterol 229mg; Calcium 47mg; Fibre 0.3g; Sodium 126mg.

Summer berry crêpes

The delicate flavour of these crêpes contrasts beautifully with tangy berry fruits. You can cook the crêpes ahead and then reheat them in the oven, or a dry frying pan before serving.

Serves four

115g/4oz/1 cup self-raising (self-rising) flour
1 large egg
300ml/½ pint/1¼ cups milk
a few drops of pure vanilla extract
15g/½oz/1 tbsp butter
15ml/1 tbsp sunflower oil
5ml/1 tsp icing (confectioners') sugar,
    for dusting

For the fruit
300ml/½ pint/1¼ cups unsweetened
    apple juice
juice of 2 oranges
thinly pared rind of ½ orange
350g/12oz/3 cups mixed summer berries,
    such as sliced strawberries, yellow
    raspberries, blueberries and redcurrants
30ml/2 tbsp brandy

1 Preheat the oven to 150°C/300°F/ Gas 2. To make the crêpes, sift the flour into a large bowl and make a well in the centre. Break in the egg and gradually whisk in the milk to make a smooth batter. Stir in the vanilla extract. Set the batter aside in a cool place for up to half an hour.

EAT WELL
Boiling unsweetened apple juice until it is reduced and concentrated creates an excellent alternative to sugar-water syrups. Reduced juice is not necessarily as sweet but it compensates with lots of flavour.

2 Heat the butter and oil together in an 18cm/7in non-stick frying pan. Swirl to grease the pan, then pour off the excess fat into a small bowl.

3 If the batter has been allowed to stand, whisk it until smooth. Pour a little of the batter into the hot pan, swirling to cover the base of the pan evenly. Cook until the crêpe comes away from the sides and is golden underneath.

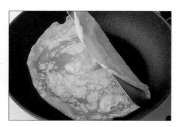

4 Flip over the crêpe with a large palette knife and cook the other side briefly until golden.

5 Slide the crêpe on to a plate, cover it with some foil or another plate and keep warm in the oven. Make seven more crêpes, greasing the pan again as needed, and keeping warm.

Tips and twists
For safety, when igniting a mixture for flambéing, use a long taper or long wooden match. Stand back as you set the mixture alight.

6 To prepare the fruit, bring the apple juice to the boil in a pan. Boil until reduced by half. Add the orange juice and rind and cook until slightly syrupy.

7 Add the fruits and warm through, then add the brandy and set it alight. Shake the pan to incorporate the liqueur until the flame dies down.

8 Fold the pancakes into quarters and arrange two on each plate. Spoon some of the fruit mixture over and dust lightly with icing sugar. Serve any of the remaining fruit mixture separately.

Energy 260kcal/1099kJ; Protein 8g; Carbohydrate 45.9g, of which sugars 24.6g; Fat 3.5g, of which saturates 0.9g; Cholesterol 51mg; Calcium 235mg; Fibre 2.4g; Sodium 184mg.

Summer berries in sabayon glaze

This luxurious combination of summer berries under a light and fluffy liqueur sauce is lightly grilled to form a crisp, caramelized topping. Fresh or frozen berries can be used.

Serves four

450g/1lb/4 cups mixed summer berries, or
   other soft fruit
4 egg yolks
50g/2oz/¼ cup vanilla sugar or caster
   (superfine) sugar
120ml/4fl oz/½ cup liqueur, such as Cointreau
   or Kirsch, or a sweet dessert wine

1 Arrange the mixed summer berries or other fruit in four individual flameproof dishes. Preheat the grill (broiler).

Tips and twists
If you want to omit the liqueur, use mango or orange juice instead.

2 Whisk the egg yolks in a heatproof bowl with the sugar and liqueur or wine. Place over a pan of hot water and whisk until thick, fluffy and pale.

3 Pour equal quantities of the yolk mixture into each dish. Place under the grill (broiler) for 1–2 minutes, add a splash of liqueur and serve immediately.

Energy 235kcal/984kJ; Protein 3.9g; Carbohydrate 27.1g, of which sugars 27.1g; Fat 5.6g, of which saturates 1.6g; Cholesterol 202mg; Calcium 48mg; Fibre 1.2g; Sodium 18mg.

Fresh fig filo tart

Figs taste superb in this crisp and creamy tart, and because they are rich in calcium, iron, phosphorus and potassium, and are a good source of fibre, it is also a healthy dessert.

Serves six to eight

five 35 x 25cm/14 x 10in sheets filo pastry, thawed if frozen
25g/1oz/2 tbsp butter, melted, plus extra for greasing
6 fresh figs, cut into wedges
75g/3oz/¾ cup plain (all-purpose) flour
15ml/1 tbsp caster (superfine) sugar
4 eggs
450ml/¾ pint/1¾ cups creamy milk
2.5ml/½ tsp almond extract
icing (confectioners') sugar, for dusting
whipped cream or yogurt, to serve

1 Preheat the oven to 190°C/375°F/ Gas 5. Grease a 25 x 16cm/10 x 6¼in baking tin (pan) with butter.

2 Brush each filo sheet in turn with melted butter and use to line the prepared tin.

3 Using scissors, cut off any excess pastry, leaving a little overhanging the edge. Arrange the figs in the filo case.

4 Sift the flour into a bowl and stir in the caster sugar. Add the eggs and a little of the milk and whisk until smooth.

5 Gradually whisk in the remaining milk and the almond extract. Pour the mixture over the figs; bake for 1 hour or until the batter has set and is golden.

6 Remove the tart from the oven and allow it to cool in the tin on a wire rack for 10 minutes. Dust lightly with the icing sugar and serve with whipped cream or yogurt.

Tips and twists
Select plump figs that have a little give when touched. Avoid any that are hard, mushy, or dry or split.

Energy 228kcal/964kJ; Protein 7.4g; Carbohydrate 36.9g, of which sugars 22.6g; Fat 6.8g, of which saturates 3g; Cholesterol 105mg; Calcium 152mg; Fibre 1.7g; Sodium 89mg.

Apple and blackberry crumble

Fruit crumbles are an excellent choice for low-sugar desserts. Sweet dessert apples retain their shape during cooking or they can be stewed first for a soft result. Wholemeal flour and oatmeal help to balance the rate at which the sugar in the topping is digested.

Serves six to eight

900g/2lb sweet eating apples
450g/1lb/4 cups blackberries

For the topping
115g/4oz/½ cup butter
115g/4oz/1 cup wholemeal (whole-wheat) flour
50g/2oz/½ cup fine or medium
 pinhead oatmeal
30ml/2 tbsp soft light brown sugar
a little grated lemon rind (optional)

EAT WELL
Relying on naturally sweet flavours helps to cultivate a taste for less-sweet dishes but sugar (for those who are not avoiding it) or sweetener can be added to individual portions at the table.

1 Preheat the oven to 200°C/400°F/Gas 6. To make the crumble topping, rub the butter into the flour until it resembles fine breadcrumbs.

2 Add the oatmeal and brown sugar and continue to rub in until the mixture begins to stick together.

3 Mix the grated lemon rind, if using, in to the crumble mixture. Peel, core and slice the apples into wedges.

4 Put the apples, blackberries, lemon juice (if using), 30ml/2 tbsp water and the sugar into a shallow ovenproof dish, about 2 litres/3½ pints/9 cups capacity.

5 Cover the fruit with the topping. Sprinkle with a little cold water. Bake in the oven for 15 minutes, then reduce the heat to 190°C/375°F/Gas 5 and cook for another 15–20 minutes until crunchy and brown on top. Serve the crumble warm.

Energy 336kcal/1413kJ; Protein 4g; Carbohydrate 53.1g, of which sugars 30.8g; Fat 13.4g, of which saturates 6.8g; Cholesterol 27mg; Calcium 72mg; Fibre 3g; Sodium 81mg.

Summer fruit cobbler

This luscious dessert incorporates sweet strawberries and raspberries with low-fat curd cheese and a scone topping. Many other fruits can be used in this easy recipe, try plums, apricots or peaches. Served with cream or custard, it is the perfect finish to a Sunday lunch.

Serves four

450g/1lb/4 cups strawberries
250g/9oz/1½ cups raspberries
15ml/1 tbsp sugar, optional

For the scone topping
175g/6oz/1½ cups self-raising (self-rising) flour
5ml/1 tsp baking powder
15ml/1 tbsp soft light brown sugar
grated rind of 1 lemon
50g/2oz/¼ cup butter, melted
1 egg, beaten
250g/9oz low-fat curd cheese

1 Preheat the oven to 220°C/425°F/ Gas 7. Mix the fruit with the sugar, if using. Place in an ovenproof dish.

2 For the scone topping, combine the flour, baking powder and sugar in a large bowl together with the grated lemon rind, then add the melted butter and stir through. Add the beaten egg and mix thoroughly.

3 Dot spoonfuls of the curd cheese over the top of the fruit.

4 Place a scoop of the scone dough on top of each spoon of curd cheese. Bake for about 20 minutes. The curd cheese should be oozing out of the scone topping. Serve immediately.

EAT WELL
Scones and crumbles do not rely on sugar for success during baking. Getting used to eating desserts that are less sweet is important for good long-term blood glucose balance, with fewer fluctuations. Adding chopped dried fruit, such as apricots, adds natural sugar, which is all carbohydrate, but they are also full of nutrients and fibre, which also helps to slow down the sugar digestion.

Energy 385kcal/1615kJ; Protein 15.9g; Carbohydrate 46.3g, of which sugars 13.8g; Fat 17.3g, of which saturates 10.3g; Cholesterol 89mg; Calcium 257mg; Fibre 2.8g; Sodium 532mg.

Fresh cherry and hazelnut strudel

Crisp filo pastry is a slightly lighter alternative to puff pastry. Sweet cherries and full-flavoured nuts bring lots of flavour to a low-sugar version of this classic pastry.

4 Continue until all the filo has been layered and buttered, reserving some of the melted butter. Scatter half the nuts over the top, leaving a 5cm/2in border around the outside. Spread the ricotta over the nuts, then add the cherries.

5 Fold in the filo pastry border and use the dish towel to carefully roll up the strudel, Swiss-roll style, beginning from one of the long sides of the pastry. Grease a baking sheet with the remaining melted butter.

6 Place the strudel on the baking sheet and scatter the nuts over the surface. Bake for 35–40 minutes until golden and crisp. Dust with icing sugar and serve with a dollop of crème fraîche.

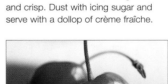

Serves six to eight

75g/3oz/6 tbsp butter
30ml/2 tbsp muscovado (molasses) sugar
3 egg yolks
grated rind of 1 lemon
1.5ml/¼ tsp grated nutmeg
250g/9oz/generous 1 cup ricotta cheese
8 large sheets filo pastry, thawed if frozen
60ml/4 tbsp chopped hazelnuts
450g/1lb/2½ cups cherries, stoned (pitted)
icing (confectioners') sugar, for dusting
crème fraîche, to serve

1 Preheat the oven to 190°C/375°F/ Gas 5. Soften 15g/½oz/1 tbsp of the butter in a bowl with the back of a mixing spoon or a fork.

2 Beat the sugar and egg yolks into the butter until light and fluffy. Beat in the lemon rind, nutmeg and ricotta.

3 Melt the remaining butter in a pan. Place a sheet of filo on a dish towel and brush it with butter. Place a second sheet on top and repeat the process.

Energy 317kcal/1326kJ; Protein 6.5g; Carbohydrate 34.2g, of which sugars 22.9g; Fat 18.1g, of which saturates 9.1g; Cholesterol 109mg; Calcium 54mg; Fibre 1.2g; Sodium 93mg.

Apricot filo parcels

These little filo parcels contain an apricot and mincemeat filling. Use home-made sugar-free mincemeat and offer these as an alternative to sugar-rich traditional mince pies.

Makes eight

350g/12oz filo pastry, thawed if frozen
25g/1oz/2 tbsp butter, melted
8 apricots, halved and stoned (pitted)
45ml/3 tbsp mincemeat
120ml/8 tbsp ground almonds
icing (confectioners') sugar, for dusting

Tips and twists

Filo pastry dries out quickly, so keep any squares not currently being used covered under a clean damp dish towel, and work quickly. If the filo should turn dry and brittle, simply brush it with a little butter.

1 Preheat the oven to 200°C/400°F/ Gas 6. Cut the filo pastry into 32 x 18cm/7in squares. Brush four of the squares sparingly with melted butter and stack them, giving each layer a quarter turn so that the stack acquires a star shape. Repeat to make eight stars.

2 Place an apricot half, hollow up, in the centre of each pastry star. Mix the mincemeat and ground almonds and spoon a little of the mixture into the hollow in each apricot.

3 Top with another apricot half, then bring the corners of each pastry together and squeeze to make a gathered purse.

4 Place the purses on a baking sheet and brush each with a little melted butter. Bake for 15–20 minutes or until the pastry is golden and crisp. Lightly dust with icing sugar to serve. Whipped cream, flavoured with a little brandy, makes an ideal accompaniment.

Energy 204kcal/853kJ; Protein 5.7g; Carbohydrate 21.3g, of which sugars 4.2g; Fat 11.3g, of which saturates 2.3g; Cholesterol 7mg; Calcium 74mg; Fibre 2.6g; Sodium 23mg.

Lemon and lime cheesecake

For special-occasion desserts, non-sugar sweeteners can be used in this type of uncooked recipe but it is best to avoid using them regularly. Alternatively, a small amount of sugar can be used but remember that the biscuit base is also sweetened.

Makes eight slices

150g/5oz/1½ cups digestive biscuits
  (graham crackers)
40g/1½oz/3 tbsp butter

For the topping
grated rind and juice of 2 lemons
10ml/2 tsp powdered gelatine
250g/9oz/generous 1 cup ricotta cheese
caster (superfine) sugar or sweetener, to taste
150ml/¼ pint/⅔ cup double (heavy) cream
2 eggs, separated

For the lime dressing
finely pared rind of 3 limes
150ml/¼ pint/⅔ cup unsweetened apple juice
5ml/1 tsp arrowroot mixed with a little water
a little green food colouring (optional)

1 Lightly grease a 20cm/8in round springform cake tin (pan). Place the biscuits in a food processor or blender and process until they form fine crumbs. Melt the butter in a large pan, then stir in the crumbs until well coated. Spoon into the prepared cake tin, press the crumbs down well in an even layer, then chill.

2 Make the topping. Place the lemon rind and juice in a pan and sprinkle over the gelatine. Leave for 5 minutes, then heat gently until the gelatine has melted. Set the mixture aside to cool slightly. Beat the ricotta cheese and sugar or sweetener in a bowl. Stir in the cream and egg yolks, then whisk in the cooled gelatine.

3 Whisk the egg whites in a grease-free bowl until they form soft peaks. Fold them into the cheese mixture. Spoon on to the biscuit base, level the surface and chill for 2–3 hours.

4 Meanwhile, make the lime dressing. Place the lime rind and apple juice in a small pan. Bring to the boil, stirring, then boil for 1 minute. Stir in the arrowroot mixture and continue to stir until the syrup boils again and thickens slightly. Remove from the heat immediately. Tint green with food colouring, if you like. Cool, then chill until required. Spoon the lime dressing over the set cheesecake. Remove from the tin and cut into slices to serve.

Energy 366kcal/1526kJ; Protein 6g; Carbohydrate 33.8g, of which sugars 23.5g; Fat 23.9g, of which saturates 13.8g; Cholesterol 105mg; Calcium 44mg; Fibre 0.4g; Sodium 166mg.

Tofu berry torte

This is a relatively low-sugar dessert, with the redcurrant jelly being the only source of straight sugar. Sugar in the fruit and apple juice sweetens the torte, while the low-fat tofu and yogurt make it deliciously creamy, a perfect foil to the summer fruit.

Serves six

425g/15oz firm tofu
300g/11oz natural (plain) yogurt
25ml/1½ tbsp/1½ sachets powdered gelatine
90ml/6 tbsp apple juice
175g/6oz/1¾ cups soft fruits, such as
　raspberries, strawberries and blueberries
30ml/2 tbsp redcurrant jelly
30ml/2 tbsp hot water

For the base
50g/2oz/¼ cup dairy-free, low-fat spread
　or margarine
30ml/2 tbsp apple juice
115g/4oz/6 cups unsweetened bran flakes

1 To make the base, place the low-fat spread or margarine and apple juice in a pan and heat them gently until the spread or margarine has melted. Crush the bran flakes and stir them into the apple juice mixture.

2 Tip the mixture into a 23cm/9in loose-based round flan tin (pan) and press down firmly with your fingers. Leave base to cool, then chill until set.

3 To make the filling, place the tofu and yogurt in a food processor and process them until smooth. Soak the gelatine in the apple juice, then heat to dissolve. Stir into the tofu mixture.

4 Spread the tofu mixture over the base, smoothing it evenly. Chill for 1–2 hours, until the filling has set.

EAT WELL
Made from soya beans, tofu is an excellent source of protein and it is low fat, making this dessert a well-balanced dish, with vitamins and health-giving nutrients in the fruit and fibre in the bran-flake base. It is useful for anyone allergic to dairy foods as a non-dairy cream or soya yogurt can be used instead of the ordinary yogurt.

5 Carefully remove the flan tin and place the cheesecake on a serving plate.

6 Arrange the soft fruits on top of the cheesecake. Place the redcurrant jelly in a small bowl and add the hot water. Stir well until the jelly has melted. Leave it to cool and then spoon or lightly brush it over the fruit to serve.

Energy 204kcal/854kJ; Protein 7.7g; Carbohydrate 23.2g, of which sugars 13.8g; Fat 9.5g, of which saturates 0.5g; Cholesterol 0mg; Calcium 311mg; Fibre 2.8g; Sodium 253mg.

Red grape and cheese tartlets

Fruit and cheese is a natural combination in this low-sugar recipe. Look out for the pale, mauve-coloured or red grapes that tend to be slightly smaller than black grapes. These are often seedless and have the added advantage of being sweeter.

1 Preheat the oven to 200°C/400°F/ Gas 6. Roll out the pastry and line six deep 9cm/3½in tartlet tins (muffin pans). Prick the bases and line with baking parchment and baking beans.

2 Bake the tartlets for 10 minutes, remove the paper and beans, then return the cases to the oven for 5 minutes until golden and fully cooked. Remove the pastry cases from the tins and cool on a wire rack.

3 Meanwhile, beat the curd cheese, yogurt, vanilla extract and caster sugar in a bowl.

4 Divide the curd cheese mixture among the pastry cases. Smooth the surfaces flat and arrange the halved grapes on top.

5 Mix the arrowroot in a small pan with the apple juice. Bring to the boil, then remove from the heat. Cool, stirring occasionally. Spoon the arrowroot over the grapes. Cool, then chill until set in the refrigerator before serving.

Makes six

350g/12oz shortcrust pastry, thawed if frozen
225g/8oz/1 cup curd cheese
150ml/¼ pint/⅔ cup natural (plain) yogurt
2.5ml/½ tsp pure vanilla extract
15ml/1 tbsp caster (superfine) sugar
200g/7oz/2 cups red grapes, halved, seeded
   if necessary
5ml/1 tsp arrowroot
90ml/6 tbsp unsweetened apple juice

Tips and twists
Use cranberry jelly or redcurrant jelly for the glaze. There will be no need to strain either of these. Also vary the fruit topping, if you like. Try blackberries, blueberries, raspberries, sliced strawberries, kiwi fruit slices, banana slices or well-drained pineapple slices.

Energy 559kcal/2330kJ; Protein 10.4g; Carbohydrate 45.1g, of which sugars 19.7g; Fat 39.3g, of which saturates 23.9g; Cholesterol 164mg; Calcium 123mg; Fibre 1.3g; Sodium 331mg.

Apple and barley flummery

The Celtic countries share this old dish, which is usually a cooked cold dessert based on oatmeal. This Irish version is based on barley and also includes apples – sweet dessert apples do not need additional sugar; sago or tapioca could replace the barley.

Serves four to six

90ml/6 tbsp pearl barley
1kg/2lb eating apples
juice of 1 lemon
45–60ml/3–4 tbsp double (heavy) cream

EAT WELL
Barley has a low GI value and combining it with eating apples (rather than cooking apples, which need added sugar) makes an excellent traditional-style pudding. Lemon juice accentuates the flavour of the apples and brings a refreshing tang to this healthy dessert. Yogurt is a low-fat alternative to cream – good for everyday meals.

1 Put 1 litre/1¾ pints/4 cups of water into a pan. Add the barley and bring gently to the boil. Peel, core and chop the apples. Add them to the pan and continue cooking gently until the barley is soft and the apples are cooked.

2 Liquidize (blend) the mixture, or press through a sieve (strainer), and return to the rinsed pan. Add the lemon juice and bring back to the boil. Remove from the heat and allow to cool. Turn into individual glasses and chill until required. Stir in the cream and serve.

Tips and twists
For a special occasion add 30ml/2 tbsp Irish whiskey to the flummery with the double (heavy) cream.

Energy 245kcal/1040kJ; Protein 2.5g; Carbohydrate 47.1g, of which sugars 28.3g; Fat 6.6g, of which saturates 3.8g; Cholesterol 15mg; Calcium 23mg; Fibre 2.7g; Sodium 7mg.

Apple and bilberry fool

Mousses, creams and fools are easily adapted to reduce sugar quantities or omit them completely. Using dessert apples instead of cooking apples introduces a naturally sweet flavour and makes added sugar superfluous.

Serves six to eight

450g/1lb sweet dessert apples
450g/1lb/4 cups bilberries or blueberries
1 sachet powdered gelatine
2 egg whites
60ml/4 tbsp double (heavy) cream, to serve

1 Peel, core and slice the cooking apples, then put them into a large pan with the bilberries, 150ml/¼ pint/⅔ cup water and 75g/3oz/scant ½ cup of the sugar. Cook gently for 15 minutes, until tender. Remove from the heat.

2 Strain the lemon juice into a cup, sprinkle the gelatine over and leave it to soak. When the gelatine has dissolved mix it into the fruit.

3 Turn the fruit mixture into a nylon sieve (strainer) over a large mixing bowl and press the fruit through it to make a purée; discard anything that is left in the sieve. Leave the purée to stand until it is cool and beginning to set.

4 Whisk the egg whites until they are standing in soft peaks.

5 Using a metal spoon, fold the whites gently into the fruit purée to make a smooth mousse. Turn into serving glasses and chill until set. Serve topped with double cream.

Tips and twists
Bilberries grow prolifically in British moorland areas in late summer. This recipe stretches a modest amount of wild fruit. Blueberries are related and they work very well in this recipe. Yogurt can be substituted for cream.

EAT WELL
Remember that uncooked eggs are not recommended for anyone who is pregnant, elderly or unwell.

Energy 92kcal/385kJ; Protein 1.6g; Carbohydrate 13g, of which sugars 10.8g; Fat 4.1g, of which saturates 2.5g; Cholesterol 10mg; Calcium 6mg; Fibre 2g; Sodium 18mg.

Red fruit and wine jelly

In 17th-century England, when making jelly was a lengthy process that involved the boiling of calf's hoof, hartshorn or isinglass, it was a centrepiece at high-class banquets. Though jelly now tends to be associated with children's parties, it can still make a light and elegant dessert. You need to allow plenty of time for straining the fruit and cooling the jelly.

2 Remove the pan from the heat, tip the mixture into a fine nylon sieve (strainer) over a large bowl, and leave to strain – this will take some time but it is important not to squeeze the fruit or the resulting juice may be cloudy.

3 When the juice from the fruit has drained into the bowl, make it up to 600ml/1 pint/2½ cups with water if necessary. Soak the gelatine in cold water for about 5 minutes to soften it.

4 Heat half the juice until very hot but not quite boiling. Remove from the heat. Squeeze the softened gelatine to remove excess water, then stir it into the hot juice until dissolved.

5 Stir the remaining raspberry juice and the wine into the hot juice.

6 Pour the jelly into stemmed glasses and chill until set. Alternatively, pour the jelly into a wetted mould, chill, and turn out on to a pretty plate for serving when it has set.

Serves six

600g/1lb 6oz fresh raspberries
50g/2oz/¼ cup sugar
300ml/½ pint/1¼ cups dry white wine
5 sheets of gelatine (6 if the jelly is to be set
   in a mould and turned out)

Tips and twists
Instead of making your own fruit juice, use a carton of juice, such as mango, cranberry or orange, sweetened to taste.

1 Put the raspberries and sugar in a pan with 100ml/3½fl oz/ scant ½ cup water and heat gently until the raspberries release their juices and become very soft, and the sugar has dissolved.

Energy 182kcal/775kJ; Protein 8.6g; Carbohydrate 30.5g, of which sugars 30.5g; Fat 0.3g, of which saturates 0.1g; Cholesterol 0mg; Calcium 43mg; Fibre 2.5g; Sodium 10mg.

Nectarines baked with nuts

Fresh nectarines filled with ground almonds and chopped pistachio nuts are meltingly tender when baked and delicious with passion fruit sauce. You can also use peaches for this dish, and the advantage of baking the fruit means that even under-ripe or early season nectarines or peaches will become sweet and full of flavour.

Serves four

50g/2oz/½ cup ground almonds
15ml/1 tbsp caster (superfine) sugar
1 egg yolk
50g/2oz/½ cup unsalted, shelled pistachio
  nuts, chopped
4 nectarines
200ml/7fl oz/scant 1 cup orange juice
2 ripe passion fruit
45ml/3 tbsp Cointreau or other orange liqueur

1 Set the oven to 200°C/400°F/Gas 6. Mix the ground almonds, sugar and egg yolk together in to a paste, then stir in the pistachio nuts.

2 Cut the nectarines in half and carefully remove the stones (pits). Pile the ground almond and pistachio filling into the nectarine halves, packing in plenty of filling,

3 Place the nectarines in a single layer in the base of an ovenproof dish. Pour the orange juice around the nectarines, then cover with foil. Cook in the oven for 15 minutes.

4 Remove the lid from the pot or dish. Some juices should have collected at the bottom of the dish, but if the nectarines are looking a little dry, add another splash of orange juice to help them tenderize. Bake, uncovered, for a further 5–10 minutes until soft.

5 Transfer the nectarines to individual, warmed serving plates and keep warm.

6 Cut the passion fruit in half, scoop out the seeds and stir them into the cooking juices in the dish with the liqueur. Place the nectarines on serving plates and spoon the sauce over and around them.

Energy 277kcal/1159kJ; Protein 7.8g; Carbohydrate 21.9g, of which sugars 21.3g; Fat 15.5g, of which saturates 1.9g; Cholesterol 50mg; Calcium 66mg; Fibre 3.5g; Sodium 78mg.

Spiced fruit platter

A simple fresh fruit platter sprinkled with spices makes a healthy dessert. It is low in fat and offers a range of essential vitamins and minerals that are needed for good health. Selecting some naturally sweet fruit means added sugar is redundant. This platter of fruit makes a good start to a summer breakfast, as well as an end to a main meal.

Serves six

1 pineapple
2 papayas
1 small melon
juice of 2 limes
2 pomegranates
ground ginger and ground nutmeg,
    for sprinkling
mint sprigs, to decorate

1 Peel the pineapple. Remove the core and any remaining eyes, then cut the flesh lengthways into thin wedges.

2 Peel the papayas, cut them in half, and then into thin wedges lengthways. Halve the melon and scrape away the seeds. Cut into thin wedges and then remove the skin.

3 Arrange the fruit on six individual plates and sprinkle with the lime juice.

4 Cut the pomegranates in half using a sharp knife, then scoop out the seeds, discarding any pith. Sprinkle the seeds over the fruit, then sprinkle the salad with a little ginger and nutmeg to taste. Decorate with sprigs of fresh mint and serve immediately.

EAT WELL
Common everyday fruits such as apples, bananas and oranges, take on a new image when served as a platter. It is a good idea to start thinking of these fruits as part of a meal, as well as snacks.

Tips and twists
The selection of fruit used in this spicy platter can be varied according to what is available. Ginger complements melon wonderfully, but guava and mango make an exotic combination and oranges and plums are also good.

Energy 91kcal/389kJ; Protein 1.2g; Carbohydrate 22.1g, of which sugars 22.1g; Fat 0.4g, of which saturates 0g; Cholesterol 0mg; Calcium 48mg; Fibre 3.4g; Sodium 32mg.

Poached pears

Pears are naturally sweet, and when cooked become more so, therefore only a little sugar is needed for this dish to give the pears their glossy sheen. You can, however, dispense with it altogether if you prefer to avoid sugar entirely. The pears can be served warm, at room temperature, or chilled, and make a pretty finish to a dinner party.

Serves four

25g/1 oz/2 tbsp caster (superfine) sugar
grated rind and juice of 1 lemon
2.5ml/½ tsp ground ginger
1 small cinnamon stick
2 whole cloves
4 firm ripe pears

1 Put the sugar in a pan with 300ml/
½ pint/1½ cups water.

Tips and twists
Omit the spices and flavour the water with elderflower cordial. Use white wine in place of water.

2 Add the lemon rind and juice, ginger and spices to the pan. Heat gently, stirring continuously, until the sugar has completely dissolved.

3 Peel each of the pears, cut them in half lengthways and remove their cores. Leave the stalk intact on one half.

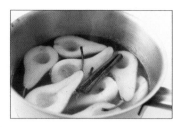

4 Add the pear halves to the pan and bring just to the boil. Cover and simmer gently for about 5 minutes or until the pears are tender, turning them over in the syrup occasionally during cooking.

5 Remove from the heat and leave to cool in the syrup before serving.

Energy 374kcal/1597kJ; Protein 1.8g; Carbohydrate 95.7g, of which sugars 95.7g; Fat 0.9g, of which saturates 0g; Cholesterol 0mg; Calcium 82mg; Fibre 9.9g; Sodium 24mg.

Frozen melon

Artificial sweeteners do not work well in sorbets and ice creams, so these desserts should be reserved for small portions or rare treats. To extend a small portion of sweet sorbet, whizz it with yogurt in a food processor.

Serves 6

75ml/5 tbsp caster (superfine) sugar
15ml/1 tbsp lemon juice
60ml/4 tbsp water
1 medium cantaloupe melon or Charentais melon, about 1kg/2¼lb
crushed ice, cucumber slices and borage flowers, to decorate

1 Put the sugar, lemon juice and water in a heavy pan and heat gently until the sugar dissolves. Bring to the boil, and boil for 1 minute, without stirring, to make a syrup. Leave to cool.

2 Cut the melon in half and discard the seeds. Carefully scoop out the flesh using a metal spoon or melon baller and place in a food processor, taking care to keep the halved shells intact.

3 Process the melon flesh until smooth, then transfer to a mixing bowl. Stir in the cooled sugar syrup and chill until very cold. Invert the melon shells and leave them to drain on kitchen paper, then transfer them to the freezer.

4 If making by hand, pour the mixture into a plastic container and freeze for about 3–4 hours, beating twice with a fork or a whisk, or processing in a food processor, to break up the ice crystals and produce a smoother texture. If using an ice cream maker, churn the melon mixture until the sorbet holds its shape.

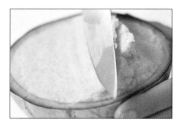

5 Remove the frozen melon shells from the freezer, pack the sorbet tightly into the melon shells and level the surface with a sharp knife.

6 Use a dessertspoon to scoop out the centre of each filled melon shell to simulate the seed cavity, then freeze the prepared fruit overnight until firm.

7 To serve, use a large knife to cut each melon half into three large wedges. Serve on a bed of crushed ice, either on a large platter or individual plates, and decorate with the cucumber slices and borage flowers.

Energy 67kcal/288kJ; Protein 0.6g; Carbohydrate 16.6g, of which sugars 16.6g; Fat 0.3g, of which saturates 0.1g; Cholesterol 0mg; Calcium 12mg; Fibre 0.1g; Sodium 3mg.

Peach and cardamom yogurt ice

Low-fat frozen desserts that rely on natural fruit for their sweetness make the perfect dessert for anyone with diabetes. This yogurt ice provides a useful source of calcium and vitamin C.

Serves four

8 cardamom pods
6 peaches, total weight about 500g/1¼lb,
  halved and stoned (pitted)
30ml/2 tbsp water
200ml/7fl oz/scant 1 cup bio natural
  (plain) yogurt

1 Put the cardamom pods on a board and crush them with the base of a ramekin, or use a mortar and pestle.

2 Chop the peaches and put them in a pan. Add the crushed cardamom pods, with their black seeds, and the measured water. Cover and simmer gently for about 10 minutes, or until the fruit is tender. Remove the pan from the heat and leave to cool.

3 Pour the peach mixture into a food processor or blender, process until smooth, then press through a sieve (strainer) placed over a bowl.

Tips and twists
Use bio natural (plain) yogurt for its extra mild taste. Greek (US strained plain) yogurt or ordinary natural yogurt are both much sharper, and tend to overwhelm the delicate taste of peach.

4 Add the yogurt to the purée and mix. Pour into a freezerproof tub and freeze for about 6 hours, beating once or twice with a whisk or in a food processor. To serve, scoop the ice cream on to a platter or into bowls.

EAT WELL
Try mango and strawberry instead of the peaches.

Energy 69kcal/296kJ; Protein 3.8g; Carbohydrate 13.3g, of which sugars 13.3g; Fat 0.6g, of which saturates 0.3g; Cholesterol 1mg; Calcium 104mg; Fibre 1.9g; Sodium 43mg.

Date and tofu ice

Generously spiced with cinnamon, this unusual ice cream is packed with soya protein and it contains no added sugar; it is also low in fat.

Serves four

250g/9oz/1½ cups stoned (pitted) dates
600ml/1 pint/2½ cups apple juice
5ml/1 tsp ground cinnamon
285g/10½oz pack chilled tofu, drained
   and cubed
150ml/¼ pint/⅔ cup unsweetened soya milk

1 Put the dates in a pan. Pour in 300ml/½ pint/1¼ cups of the apple juice and leave to soak for 2 hours. Simmer for 10 minutes, then leave to cool. Using a slotted spoon, lift out one-quarter of the dates, chop roughly and set aside.

2 Purée the remaining dates in a food processor or blender. Add the cinnamon and process with enough of the remaining apple juice to make a smooth paste.

3 Add the cubes of tofu to the food processor, a few at a time, processing after each addition. Finally, add the remaining apple juice and the soya milk and mix well to combine.

Tips and twists
You could make this tasty ice cream with any soft dried fruits; dried figs, apricots or peaches would be especially good. Alternatively you could use a combination for a vitamin- and fibre-packed feast.

4 Churn the mixture in an ice cream maker until very thick, but not thick enough to scoop. Scrape into a plastic tub.

5 Stir in most of the chopped dates, retaining a few pieces for garnishing, and freeze for 2–3 hours until firm.

6 Scoop into dessert glasses and decorate with the remaining chopped dates.

EAT WELL
Remember that dried fruits are naturally high in sugar and they can cause fluctuations in blood sugar levels. This tofu and date ice does not have added sugar and it can be served with fresh fruit or have fresh fruit mixed in at the last minute – try fresh strawberries, raspberries or cherries to bulk out the ice (making portions smaller and the sugar content less).

Energy 290kcal/1232kJ; Protein 9.1g; Carbohydrate 58.2g, of which sugars 57.9g; Fat 3.9g, of which saturates 0.5g; Cholesterol 0mg; Calcium 407mg; Fibre 2.5g; Sodium 24mg.

Mango and lime fool

Canned fruit is practical for everyday dessert goodness. This fool tastes even better if made with fresh fruit. Choose a delicious, fragrant variety like the voluptuous Alphonso mango.

Serves four

400g/14oz can sliced mango
grated rind of 1 lime
juice of ½ lime
150ml/¼ pint/⅔ cup low-fat crème fraîche
90ml/6 tbsp low-fat Greek (US strained
    plain) yogurt
fresh mango slices, to decorate (optional)

1 Drain the mango slices and place them in the bowl of a food processor or in a blender. Add the grated lime rind and the freshly squeezed lime juice. Process or blend until the mixture forms a smooth mango purée.

2 Alternatively, mash the mango slices with a fork or a potato masher, then press the mixture through a sieve (strainer) with a wooden spoon until you achieve a smooth purée.

3 Pour the crème fraîche into a bowl and add the Greek yogurt.

4 Whisk the mixture with a balloon whisk until it is thick and then fold in the mango purée. Spoon the mango and lime fool into four small cups or glasses and chill for approximately 1–2 hours.

5 When serving, decorate each glass with fresh mango slices, if you like.

> **EAT WELL**
> Canned fruit in juice makes a good basis for a fruit salad, for example, pineapple pieces or peach slices are excellent with orange, apple and grapes. Serve fruit salads topped with roasted seeds (sunflower, sesame and pumpkin) with a dollop of yogurt for a great dessert or breakfast.

Energy 289kcal/1203kJ; Protein 2.4g; Carbohydrate 21.4g, of which sugars 21.3g; Fat 22.4g, of which saturates 13.7g; Cholesterol 51mg; Calcium 62mg; Fibre 0.7g; Sodium 27mg.

Rhubarb and ginger yogurt ice

Frozen yogurt flavoured with fruit makes a good alternative to very sweet, commercial ice cream. It is low in fat and high in calcium, which is essential for good bone health.

Serves six

300g/11oz/scant 1½ cups set bio natural
   (plain) live yogurt
200g/7oz/scant 1 cup mascarpone
350g/12oz/3 cups chopped rhubarb
30ml/2 tbsp clear honey
3 pieces preserved stem ginger,
   finely chopped

1 Whisk together the yogurt and mascarpone. Pour the mixture into a shallow freezerproof container and freeze for about 1 hour.

2 Put the rhubarb and honey in a pan and add 45ml/3 tbsp water. Cook over a very low heat, stirring occasionally, for 15 minutes, or until the rhubarb is soft. Remove the pan from the heat and set aside to cool. When the fruit has cooled, place it in a food processor or blender and process to a purée.

3 Remove the semi-frozen yogurt mixture from the freezer and fold in the rhubarb purée. Beat well until smooth, breaking up the ice crystals, then fold in the chopped ginger.

4 Return the yogurt ice to the freezer and freeze for 2 hours. Remove from the freezer and beat again, then freeze until solid. To serve, scoop the yogurt ice into individual serving bowls.

EAT WELL

The problem with ices is that they need a lot of sugar (or fat, or both) to soften their set. Preserved stem ginger in syrup is sweet and sugar-rich, so for an alternative, omit the stem ginger and add a large knob of peeled chopped fresh ginger.

Energy 106kcal/446kJ; Protein 6.2g; Carbohydrate 9.1g, of which sugars 9.1g; Fat 5.4g, of which saturates 3.3g; Cholesterol 15mg; Calcium 150mg; Fibre 0.8g; Sodium 44mg.

Cakes, Cookies and Bread

Lots of brilliant bakes fit well into a healthy diet for balancing blood-sugar levels, with naturally sweet foods used instead of huge amounts of sugar. High-fibre and low GI value foods are important for making tempting alternatives to commercial sugar-laden goods. Bake, slice and freeze for everyday eating or make a special treat to share with family and friends.

Courgette and ginger cake

Whisked sponges require less sugar in the baking process than creamed-fat mixtures – the whisked mixture is adapted into a spicy teabread in this light recipe.

Serves eight to ten

3 eggs
60ml/4 tbsp caster (superfine) sugar
120ml/4fl oz/½ cup sunflower oil
5ml/1 tsp vanilla extract
225g/8oz courgettes (zucchini), grated
5cm/2in piece fresh root ginger, peeled and grated
350g/12oz/3 cups unbleached plain (all-purpose) flour
5ml/1 tsp baking powder
pinch of salt
5ml/1 tsp ground cinnamon
1 piece stem ginger, chopped
15ml/1 tbsp demerara (raw) sugar

1 Preheat the oven to 190°C/325°F/ Gas 5. Whisk the eggs and sugar until creamy. Slowly beat in the oil until the mixture forms a batter. Mix in the vanilla extract, then add the grated courgettes and fresh ginger.

2 Sift together the flour, baking powder and salt into a large bowl. Add the cinnamon and mix, then stir the dried ingredients into the courgette mixture.

3 Lightly grease a 900g/2lb loaf tin and pour in the courgette mixture. Smooth and level the top, then sprinkle the chopped ginger and demerara sugar over the surface.

4 Bake for 1 hour until a skewer inserted into the centre comes out clean. Leave the cake in the tin to cool for about 20 minutes, then turn out on to a wire rack.

EAT WELL
Courgettes (zucchini) make moist bakes, contributing vegetable goodness to semi-sweet mixtures. Select firm young courgettes, trim off the ends and keep the nutritious skin for added flavour and colour.

Energy 252kcal/1060kJ; Protein 5.6g; Carbohydrate 35.6g, of which sugars 8.8g; Fat 10.7g, of which saturates 1.6g; Cholesterol 57mg; Calcium 73mg; Fibre 1.3g; Sodium 82mg.

Chocolate and prune cake

Thanks to gram flour, this delicious cake is high in soluble fibre but it is also quite high in sugar from the prunes, so enjoy it as an occasional treat.

Makes a 20cm/8in cake

300g/11oz dark (bittersweet) chocolate
150g/5oz/²⁄₃ cup low-fat spread
200g/7oz/generous 1 cup ready-to-eat stoned
   (pitted) prunes, quartered
3 eggs, beaten
150g/5oz/1¼ cups gram flour, sifted with
   10ml/2 tsp baking powder
120ml/4fl oz/¼ cup soya milk

1 Preheat the oven to 180°C/350°F/ Gas 4. Grease and base-line a deep 20cm/8in round cake tin (pan). Melt the chocolate in a heatproof bowl over a pan of hot water.

2 Mix the low-fat spread and prunes in a food processor. Process until light and fluffy, then scrape into a bowl.

Tips and twists
Use dark (bittersweet) chocolate with a high proportion of cocoa solids (70 per cent). You can substitute ready-to-eat apricots in place of the prunes, if you wish.

3 Gradually fold in the melted chocolate and eggs, alternately with the flour mixture. Beat in the soya milk.

4 Spoon the mixture into the cake tin, level the surface with a spoon, then bake for 20–30 minutes or until the cake is firm to the touch. A fine skewer inserted in the cake should come out clean. Leave to cool on a wire rack.

EAT WELL
Chickpea flour or besan can be used instead of gram flour – both contribute protein and fibre.

Energy 3173kcal/13294kJ; Protein 65g; Carbohydrate 376.8g, of which sugars 259.8g; Fat 166.1g, of which saturates 72.6g; Cholesterol 598mg; Calcium 537mg; Fibre 23.6g; Sodium 1268mg.

Chunky chocolate and banana muffins

American muffins are simple and quick to make and they work well with less sugar than usual.
Serve warm while the chocolate is still gooey.

Makes twelve

90ml/6 tbsp milk
2 eggs
150g/5oz/10 tbsp unsalted butter, melted
225g/8oz/2 cups unbleached plain
    (all-purpose) flour
pinch of salt
5ml/1 tsp baking powder
30ml/2 tbsp golden caster (superfine) sugar
105g/4oz plain (semisweet) chocolate
2 small firm bananas, mashed

1 Place 12 large paper muffin cases in
a deep muffin tin (pan). Preheat the
oven to 200°C/400°F/Gas 6.

2 Whisk together the milk, eggs and
butter in a bowl until combined.

3 Sift together the flour, salt and baking
powder into a separate bowl. Chop the
chocolate into small pieces, add to the
flour mixture together with the sugar
and then stir to combine.

4 Slowly stir in the milk mixture, but
do not beat it. Gently fold in the
mashed bananas.

5 Spoon the mixture into the paper
cases. Bake for 20 minutes until
golden. Cool on a wire rack.

Apricot and hazelnut oat cookies

These cookies have a lovely chewy texture. Any combination of dried fruit and nuts can be used.

Makes nine

115g/4oz/½ cup unsalted butter, plus extra
    for greasing
30ml/2 tbsp golden caster (superfine) sugar
30ml/2 tbsp orange juice
115g/4oz/1 cup self-raising (self-rising)
    flour, sifted
115g/4oz/1 cup rolled oats
75g/3oz/scant ½ cup ready-to-eat dried
    apricots, chopped

For the topping
25g/1oz/2 tbsp ready-to-eat dried
    apricots, chopped
25g/1oz/¼ cup hazelnuts, toasted

> **EAT WELL**
> Oats provide soluble fibre, which is
> helpful for regulating blood glucose
> and cholesterol levels.

1 Spread the nuts on a baking tray and
place under a grill (broiler) until toasted.
You could also do this in a frying pan or
in the oven. Chop when cool.

2 Preheat the oven to 170°C/325°F/
Gas 3. Lightly grease a large baking
sheet. Put the butter, sugar and orange
juice in a small heavy pan and cook
over a gentle heat, until the butter has
melted and the sugar has dissolved,
stirring occasionally. Remove the pan
from the heat.

3 Put the flour, oats and apricots in a
bowl, add the butter mixture and mix
with a wooden spoon to form a sticky
dough. Divide the dough into nine
pieces and place on the baking sheet.
Press into 1cm/½in thick rounds.
Scatter over the apricots and hazelnuts
and press into the dough.

4 Bake for 15 minutes until golden and
slightly crisp. Leave to cool on the
baking sheet for 5 minutes, then
transfer to a wire rack.

Energy 240kcal/1003kJ; Protein 3.7g; Carbohydrate 26.3g, of which sugars 11.6g; Fat 14.1g, of which saturates 8.4g; Cholesterol 59mg; Calcium 47mg; Fibre 1g; Sodium 92mg.
Energy 262kcal/1098kJ; Protein 3.7g; Carbohydrate 33.2g, of which sugars 14.4g; Fat 13.6g, of which saturates 6.8g; Cholesterol 27mg; Calcium 71mg; Fibre 2.1g; Sodium 130mg.

Fruit malt bread

Malt extract and dried fruit sweeten and flavour this simple yeast-free loaf, which makes a good alternative to cake as a tea-time treat.

3 Heat the malt extract and milk, until the malt extract has dissolved. Add to the dry ingredients and mix.

4 Spoon the mixture into the prepared tin. Bake for 45 minutes or until a fine skewer inserted in the loaf comes out clean. Cool on a wire rack.

EAT WELL
For a breakfast bread add chopped apricots, roasted sunflower seeds, chopped unsalted nuts or fresh blueberries. Freeze the bread in thick slices for thawing one by one.

Makes 1 loaf

250g/9oz/2¼ cups self-raising (self-rising) wholemeal (whole-wheat) flour
pinch of salt
2.5ml/½ tsp bicarbonate of soda
175g/6oz/1 cup dried fruit
15ml/1 tbsp malt extract
250ml/8fl oz/1 cup skimmed milk
low-fat spread, to serve (optional)

1 Grease the base and sides of a 23 x 13cm/9 x 5in loaf pan, and line the base with baking parchment.

2 Preheat the oven to 160°C/325°F/ Gas 3. Sift the flour, salt and the bicarbonate of soda into a bowl. Stir in the dried fruit.

Tips and twists
Use any combination of dried fruit you like for this bread, choose from sultanas (golden raisins), raisins and currants, or include chopped dried pears, apricots, pineapple, peaches or mangoes.

Energy 1818kcal/7724kJ; Protein 36.7g; Carbohydrate 410.4g, of which sugars 177g; Fat 14.6g, of which saturates 1.9g; Cholesterol 5mg; Calcium 681mg; Fibre 12.6g; Sodium 267mg.

Spiced teabread

Semi-sweet fruited breads and teabreads are excellent alternatives to cakes made with lots of sugar. Serve this bread warm and thickly sliced; spread with butter or eat on its own.

Makes 2 loaves

450g/1lb/4 cups plain (all-purpose) flour
5ml/1 tsp mixed (apple pie) spice
2.5ml/½ tsp salt
2 sachets easy blend (rapid-rise) dried yeast
115g/4oz/½ cup butter, melted
300ml/½ pint/1¼ cups tepid milk
1 egg, lightly beaten
375g/13oz/generous 2 cups dried mixed fruit
25g/1oz/⅓ cup mixed chopped (candied) peel
15ml/1 tbsp caster (superfine) sugar

1 Grease two 450g/1lb loaf tins (pans). Mix the flour, mixed spice, salt and yeast in a large bowl and make a well in the centre.

2 Mix the butter with the tepid milk and lightly beaten egg and add to the flour mixture. Add the mixed fruit and peel to the bowl and mix well.

3 Turn the cake mixture into the loaf tins. Leave in a warm place for about 30 minutes to rise. Meanwhile, preheat the oven to 200°C/400°F/Gas 6.

4 When the dough has doubled in size, bake in the hot oven for about 45 minutes, or until the loaves begin to shrink slightly from the sides of the tins; when turned out and tapped underneath they should sound hollow.

5 To make the glaze, add the caster sugar to a bowl together with 30ml/2 tbsp water from a freshly boiled kettle. Mix until the sugar is dissolved.

6 Remove the loaves from the oven and brush over with the glaze. Return them to the oven for 3 minutes, or until the tops are a rich shiny brown. Turn on to a wire rack to cool.

Energy 1832kcal/7735kJ; Protein 34.1g; Carbohydrate 317.3g, of which sugars 145.9g; Fat 56.4g, of which saturates 32.8g; Cholesterol 227mg; Calcium 673mg; Fibre 11.7g; Sodium 580mg.

Iced carob cookies

These heavenly cookies, with their creamy topping, are made with wholemeal flour and rolled oats, with a relatively modest amount of sugar.

Makes twelve to sixteen

115g/4oz/½ cup butter
10ml/2 tsp carob powder
115g/4oz/1 cup wholemeal (whole-wheat) flour
5ml/1 tsp baking powder
45ml/3 tbsp muscovado (molasses) sugar
50g/2oz/generous ½ cup rolled oats

For the topping
50g/2oz carob bar, coarsely chopped
45ml/3 tbsp double (heavy) cream
15ml/1 tbsp chopped ready-to-eat dried apricots

1 Preheat the oven to 190°C/375°F/Gas 5.

2 Put the butter in a large pan and add the carob powder. Stir over a low heat until the mixture is smooth and combined. Stir in the remaining ingredients and mix well.

3 Line the base and sides of an 18cm/7in square shallow cake tin (pan) with baking parchment.

4 Press the mixture into the prepared tin and bake for about 20–25 minutes until just set. Mark into squares or bars while still hot. Leave to cool in the tin.

5 To make the topping, stir the carob and cream in a small pan over a low heat. Spread over the cookies and sprinkle the apricots on top.

Energy 133kcal/554kJ; Protein 1.7g; Carbohydrate 12.3g, of which sugars 5.5g; Fat 8.9g, of which saturates 5.3g; Cholesterol 19mg; Calcium 11mg; Fibre 1.1g; Sodium 52mg.

Lemon shortbread

This shortbread recipe has slightly less sugar than usual, which is lower than most sweet biscuits, but it is high in fat, so is best reserved for an occasional indulgence.

Makes about 48 fingers

275g/10oz/2½ cups plain (all-purpose) or
   wholemeal (whole-wheat) flour
50g/2oz/½ cup ground almonds
175g/6oz/¾ cup butter, softened
60ml/4 tbsp caster (superfine) sugar
grated rind of 1 lemon

1 Preheat the oven to 180°C/350°F/
Gas 4 and oil a large Swiss roll tin
(jelly roll pan) or baking tray.

2 To make in a food processor: put the
flour, ground almonds, softened butter,
caster sugar and lemon rind into the
food processor and process until the
mixture comes together. (To make by
hand, see right.)

3 Place the mixture in the tin and flatten
it out. Bake in the preheated oven for
20 minutes, or until pale golden brown.

Eat well

Using wholemeal flour gives added
fibre. Reduce the sugar if you want.

---

4 Remove from the oven and
immediately mark the shortbread into
fingers or squares while the mixture is
soft. Allow to cool a little, and then
transfer to a wire rack and leave until
cool before storing, although it is
delicious eaten when still warm from
the oven. If stored in an airtight
container, the shortbread should keep
for up to two weeks.

To make by hand Sift the flour and
almonds on to a pastry board or work
surface. Cream the butter and sugar
together in a mixing bowl, until it is soft
and light. Turn the creamed mixture on
to the flour and almonds and work it
together by hand to make a smooth
dough. Continue as from step 3.

Energy 57kcal/239kJ; Protein 0.8g; Carbohydrate 5.6g, of which sugars 1.2g; Fat 3.7g, of which saturates 2g; Cholesterol 8mg; Calcium 12mg; Fibre 0.3g; Sodium 22mg.

Oatmeal biscuits

Although not as neat as bought ones, these unsweetened home-made oatmeal biscuits make up in flavour and interest anything they might lose in presentation. Serve them with full-flavoured cheeses instead of commercial crackers.

Makes about eighteen

75g/3oz/⅔ cup plain (all-purpose) flour
2.5ml/½ tsp salt
1.5ml/¼ tsp baking powder
115g/4oz/1 cup fine pinhead oatmeal
65g/2½oz/generous ¼ cup butter

1 Preheat the oven to 200°C/400°F/ Gas 6 and grease a baking sheet.

2 Sift the flour, salt and baking powder into a mixing bowl. Add the oatmeal and mix well. Rub in the fat to make a crumbly mixture, then blend in enough water to make a stiff dough.

3 Turn on to a worktop sprinkled with fine oatmeal and knead until smooth and manageable. Roll out to about 3mm/⅛in thick and cut into rounds, squares or triangles. Place on the baking sheet.

4 Bake in the preheated oven for about 15 minutes, until crisp. Cool the biscuits on a wire rack.

5 When cold, store the biscuits in an airtight container lined with baking parchment. Check for crispness before serving; reheat for 4–5 minutes at 200°C/400°F/Gas 6 to crisp.

Tips and twists
Spread with low-fat soft cheese and top with sweet dessert apple for a quick but healthy snack.

Energy 67kcal/279kJ; Protein 1.2g; Carbohydrate 7.9g, of which sugars 0.1g; Fat 3.6g, of which saturates 1.3g; Cholesterol 1mg; Calcium 10mg; Fibre 0.6g; Sodium 31mg.

Drop scones

Variously known as girdlecakes, griddlecakes and Scotch pancakes, these light drop scones make a quick and easy breakfast, elevenses or teatime snacks served with butter and traditionally drizzled with honey, although this is of course optional.

Makes eight to ten

115g/4oz/1 cup plain (all-purpose) flour
5ml/1 tsp bicarbonate of soda (baking soda)
5ml/1 tsp cream of tartar
25g/1oz/2 tbsp butter, diced
1 egg, beaten
about 150ml/¼ pint/⅔ cup milk

1 Sift the flour, bicarbonate of soda and cream of tartar together into a mixing bowl. Add the diced butter and rub it into the flour with your fingertips until the mixture resembles fine, evenly textured breadcrumbs.

2 Lightly grease a griddle pan or heavy frying pan, then preheat it. Make a well in the centre of the flour mixture, then stir in the egg. Add the milk a little at a time, stirring it in to check consistency.

3 When you have added enough milk to give a thick creamy consistency, cook the scones in batches. Drop three or four evenly sized spoonfuls of the mixture, spaced slightly apart, on the griddle or frying pan. Cook over a medium heat for 2–3 minutes, until bubbles rise to the surface and burst.

4 Turn the scones over and cook for a further 2–3 minutes. Place the cooked scones between the folds of a clean dish towel while cooking to keep warm. Serve with butter and honey.

Tips and twists
Placing the cooked scones in a clean, folded dish towel keeps them warm, soft and moist. Bring to the table like this and ask your guests to pull them out.

EAT WELL
For a dessert top the scones with fruit and low-fat soft cheese. Try fresh berries or diced mango, or cook sliced dessert apple in a little butter in a frying pan until browned.

Energy 59kcal/249kJ; Protein 2g; Carbohydrate 10.9g, of which sugars 1.8g; Fat 1.1g, of which saturates 0.2g; Cholesterol 11mg; Calcium 65mg; Fibre 0.4g; Sodium 56mg.

Chelsea buns

Chelsea buns are said to have been invented in London at the end of the 17th century. They make a good between-meals snack, as an occasional treat.

Makes twelve buns

500g/1¼lb/4½ cups unbleached white
    bread flour
2.5ml/½ tsp salt
50g/2oz/¼ cup butter, softened
5ml/1 tsp fast action, easy-blend dried yeast
225ml/8fl oz/scant 1 cup hand-hot milk
1 egg, beaten

For the filling
25g/1oz/2 tbsp butter, melted
115g/4oz/⅔ cup sultanas (golden raisins)
25g/1oz/3 tbsp mixed chopped (candied) peel
25g/1oz/2 tbsp currants
5ml/1 tsp mixed (apple pie) spice

For the glaze
50g/2oz/2oz/¼ cup caster (superfine) sugar
60ml/4 tbsp water
5ml/1 tsp orange flower water

1 Place the flour in a bowl. Add the salt and then rub in the butter. Stir in the yeast. Make a well in the middle of the dry ingredients. Pour the milk into the bowl and stir in some of the flour mixture, then add the egg and mix everything to a firm dough.

2 Turn the dough out on to a floured surface and knead it thoroughly for about 10 minutes, until it is smooth and elastic.

3 Roll out the dough to form a square that is approximately 30cm/12in, and brush with melted butter.

4 Sprinkle the buttered dough with the sultanas, mixed peel, currants and mixed spice, leaving a 1cm/½in border along one edge. Starting at a covered edge, roll the dough up. Press the edges together to seal.

5 Lightly grease a 23cm/9in square cake tin (pan). Cut the roll into 12 slices and then place these cut sides uppermost in the prepared tin.

6 Cover with oiled clear film (plastic wrap). Leave to rise in a warm place for about 1 hour, or until the buns have doubled in size. Meanwhile, preheat the oven to 200°C/400°F/Gas 6.

7 Bake the buns for 15–20 minutes, or until they have risen well and are evenly golden all over. Once they are baked, leave them to cool slightly in the tin before turning them out on to a wire rack to cool further.

8 Make the glaze. Mix the caster sugar and water in a small pan. Heat, stirring occasionally, until the sugar is completely dissolved. Then boil the mixture rapidly for 1–2 minutes without stirring, until syrupy.

9 Stir the orange flower water into the glaze and then brush the mixture over the warm buns. Serve the Chelsea buns when they are still fresh, they are delicious when still slightly warm.

Energy 287kcal/1208kJ; Protein 6.1g; Carbohydrate 43.5g, of which sugars 16.6g; Fat 11.1g, of which saturates 2.3g; Cholesterol 26mg; Calcium 85mg; Fibre 1.3g; Sodium 243mg.

Barley bannocks

Bannocks are Scottish, but similar cakes, or breads, were made in many pre-industrial cultures. They were traditionally cooked on a griddle on top of a stove or open fire, but baking them in the oven works very well. They make an excellent source of slow-release carbohydrate.

Serves six

225g/8oz/2 cups barley flour
50g/2oz/½ cup plain (all-purpose) flour
5ml/1 tsp cream of tartar
2.5ml/½ tsp salt
5ml/1 tsp bicarbonate of soda (baking soda)
250ml/8fl oz/1 cup buttermilk or natural (plain) yogurt

1 Preheat the oven to 180°C/350°F/ Gas 4. Mix the barley flour, the plain flour, cream of tartar and salt together in a bowl.

2 Mix the bicarbonate of soda with the buttermilk or yogurt then pour this mixture into the dry ingredients. Mix to a soft dough like a scone mix.

3 Turn the dough out on to a floured surface and press down with your hands to make the whole dough, about 1cm/½in thick.

4 Cut the dough into six segments and place on an oiled baking sheet. Bake in the oven for about 15 minutes.

EAT WELL
Yeast-free breads of this type are easy to make and freeze well.

Energy 344kcal/1452kJ; Protein 10.4g; Carbohydrate 54.6g, of which sugars 4.8g; Fat 11g, of which saturates 6.1g; Cholesterol 27mg; Calcium 157mg; Fibre 8.4g; Sodium 552mg.

Wholemeal soda bread

Soda bread is best eaten on the day of baking, but it slices better if left to cool and "set" for a few hours. It freezes well, either whole or cut into chunks ready for a quick snack with cheese and celery or a bowl of home-made soup.

Makes one loaf
450g/1lb/4 cups wholemeal
  (whole-wheat) flour
175g/6oz/1½ cups plain (all-purpose) flour
7.5ml/1½ tsp bicarbonate of soda
  (baking soda)
5ml/1 tsp salt
about 450ml/¾ pint/scant 2 cups buttermilk

1 Preheat the oven to 200°C/400°F/ Gas 6, and grease a baking sheet. Combine the dry ingredients in a mixing bowl and stir in enough buttermilk to make a fairly soft dough. Turn on to a work surface dusted with wholemeal flour and knead lightly until smooth.

EAT WELL
Use the basic wholemeal (whole-wheat) soda bread recipe as a basis for making semi-sweet fruit loaves. Add raisins or mixed dried fruit; or try chopped ready-to-eat dried apricots or dates. Chopped nuts are good, as are lightly roasted sunflower, sesame and pumpkin seeds. For savoury nutty or seeded breads, chopped fresh herbs go well.

The chemical reaction that the heat of the oven has on the buttermilk is what makes the bread rise. It is important that as soon as it is ready, the dough is placed in a hot oven straight away before the gases escape.

2 Form the dough into a circle, about 4cm/1½in thick. Lay on the baking sheet and mark a deep cross in the top with a floured knife.

3 Bake for about 45 minutes, or until the bread is browned and sounds hollow when tapped on the base. Cool on a wire rack. If a soft crust is preferred, wrap the loaf in a clean dish towel while cooling.

Tips and twists
Instead of buttermilk, mix the same amount of fresh milk with the juice of half a lemon to create the same chemical reaction.

Energy 2264kcal/9627kJ; Protein 74.5g; Carbohydrate 502g, of which sugars 30.5g; Fat 9.5g, of which saturates 1.9g; Cholesterol 18mg; Calcium 1454mg; Fibre 19.2g; Sodium 2933mg.

Oven-baked potato cakes

Potato cakes come in a variety of forms, but they're all at their best if made with freshly cooked potatoes, preferably while still warm. They are good served straight out of the oven, as a base for roasted peppers, with poached eggs for breakfast, or with a mixed salad for a snack.

Makes about twelve

225g/8oz/2 cups self-raising (self-rising) flour
2.5ml/½ tsp baking powder
50g/2oz/¼ cup butter, diced
a pinch of salt
175g/6oz freshly cooked mashed potato
15ml/1 tbsp chopped fresh chives
200ml/7fl oz/scant 1 cup buttermilk

1 Preheat the oven to 220°C/425°F/ Gas 7 and lightly grease a baking tray with butter. Sift the flour and the baking powder into a bowl and rub in the butter. Season with salt.

2 Add the mashed potato and chives. Mix well, and then incorporate enough buttermilk to make a soft dough. Turn on to a floured work surface, knead lightly into shape, then quickly roll out.

3 Cut into squares with a sharp knife, then place on the baking tray and bake in the preheated oven for about 20 minutes or until well risen, golden brown and crisp.

Energy 108kcal/455kJ; Protein 2g; Carbohydrate 16.5g, of which sugars 0.4g; Fat 4.3g, of which saturates 2.6g; Cholesterol 11mg; Calcium 68mg; Fibre 0.7g; Sodium 99mg.

Wholemeal sunflower bread

Sunflower and sesame seeds add protein, calcium and a nutty crunchiness to this wholemeal loaf. The bread is a good accompaniment to cheese and chutney or soup, and is also excellent for a packed-lunch sandwich or breakfast toast.

Makes one loaf

450g/1lb/4 cups strong wholemeal (whole-
wheat) flour
2.5ml/½ tsp easy-blend dried yeast
2.5ml/½ tsp salt
50g/2oz/½ cup sunflower seeds, plus extra
for sprinkling

1 Grease and lightly flour a 450g/1lb loaf tin (pan). Mix the flour, yeast, salt and sunflower seeds in a large bowl. Make a well in the centre and stir in 300ml/½ pint/1¼ cups warm water.

2 Mix the water and flour vigorously with a wooden spoon to form a soft, sticky dough. The dough should be quite wet, so don't be tempted to add any extra flour.

3 Cover the bowl with a damp dish towel and leave the dough to rise in a warm place for 45–50 minutes or until doubled in size.

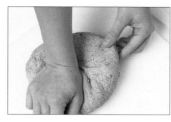

4 Preheat the oven to 200°C/400°F/ Gas 6. Turn out the dough on to a floured work surface and knead for 10 minutes – it will still be quite sticky. Form the dough into a rectangle.

5 Place in the loaf tin. Sprinkle the top with sunflower seeds. Cover with a damp dish towel and leave to rise again for a further 15 minutes.

6 Bake for 40–45 minutes until golden – the loaf should sound hollow when tapped underneath. Leave for 5 minutes, then turn out of the tin and leave to cool on a wire rack.

Energy 1686kcal/7136kJ; Protein 67g; Carbohydrate 296.9g, of which sugars 10.3g; Fat 33.6g, of which saturates 3.6g; Cholesterol 0mg; Calcium 226mg; Fibre 43.5g; Sodium 998mg.

Spicy millet bread

This is a delicious spicy bread with a golden crust. Cut into wedges, as you would a cake, and serve warm with a thick vegetable soup.

Makes 1 loaf

90g/3½oz/½ cup millet
550g/1lb 6oz/5½ cups strong unbleached plain (all-purpose) flour
10ml/2 tsp salt
5ml/1 tsp sugar
5ml/1 tsp dried chilli flakes (optional)
7g/¼oz sachet easy-blend dried yeast
25g/1oz/2 tbsp unsalted butter
1 onion, roughly chopped
15ml/1 tbsp cumin seeds
5ml/1 tsp ground turmeric

1 Bring 200ml/7fl oz/scant 1 cup water to the boil, add the millet, cover and simmer gently for 20 minutes until the grains are soft and the water is absorbed. Remove from the heat and leave to cool until just warm.

3 Turn out the dough on to a floured work surface and knead for 10 minutes. If the dough seems a little dry, knead well until the dough becomes smooth and elastic.

4 Place the dough in an oiled bowl and cover with oiled clear film (plastic wrap) or a dish towel. Leave to rise in a warm place for 1 hour until doubled in bulk.

6 Knock back the dough by pressing down with your knuckles to deflate the dough, then shape into a round. Place the onion mixture in the middle of the dough and bring the sides over the filling to make a parcel, then seal well.

7 Place the loaf on an oiled baking sheet, seam side down, cover with oiled clear film and leave in a warm place for 45 minutes until doubled in bulk. Preheat the oven to 220°C/425°F/Gas 7.

8 Bake the bread for 30 minutes until golden. It should sound hollow when tapped underneath. Leave to cool on a wire rack.

2 Mix together the flour, salt, sugar, chilli flakes, if using, and yeast in a large bowl. Stir in the millet, then add 350ml/12fl oz/1½ cups warm water and mix to form a soft dough.

5 Meanwhile, melt the butter in a heavy-based frying pan, add the onion and fry for 10 minutes until softened, stirring occasionally. Add the cumin seeds and turmeric, and fry for a further 5–8 minutes, stirring constantly, until the cumin seeds begin to pop. Set the pan aside.

EAT WELL

With a freezer stock of simple soups and interesting breads, packed in individual portions ready for thawing and reheating in the microwave, you will always have supplies for a healthy lunch or supper ready in minutes. This is the key to well-balanced eating and good diabetes control.

HEALTH BENEFITS

Millet is a versatile – and much underrated – grain. If eaten on a regular basis as part of a varied healthy diet, it can help lower the risk of heart disease and avoid certain cancers.

Tips and twists

To test if a dough has risen properly, make a small indentation in the top with your index finger. If the indentation does not spring back entirely, then rising is complete; if it springs back at once, the dough is not ready and should be left for another 15 minutes before retesting.

Energy 2464kcal/10426kJ; Protein 59.7g; Carbohydrate 509.5g, of which sugars 15.9g; Fat 31.5g, of which saturates 14.1g; Cholesterol 53mg; Calcium 957mg; Fibre 22.5g; Sodium 4209mg.

Muesli and date bread

This loaf is a good example of how home baking allows you to make low-GI breads with less salt than shop-bought bread. Use homemade, unsweetened muesli for best results.

Makes one loaf

75g/3oz/³/₄ cup wholemeal (whole-wheat) bread flour
300g/10¹/₂oz/2²/₃ cups unbleached white bread flour
2.5ml/¹/₂ tsp salt
45ml/3 tbsp skimmed milk powder (non fat dry milk)
7.5ml/1¹/₂ tsp fast action, easy-blend dried yeast
150g/5¹/₂oz/generous 1¹/₂ cups unsweetened fruit and nut muesli
65g/2¹/₂oz/scant ¹/₂ cup dates, chopped
260ml/9fl oz/scant 1¹/₈ cups hand hot water
30ml/2 tbsp sunflower oil
15ml/1 tbsp clear honey

1 Mix the wholemeal flour and white flour in a bowl with the salt, milk powder and yeast. Stir in the muesli and dates, make a well in the middle and pour in the water, oil and honey.

2 Mix the dry ingredients and liquid to make a firm dough. Turn this dough out on to a floured surface and knead it thoroughly for about 10 minutes, until it is smooth and elastic. Lightly oil a baking sheet.

3 Shape the dough into a plump round and place it on the prepared baking sheet. Using a sharp knife make three cuts on the top about 1cm/¹/₂in deep, to divide the bread into six sections.

4 Cover the loaf with lightly oiled clear film and leave to rise for about an hour, or until it has almost doubled in size.

5 Preheat the oven to 200°C/400°F/ Gas 6. Bake the loaf for 30–35 minutes until it is golden and hollow sounding when tapped underneath. Transfer it to a wire rack to cool.

EAT WELL
Baking your own bread is very satisfying, and means you are in total control of the salt and sugar levels of your loaves. If you don't have the time to hand bake, consider buying a bread machine.

Barley-enriched farmhouse loaf

Barley adds a very distinctive, earthy, slightly nutty flavour to this crusty loaf and it also helps to lower the GI value of a standard white loaf.

Makes one loaf

400g/14oz/3¹/₂ cups unbleached white bread flour
115g/4oz/1 cup barley flour
5ml/1 tsp salt
7.5ml/1¹/₂ tsp easy-blend dried yeast
10ml/2 tsp sugar
200g/7fl oz/1¹/₈ cups hand-hot water
100ml/31/2fl oz/¹/₂ cup hand-hot milk
25g/1oz/2 tbsp pumpkin or sunflower seeds
flour, for dusting

1 Mix the white and barley flours in a bowl. Stir in the salt, yeast and sugar, then make a well in the centre. Pour in the water and milk, and mix the ingredients to a firm dough.

2 Turn the dough out on to a floured surface and knead it for about 10 minutes, until it is smooth and elastic. Knead the seeds into the dough.

3 Lightly oil a 900g/2lb loaf tin (pan) measuring 18.5 x 12cm/7¹/₄ x 4¹/₂in. Shape the dough into a rectangle the same length as the tin.

4 Roll up the dough lengthwise, tuck the ends under, and place in the tin with the seam underneath. Cover with lightly oiled clear film (plastic wrap). Leave to rise for 1 hour until the dough reaches the top of the tin. Preheat the oven to 220°C/425°F/Gas 7.

5 Dust the top of the loaf with flour, and make a deep lengthways cut along the top. Leave to rest for 10 minutes. Bake for 15 minutes, reduce the oven to 200°C/400°F/Gas 6 and bake for 20–25 minutes more, until the bread sounds hollow when tapped on the base. Cool on a wire rack.

Energy 2283kcal/9675kJ; Protein 70.8g; Carbs 437.3g, of which sugars 85.2g; Fat 39.6g, of which saturates 5.9g; Cholesterol 5mg; Calcium 1111mg; Fibre 28.6g; Sodium 335mg.
Energy 2009kcal/8531kJ; Protein 55.1g; Carbohydrate 426.7g, of which sugars 21.6g; Fat 20.7g, of which saturates 3g; Cholesterol 6mg; Calcium 737mg; Fibre 13.9g; Sodium 2025mg.

Chickpea and peppercorn bread

Bread may be a basic food, but it certainly isn't boring, as this exciting combination proves.
Chickpeas add flavour, moisture and texture. This loaf works well made with wholemeal flour.

Makes one loaf

500g/1lb 2oz/4¹/₂ cups unbleached white
bread flour
10ml/2 tsp drained fresh pink peppercorns
in brine
10ml/2 tsp drained fresh green peppercorns
in brine
22ml/1¹/₂ tbsp skimmed milk powder (non fat
dry milk)
5 ml/1 tsp salt
10ml/2 tsp sugar
7.5ml/1¹/₂ tsp easy-blend, fast-action dried
yeast
175g/6oz/1 cup canned chickpeas
250ml/9fl oz/generous 1 cup hand-hot water
30ml/2 tbsp extra virgin olive oil
milk, for brushing (optional)

1 Mash the chickpeas with a fork so
that they are well crushed. You can also
do this in a food processor, but don't
over-process to a paste.

2 In a large bowl, mix the flour, both
types of peppercorn, milk powder,
sugar and yeast. Make a well in the
middle of the ingredients.

3 Add the crushed chickpeas to the
four mixture, then pour in the water and
olive oil. Mix all the ingredients to form
a stiff dough.

4 Turn the dough on to a floured work
surface and knead thoroughly, for about
10 minutes, until smooth and elastic.

5 Lightly oil a 900g/2lb loaf tin (pan)
measuring 18.5 x 12cm/7¹/₄ x 4¹/₂in.
Shape the dough to fit in the tin, the
cover loosely with oiled clear film
(plastic wrap).

6 Leave the dough in a warm place for
1¹/₂–2 hours, until the dough has
doubled in size. Preheat the oven to
220°C/425°F/Gas 7.

7 Bake for 15 minutes, then reduce the
oven to 200°C/400°F/Gas 6 and bake
for a further 20–25 minutes until the
bread is golden and sounds hollow
when turned out and tapped on the
base. Cool on a wire rack.

Energy 2220kcal/9410kJ; Protein 67.6g; Carbohydrate 438.8g, of which sugars 30.3g; Fat 33.7g, of which saturates 4.8g; Cholesterol 3mg; Calcium 1062mg; Fibre 22.7g;
Sodium 2487mg.

Courgette and three-seed bread

The grated courgette combines with the flour during kneading to make a succulent half-wholemeal bread, while the seeds add texture and flavour.

Makes one loaf

375g/13oz/3¹/₄ cups unbleached white
   bread flour
75g/3oz/³/₄ cup wholemeal (whole-wheat)
   bread flour
40g/1¹/₂oz/3 tbsp butter
22ml/1¹/₂ tbsp sunflower seeds
22ml/1¹/₂ tbsp pumpkin seeds
10ml/2 tsp millet seeds
7.5ml/1¹/₂ tsp salt
7.5ml/1¹/₂ tsp sugar
7.5ml/1¹/₂ tsp easy-blend fast-action
   dried yeast
175g/6oz/1 cup grated courgette (zucchini)
75ml/5 tbsp buttermilk
55ml/2fl oz/¹/₄ cup water
cornmeal, for sprinkling

1 Mix the white and wholemeal flours in a bowl. Rub in the butter and then mix in the sunflower, pumpkin and millet seeds, with the salt, sugar and yeast. Make a well in the middle.

2 Add the courgette and buttermilk, then pour in the water. Mix in the dry ingredients to form a stiff dough. Turn out the dough on to a floured surface and knead it thoroughly, for about 10 minutes, until it is smooth and elastic.

3 Lightly oil a 900g/2lb loaf tin (pan) measuring measuring 18.5 x 12cm/ 7¹/₄ x 4¹/₂in. Shape the dough to fit in the tin, then cover loosely with oiled clear film (plastic wrap).

4 Leave to rise in a warm place for about 1¹/₂-2 hours until doubled in size.

5 Preheat the oven to 220°C/425°F/ Gas 7. Bake the loaf for 15 minutes. then reduce the oven to 200°C/400°F/ Gas 6 and bake the bread for a further 25–30 minutes until the bread is well browned and sounds hollow when turned out and tapped on the base. Cool on a wire rack.

Energy 2185kcal/9216kJ; Protein 60g; Carbohydrate 369.6g, of which sugars 22.3g; Fat 61.4g, of which saturates 24.1g; Cholesterol 88mg; Calcium 752mg; Fibre 22.6g; Sodium 2025mg.

Useful addresses

AUSTRALIA
Baker IDI Heart and Diabetes Institute
PO Box 6492, Melbourne
Victoria 3004
Australia
Tel. (03) 8532 1111
www.bakeridi.edu.au

Diabetes Australia
GPO BOX 3156
Canberra, ACT 2601
Australia
Tel. (02) 6232 3800
Infoline: 1300 136 588
www.diabetesaustralia.com.au

CANADA
Canadian Diabetes Association
1400-522 University Ave.
Toronto, ON M5G 2R5
Tel. 1 416 363 3373
Contact centre tel. 1-800 226-8464
www.diabetes.ca

Diabetes Québec
8550 Pie-IX Boulevard
Suite 300
Montréal QC H1Z4G2
Tel 1 514 259 3422 ext. 233
1 800 361 3504 ext. 233
www.diabete.qc.ca

HONG KONG
Diabetes Division
Society for the Study of Endocrinology,
Metabolism and Reproduction
www.endocrine-hk.org

IRELAND
Diabetes Ireland
19 Northwood House
Northwood Business Campus
Santry, Dublin 9
Ireland
Tel. 01 842 8118
Helpline: 1850 909 909
www.diabetes.ie

NEW ZEALAND
Diabetes New Zealand
PO Box 12441
Thorndon
Wellington
New Zealand
Tel. 64 4 499 7145
Tel. toll-free: 0800 342 238
Email: admin@diabetes.org.nz
www.diabetes.org.nz

SOUTH AFRICA
Diabetes South Africa
PO Box 604
Fontainebleau 2032
South Africa
Tel. 086 111 3913
www.diabetessa.co.za

Society of Endocrine, Metabolism &
Diabetes of South Africa
PO Box 2127, Cresta 2118
South Africa
Tel. 011 340 9000
www.semdsa.org.za

UNITED KINGDOM
Diabetes UK
10 Parkway
London NW1 7AA
United Kingdom
Tel. 0345 123 2399
www.diabetes.org.uk

Juvenile Diabetes Research Foundation
17/18 Angel Gate
City Road
London EC1V 2PT
United Kingdom
Tel. 020 7713 2030
www.jdrf.org.uk

USA
American Diabetes Association
1701 North Beauregard Street
Alexandria
VA 22311
USA
Tel. 1-800-342-2383
www.diabetes.org

Juvenile Diabetes Research Foundation
26 Broadway
New York
NY 10004
USA
Tel. 1-800-533-2873
or (212) 785-9595
jdrf.org

INTERNATIONAL
International Diabetes Federation (IDF)
166 Chaussee de La Hulpe
B-1170 Brussels
Belgium
Tel. 32 2 5385511
www.idf.org
The International Diabetes Federation
(IDF) is an umbrella organization of over
230 national diabetes associations in
170 countries and territories. It
represents the interests of the growing
number of people with diabetes and
those at risk. The Federation has been
leading the global diabetes community
since 1950.

Index